Paul's Gospel

Paul's Gospel

in Romans & Galatians

Roger Forster
& Paul Marston

Contents

Preface

Why add yet another book to the many commentaries on Paul's letters to the Galatians and Romans?

The aim of this book is to rediscover Paul's gospel – the good news message that the Lord gave to him – and to challenge some of the very common interpretations put on passages due to ingrained theological traditions, which obscure Paul's message and in some cases make it contradict the Old Testament prophets. Our main objective is to encourage you the reader to look closely at what the text actually says, bearing in mind the cultural and literary backgrounds, and to question some of the assumptions commentators have made about what Paul might be saying, but which fit neither the text nor the context.

We have taken the unusual step of tackling Galatians and Romans together in the same book because, while they appear to address some similar issues, these two epistles were written into very different situations for very different purposes.

Our burden is to offer an accessible and readable book that anyone can enjoy, but which is also a scholarly, well-researched work, to encourage an informed understanding of these epistles. Our hope is not only to exposit these epistles so that they make sense in and of themselves, but also how they fit in with the whole rest of the flow of Scripture.

The structure of the book enables readers to look up a particular passage easily, though we would encourage you to read each commentary straight through to get the flow and context. At various points we have also included questions for thought or discussion, which may help to encourage individual or group study.

It was in 1967 that we began to systematically study the book of Romans, reading all the commentaries we could find, and working through the text together verse by verse looking at the Greek text in which the letter was originally written by Paul. Out of that study came our first book *God's Strategy in Human History* in 1973.

Since then, scholars like N.T. Wright and James Dunn have developed what is called the 'New Perspective on Paul': Paul's Jewish critics were not arguing that doing meritorious deeds earned a ticket to heaven, but that the way to live righteously as the people of God was through keeping the ceremonials of the Law. Other works on the meaning of 'justification', for example *Justitia Dei* by Alister McGrath and *Justification: God's Plan and Paul's Vision* by N.T. Wright, have shown that this term means being shown or declared to be in right relationship with God, rather than being 'made righteous' as once was commonly taught.

In some aspects, this and other new scholarship has confirmed points we argued in 1973, and in others it has greatly enriched our understanding. So here, nearly half a century after we started, we want to present an outline of what we believe is Paul's gospel as presented in Galatians and Romans. Romans contains a kind of systematic theological framework on which all of Paul's message fits. However, central in this are Jewish–Gentile and Law–Grace issues, and it is important to realise the different purpose for which Galatians addresses similar topics. This is why we have put both epistles together in setting out the framework for Paul's gospel. As Paul says both at the beginning and end of Romans, the gospel of Jesus the Messiah is to bring about the obedience of faith for all nations – understanding God's strategy and plan helps us to understand this purpose.

Paul and Roger

Summer 2016

Introduction

1

Introduction

The apostle Paul travelled over 10,000 miles to spread the good news of Jesus to the Gentile world. In Romans 2:16 and 16:25 Paul writes 'according to *my gospel*', but what specifically is Paul's gospel? How can we understand what it meant to the people Paul was writing to, and how can we apply it to our lives today in the twenty-first century?

How to read this book

Our primary intention in writing this book is to show how application of good principles of interpretation puts into context the drift and flow of what Paul is saying in his letters to the churches in Galatia and Rome. These two books set out a structure to understand Paul's gospel. There are also many times when understanding the cultural and theological backgrounds greatly elucidates the meaning of what Paul is saying.

In a number of places, however, especially in commentaries on *Romans*, many commentators import ideas which are neither in the text nor in the cultural background. We will argue that in such cases we should rather read what Paul actually says and make the assumption that he is not contradicting what God says through His servants and prophets in the Old Testament.

This is not going to be a detailed phrase-by-phrase commentary that considers all the alternatives for each phrase. Not everyone wants to know that ἀφωρισμένος in Romans 1:1 is a nominative, singular, masculine, perfect, passive substantival participle! These can be found in more highly technical and analytical (ie 'critical') commentaries such as those by Longenecker or Dunn. If the various alternatives for a phrase do not really affect the overall meaning we will not mention them.

In places we need to briefly explain why we have taken a particular line of interpretation. A kind of excursus will then be inserted as a block entitled 'Discussion Topic', separated from the main flow of the commentary. These will be on points which are of significance, but the commentary can be read without going into all of these if they are not a particular issue for the reader.

We have read a large number of commentaries in producing this little book, but have avoided making copious citations/quotations. Sometimes we may make citations on relevant linguistic or cultural background points, but in general once these are clarified we try to ask:

1. Does a particular interpretation make sense in the context of Paul as an Old Testament believing Jew?

2. Does it address questions Paul would be addressing in his context?

3. Does an interpretation have to import ideas which could have easily been stated but are not there in the text?

With these questions in mind we need to set out some principles for how we will approach Scripture.

Approaching Scripture

Should I skip this bit?

Some readers may just want to skip over all the 'introduction bits' and get to the commentary itself, and this is fine. We would, though, recommend at least looking through the following pages about good principles of how to approach interpreting Scripture, as they underlie all the understandings we suggest. The social and literary contexts of the two letters which we then summarise will also help in understanding some of their features.

Principles of interpretation

In order to take a proper look at what Romans says we need to set out some ground rules for how to go about this – this will include principles such as exegesis and hermeneutics.

'Exegesis' means bringing out what the text says, and 'hermeneutics' means explaining its further context and meaning for us today. Sometimes people say 'We don't need to interpret the Bible, just read its plain sense', however, this is mistaken for a couple of reasons:

1. One of the first things Jesus did after He rose again, was to apply hermeneutics to the Old Testament for two followers on the road to Emmaus – 'He *explained* to them the things concerning Himself in all the Scriptures'. The Greek word used in Luke

24:27 for 'explained' is *diermeneuo* which is where we get our word hermeneutics from. Jesus explained how the Old Testament referred to Himself coming as Messiah. We see this again when the Ethiopian official said to Philip that he needed someone to *explain* the meaning of the passage of Isaiah to him (Acts 8:30-31).

2. Human language is not all that simple. Its meaning is often given by linguistic background, context, etc. Translation itself, from the original Greek text into any language, always involves a certain amount of interpretation.

So Scripture does need to be interpreted, or 'exegeted'. Having said this, we do have to beware of commentators who make a verse completely stand on its head and say the opposite of what it seems to. An extreme example of this is when Augustine interpreted the lament of Jesus in Matthew 23:37 ('how often I wanted to gather you but you would not') to mean that actually He did gather all the ones He really wanted! Unfortunately, this kind of 'exegesis' is far from rare amongst commentators, and we will find in *Romans* that parts of the text have been forced by commentator tradition into meaning what the words simply do not say.

Exegesis

So how should we go about our exegesis of the letters Paul writes to the churches in Rome and Galatia? Klein et al. in their *Introduction to Biblical Interpretation* (p.156) usefully define five essential items for good exegesis:

1) literary context
2) historical-cultural background
3) word meanings
4) grammatical relationships
5) literary genre.

Literary context means where this particular passage comes in relation to other parts of that book, in this case the books of *Galatians* or *Romans*. The writer has a flow of thought, and each passage is related to what comes before and after it.

Historical-cultural background refers in this case to the 'thought-world' in which Paul moved. We know that Paul identifies himself as a Pharisee with a particular eschatological hope (ie of a resurrection) in Acts 23:6, which was not just a cynical ploy, and helps us to understand his worldview. In *Paul and the Faithfulness of God*, N.T. Wright has shown just how much Paul's thinking tied in with first century Jewish ideas, though of course there were also contrasts. This is also important because we cannot assume that Paul is answering questions that no one was asking. For example, if no one was supposing that a person could somehow 'live a perfect life and get to heaven' then there would be no need for Paul to address it. In what issues he does address, Paul uses language that relates to the live issues of his day.

Word meanings are obviously important. We need to beware of two possible errors. The first is to assume that a word is always used in exactly the same sense. Even the same author may sometimes use the same word differently as Paul does with the word 'flesh' (*sarx*) [see pages 169]. The second mistake is to assume that a term has a clear technical meaning when in fact it is used loosely. But, having noted this, when we are looking at a 'dead' language like New Testament Greek, then the range of meanings we find elsewhere may be our best guide to its meaning in a particular verse.

Grammatical relationships are something more specialised. Most of us have to rely on linguistic experts to tell us when there may be two possible meanings to a particular structure of grammar.

Literary genre is of general importance because poetry for example does not use language in the same way as a theological treatise. So for example, to use David's cry of lament in Psalm 51:5 to build some kind of doctrine of being born guilty, is as silly as it would be to take 51:4 to mean that we can only sin against God and not against other people – but that is what some theologians have tried to do. In terms of genre, Galatians is an impassioned theological plea to a specific group of Christians, while Romans is a carefully weighed theological treatise throughout, and should be read as such.

Finally, in his epistle James says that if anyone lacks wisdom let him ask of God (1:5) and of course we do not approach the Scriptures as a merely academic exercise, but seeking the help and guidance of the Holy Spirit.

The Different Focus in Galatians and Romans

There is general agreement that *Galatians* was written before *Romans* (some of the questions about more precise dating and occasion are explored below). It is also obvious that, although the two letters cover some common ground about the Jewish Law and the Christian faith, the situations and reasons for writing are quite different.

The Galatian churches were ones Paul had founded. He writes because he has heard that some Jewish Christians are encouraging Gentile Christians to adopt some or all of the Jewish rites and rituals like circumcision and special days. This is not in order to become Christians, but (they say) if the Gentile Christians want to go forward in holiness. So Paul writes to these Galatian Christians, Jew and Gentile, to assert that there is no such need. He writes in urgent anguish to deal with a practical theological issue in the Galatian churches.

Paul did not found the Roman Church and writes glowingly of their faith (1:8), knowing that Aquila and Priscilla, some of his close associates, are also there. In Romans Paul gives a much more general treatment of what we call God's strategy in human history and N.T. Wright calls 'the single-saving-plan-through-Israel-for-the-world-now-fulfilled-in-the-Messiah.' Paul deals with general issues like how believers in Old Testament times were justified, the basis of our justification and Christian living, the place of Israel and the Law in God's historical dealings, and general practical implications for the Church as a whole.

So we can already see that the audiences for the two letters are very different, as are the situations that they were addressing, and in looking at them it will be very important to note what particular concerns or questions are being addressed.

To reiterate, in Galatians Paul is addressing people who are Christians – some Jews and some Gentiles – concerning their present position. He is not addressing any general question about the basis on which Old Testament saints were forgiven and accepted by God. He is not considering the place of Israel the nation (it is not mentioned). His concern on the purpose of the Law is primarily as it affects them as present Christians. In Romans, in contrast, his concerns are for a much more general treatment, presenting what he calls 'my gospel' explaining, elucidating and vindicating his whole understanding of God's dealings.

Key Terms

In *God's Strategy in Human History – Volume 2: Reconsidering Key Biblical Ideas* we look in depth at the meanings of some often misunderstood key biblical terms. Here we will simply outline some of these as they are crucial to understanding this book, but for detail please see our earlier book.

Torah: The Jewish word for 'law' or 'teaching'. It could either mean the first five books in our Bible, or it could mean the commandments (*mitzvoth*) laid down in it – later rabbis identified 613 of these!

Justification: This does *not* mean 'being made right with God' but rather 'being *declared* to be in rightstanding (before God)'. This may seem like a small difference, but as we will see it has significant implications. It can happen initially at conversion, but (as with Abraham in Genesis 15:6) also long into a person's walk with God. See also our *Reconsidering Key Biblical Ideas* chapter 2, N.T. Wright's *Justification: God's Plan and Paul's Vision* and *Justitia Dei* by McGrath.

Righteous and *Sinner*: 'Righteous' does not mean ethically perfect or without sin. In Scripture a 'righteous' person is someone in rightstanding with God. A 'sinner' does *not* mean that someone has sinned (we all have) but a person whose lifestyle is lived without God. Preachers sometimes say 'all of us here are sinners!' but in Biblical terms this would imply that no one present is living in harmony with God, so none of them are Christians, which is not what the preacher really means! See also our *God's Path to Victory* p.12ff and *Reconsidering Key Biblical Ideas* chapter 2.

Works of the Law: This does not mean good works in general. It means things specific to Torah, in particular circumcision, kosher diet, and keeping Jewish Sabbaths and festivals. These were the key distinguishing markers of being Jewish, and so to them being part of the people of God. Jews were also distinguished, of course, by a fiercely monotheistic rejection of any polytheistic rituals. This, however, might be shared by some non-Jews such as godfearers and in Paul's time Gentile Christians – without it marking them out as Jewish.

Translations

In this book we will use various translations in an effort to get the nearest to what the Greek text actually says while still flowing in English. In particular we will use two versions:

NASB: New American Standard Bible®,Copyright © 1960, 1962, 1963,

1968, 1971, 1972, 1973, 1975, 1977, 1995 by The Lockman Foundation. Used by permission.

NRSVA: New Revised Standard Version Anglicized: New Revised Standard Version Bible: Anglicized Edition, copyright © 1989, 1995 National Council of the Churches of Christ in the United States of America. Used by permission. All rights reserved.

We will also sometimes refer to the NKJV (New King James Version), the ESV (English Standard Version), the NEB (New English Bible), the NIV (New International Version), YLT (Young's Literal Translation) the CEB (Common English Bible) and CJB (Complete Jewish Bible).

Reference may also be made to the LXX (Septuagint) Greek translation of the Old Testament which was in common use in first century and is sometimes quoted in the New Testament. Sometimes it can give a good clue about Greek word meanings as used by Paul.

Christ

The Greek word *Christos* simply means 'anointed one', with the assumption that this means an anointing as a king or high priest. In Hebrew this is the word 'Messiah' מָשִׁיחַ and it had come to mean a promised deliverer (and King) for the Jewish people (and as shown in John 4 also for the Samaritans). In English the word 'Messiah' has come to mean an expected deliverer, but the word 'Christ' has no such meaning. So why do most New Testament translations simply transliterate the Greek word *Christos* rather than translate it as 'anointed one' or 'Messiah'?

Some commentators have argued that really Paul uses it as a name rather than a title, because: i) the term as a title would be meaningless to Gentiles, and ii) Paul uses it a lot. Neither argument carries any weight. Since the Church spread initially through the Jewish communities (and indeed the Gentile Christians in Rome knew the Torah, see Romans 7:1) of course they would know that Jesus was the Jewish Messiah. Later, as the Church moved further away from and even became antagonistic to its Jewish roots, so people started to think of *Christos* as a name rather than a title. Probably many Europeans today think that 'Mahatma' was Ghandi's name, but his original followers were quite clear it was an honorific title.

Paul was intensely a first-century second-Temple Jew, and it seems bizarre

9

to imagine that he would suddenly think of the Greek word for 'Messiah' as merely a name (like, say, Sidney) just in case Gentiles didn't understand it. Paul was clear that from Israel came the Messiah (Romans 9:5) who fulfilled that role prophesied in Isaiah which Israel could not. Moreover, as Dunn and Cranfield point out, if it were regarded as a name, then the occasional reversal of the order to 'Christ Jesus' (Acts 24:24, Romans 1:1, 3:24 etc) would be odd. For this reason we have no doubt that scholars like Cranfield and Wright and Dunn are correct in seeing it as a title throughout Paul, and it is tempting to replace the transliteration 'Christ' with the word it means – 'Messiah' – in all the texts. We have left the text as the NRSVA and NASB have it, but would encourage readers to think 'Messiah' when they read 'Christ'.

Settings and Dates for Galatians and Romans

There is general agreement that Galatians was written before Romans and that they have different concerns. Here we give a brief outline of the historical context and issues, but if desired the reader can skim read this section and move to the commentary on Galatians on page 17. Ideally the commentaries are meant to be read through to get the context, and ideally the one on Galatians should be read first. However, we have structured it so that you can easily look up a particular verse if you so desire.

The Area to which Paul wrote Galatians

Historically there have been two divergent views about the area to which Paul wrote the letter to the Galatians. However, it is now generally recognised that, at the time Paul wrote, the cities of Derbe, Lystra and Psidian Antioch were in the southern part of the Roman area of Galatia. In his first missionary journey with Barnabas (Acts 13–14, c48–49 AD) he had visited these cities and set up churches there, and these were the cities to which he wrote his letter. This so called 'South Galatian hypothesis' was first put forward by the great archaeologist and commentator Sir William Ramsay, and it is now overwhelmingly accepted. Further details are in Bruce, Longenecker and Dunn.

Timing of the letter

There is no universal agreement on when Galatians was written – in particular

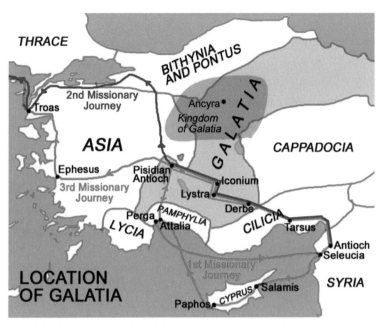

Map by kind permission of Pastor Ralph Wilson: *www.jesuswalk.com*

was it before or after the big council in Jerusalem that is recorded in Acts 15? At the end of that council a letter-decree was given to various people, including Paul and Barnabas, to take to Gentile Christians affirming that they did not have to keep the Jewish Torah (Law) to be good Christians. Since this is a major issue in the letter to the Galatians we have to agree with Witherington:

> Had Paul known of and had the Jerusalem church agreed to such a compromise before Galatians was written it is very difficult to explain why Paul did not refer to it in this letter to support his arguments. (*Grace in Galatia*, p.13)

Lyons claims that Galatians was written after the Acts 15 Council decree, but 'Paul considered it irrelevant to the Galatians', a claim that seems highly implausible, as it is very relevant.

Those like Lyons and Dunn who place Galatians after the Acts 15 letter-decree seem to make various other implausible assumptions, such as:

– Paul 'lost' his argument with Peter at Antioch, and maybe this was the real cause of the separation from Barnabas at the second missionary journey.

11

- Maybe Paul tolerated but really opposed the Acts 15 decree.
- Paul lost the support of Antioch and moved his centre to Philippi.

Actually there is no indication that Paul 'lost' the argument over table-fellowship in Antioch; rather the impression we get is that the various issues rumbled on as a dispute until Paul and Barnabas were sent off up to Jerusalem to sort it with the church leaders there.

The suggestion that the rift with Barnabas was 'really' over the Antioch controversy is also unconvincing, as is the suggestion that Paul lost the support of Antioch. Luke in Acts 15:31–36 has Paul and Barnabas in harmony in Antioch, and when Paul set out with Silas the 'believers commended him to the grace of God' (Acts 15:40). Luke is also clear that the rift between Paul and Barnabas was a personal one over John Mark and there was no theological rift between them or with Antioch.

Above all though, commentators like Bruce and Witherington and Longenecker are right to emphasize that (although Paul mentions in Galatians the earlier dispute with Peter over table-fellowship) the Galatians dispute is clearly about whether Gentiles should be circumcised to progress in holiness, and the Jerusalem letter-decree clearly said that they need not be. It would seem really strange, as Paul and Barnabas were given the letter-decree to carry, if Paul didn't mention it in his letter to the Galatians.

It is, then, overwhelmingly likely that the letter to the Galatians was written from Antioch to the cities of South Galatia, shortly *before* the Acts 15 council at Jerusalem.

Suggested sequence and timing of events

So here is an outline chronology of events. The dates cannot be precise (no one can be absolutely sure even of the year of the crucifixion), but this is our best guess:

1. After his conversion (33 AD?) and a brief spell in contemplation in Arabia Paul stayed about 3 years (it could be 2 years and 1 month in Jewish terms) in Damascus.

2. Paul escaped from a plot in Damascus and made a first Jerusalem visit (35 AD?), where Barnabas introduced him to Peter and the apostles. (Acts 9:26, Galatians 1:18). The Gentile issue did not feature large

at this time, maybe Paul was still taking his gospel 'to the Jew first' or maybe it just had not yet been taken up as an issue.

3. In Jerusalem he argued with the 'Hellenists' (Acts 9:29) – Greek speaking Jews. We don't know how long he stayed, but again he had to escape and went through Caesarea to Tarsus his home city in Asia Minor

4. It was after this time that Peter had his Acts 10 vision and accepted that Cornelius had received full forgiveness and the Holy Spirit, just as the disciples had at Pentecost, and this was while he was a Gentile. Peter said that although he had believed it 'unlawful for a Jew to associate with or visit a Gentile', God had shown him otherwise (Acts 10:28).

5. The gospel continued to spread. It was preached mainly to Jews (Acts 11:20) but then also to a group in Antioch which in some manuscripts is 'Hellenists' (ie Greek-speaking Jews) and in others 'Hellenes' (= Greeks, ie Gentiles). Given that the 'Hellenists' had received the gospel since before Acts 6:1, 'Gentiles' seems the more likely reading. So the Jerusalem church sent Barnabas to check it out, and he then went off to Tarsus to fetch Paul and they stayed in Antioch a year (Acts 11:26). A prophet came down and prophesied a famine, so the Antioch church decided to send famine relief to Jerusalem.

6. So, fourteen years after his first visit (though again in Jewish terms it could be 13 years and 1 month) Paul made a second Jerusalem visit (Acts 11:27–30, Galatians 2:1ff) with Barnabas to take famine relief to Jerusalem (48 AD?). But Paul also took the opportunity to lay before the apostles his mission to the Gentiles.

7. Returning with Barnabas to Antioch, the church there commissioned his first missionary journey (48–49 AD?) He went to the South Galatian cities of Psidian Antioch, Lystra and Derbe (Acts 13:4–25). Gentiles and Jews became Christians.

8. They returned back to Antioch (Acts 14:27) and stayed there 'for some time' (Acts 14:28).

9. During this time some brothers came down from Judaea and began to teach that Gentile converts should become Jews (Acts 15:1).

10. Also during this time Peter (Cephas) came down at some point to Antioch (Galatians 2:11) and as the controversy continued he and Barnabas began to separate themselves from Gentiles. Paul pointed out that this was inconsistent with Peter's own revelation from God (prior to seeing Cornelius) and his previous behaviour – he was play-acting in separating not from conviction but in wanting to placate the 'Judaisers'.

11. After Peter returned to Jerusalem the controversy rumbled on, and at this time Paul wrote his letter to the Galatians (50 AD?) from Antioch (the mother church for the churches in South Galatia) as some similar controversy had arisen there, ie Gentiles were being encouraged to adopt Jewish practices to join the advanced holiness group.

12. After 'no small dissension' with the Judaisers (Acts 15:2) it was decided that Barnabas and Paul should go up to the church in Jerusalem to 'discuss this issue with the apostle and elders'. Of course (as Cornelius had shown) Gentiles could become Christians without becoming Jews first, but should they then be expected to adopt circumcision and Jewish law?

13. After much debate, the council (51 AD?) decided that Gentiles did *not* have to be circumcised, but just to abstain from immorality, from meat offered to idols, and from blood (Acts 15:23–29). The letter carrying this decision was given to Paul and Barnabas, Judas Barsabas and Silas (Acts 15:22, 30). They stayed in Antioch some time (Acts 15:33–35).

14. Paul then made a second missionary journey with Silas (Acts 15:40–18:23a). During this journey he founded a church at Thessalonica (Acts 17:1) and probably wrote his letters to there later in his journey. He also visited Corinth (Acts 18:1) where he stayed with Priscilla and Aquila, probably leaving c52 AD.

15. Most commentators believe Paul wrote letters to Corinth c53–54 AD, the second from Ephesus (1 Corinthians 16:8) and probably

also the first after a brief visit to Corinth from Ephesus that is unrecorded in the Acts.

16. The letters to Corinth therefore come after the council at Jerusalem and after the second missionary journey (Acts 15:39–18:23a). The controversy about circumcision had now already been settled by the apostolic decree, but the issue of food offered to idols was still difficult to apply in practice in a place like Corinth (it was easy in Jerusalem where the leaders made the decree!).

17. Paul made a third missionary journey (54–58 AD?) (Acts 18:23b–20:3a)

18. The letter to Rome comes after his second letter to Corinth, and was written (55–56 AD?) from Cenchrea in Corinth (Romans 16:1). Again, the controversy about whether Gentiles should be circumcised was long settled, but the difficulties over living together with Jews and Gentiles were still there (Romans 14).

All this is an attempt at a reasonable reconstruction of the chronology, and it is not possible to give more accurate dates, however it does seem highly probable that the letter to the Galatians was written before the Jerusalem council and that the letter to the Romans was written some years afterwards.

The Letter to the Galatians

Introduction to Galatians

Commentaries

We have listed only the commentaries we have found useful on Galatians. Sir William Ramsay in *A Historical Commentary on St Paul's Epistle to the Galatians* (1900) first really set the epistle in context. Longenecker and Dunn are similar substantial commentaries – Dunn transliterates the Greek so is easier to follow for those who do not read Greek. *The Epistle to the Galatians* by F.F. Bruce and *Grace in Galatia* by Ben Witherington are also scholarly and useful, though the latter is hard to read if one is unfamiliar with technical rhetoric. Lyons' commentary is in the 'Wesleyan Tradition' but we found it disappointingly traditionalist in many of its points.

Background of the Letter to the Galatians

The Churches in Galatia

Paul and Barnabas had founded these Galatian churches on their first missionary journey. Gentiles as well as Jews had become Christians, but Paul had never suggested that they needed to become Jews in order to function within the church.

Date and Occasion

When Paul wrote Galatians, he and Barnabas had completed their first missionary journey and were back in Antioch, probably around 50 AD. By this time it was clear that Gentiles could become Christians without being circumcised. It was over a decade since Paul was called to be a missionary to the Gentiles and the Gentile Cornelius was given baptism by Peter who said: *'God has shown me that I should not call any man common or unclean'* (Acts 10:28). Cornelius was plainly accepted by God and given the Holy Spirit *as a Gentile*. But some still held that to go on into full *salvation in their lives and future* they needed to become Jews.

To 'be saved' was not about a ticket to a spiritual heaven, but to enter fully into being part of God's people. So we read in Acts 15:

> [1] Some men came down from Judea and began teaching the brethren, 'Unless you are circumcised according to the custom of Moses, you cannot be saved.' [2] And when Paul and Barnabas had great dissension and debate with them, the brethren determined that Paul and Barnabas and some others of them should go up to Jerusalem to the apostles and elders concerning this issue. (Acts 15:1–2, NASB)

Paul was at this time in Antioch, but the same group had presumably been saying similar things to his converts in South Galatia. So he wrote his letter to the Galatians.

Context of the Letter

There are two key things here:

1. The letter is written to Christians, those who are already a part of *the faith*, to tell them that they do not have to keep the Jewish law.

2. The core issue is whether in order to live out the Christian life someone should be circumcised and keep Jewish law – it is about holiness, not about getting initial forgiveness, rebirth and the Holy Spirit.

As noted, the letter to the Romans is in a quite different situation. The apostolic letter-decree has gone out (via Paul and Barnabas) that Gentiles have only to keep some basic rules and do not need to be circumcised or keep the Torah. Paul no longer has to argue this. In Romans, Paul writes rather to set out systematically his understanding of Christianity. Part of this is to explain the position of Israel and the Law. At the same time he realises (see also his letters to Corinth) he may have given rise to some doubt as to whether he supports the aspect of the apostolic decree that forbad eating meat offered to idols (Acts 15:29, 21:25 and 1 Corinthians 8) and he wants to put it on a more general footing about foods and mutual tolerance (Romans 14).

This means that in Romans, Paul's purpose is much more general. Galatians focuses on their position as Christians, Romans concerns the more general issues of God's dealings with mankind.

The Galatian Gentile Christians knew that it was by faith that they were accepted by God and had received the Holy Spirit (3:2). No-one seems to have been suggesting that they could 'earn' God's forgiveness by good works, or that until they were circumcised they were not really Christians. The issue was about holiness, about the ongoing salvation in their lives, about their effectiveness as part of the people of God on Earth. This is consistent with the view in the 'New Perspective on Paul' associated with Dunn, Wright and to some extent Longenecker. Pharisees in general did *not* believe that they could 'earn' God's forgiveness, but that it was through meticulous keeping of the Law that they could express the holiness God expected of His people. Dunn called this 'covenantal nomism'. Sadly, Christian holiness movements can make the same mistake, as we will note.

So, the so-called 'Judaisers' were teaching that, having become Christians, to 'go on with God' they should receive the sign of the covenant (circumcision), keep special days (4:10) and if they were like the people in Colossae, also submit to a set of dietary rules (Colossians 2:21). These three things (circumcision, diet and Sabbaths) were what marked off the Jews in the eyes of the ancient (and modern) world. They were 'social markers'. Dunn suggests that these were the most basic 'works of the Law'. They are symbolic and ceremonial, not moral, though what they symbolise are moral issues.

Concerns in the Letter to the Galatians

At risk of caricaturing it, a very 'traditional' (albeit misguided) understanding of the letter to the Galatians could be set out thus:

1. Galatians was written to tell people how to get right with God and get an individual ticket to a spiritual heaven.

2. This is what 'justification' means – it is the forgiveness received at conversion when people are 'made right with God'.

3. The 'Judaisers' were saying that through doing works of the Law (ie through doing good works) people could earn God's forgiveness and their ticket to heaven.

4. It is only through Christian faith that anyone can get forgiven and a ticket to heaven.

Virtually all of this is incorrect. In fact:

1. Galatians was written to Christians who had already received forgiveness and the Holy Spirit, and knew that they had done

this through faith not legalistic works.

2. 'Justification' means being declared to be or shown to be in right relationship with God, and it can happen at conversion or at any time in a believer's life (as with Abraham in Genesis 15 according to Romans 4:2–3 and Genesis 22 according to James 2:21).

3. The 'Judaisers' were telling people that although they became Christians through faith, to really 'go on with God' in holiness it was best to keep some or all of the Jewish ceremonial Law (particularly key 'works of the Law': circumcision, diet and Sabbath festivals).

4. The 'Judaisers' were not claiming that this earned the favour of God, but rather that it was how to show oneself to be in really good standing with God, to be 'justified' in the real sense of this term.

5. Galatians does not address whether it is only specifically *Christian* faith through which people can be right with God. Paul writes urgently *to Christians* about *their* situation, a situation since the coming of *the faith*.

Commentary on Galatians

Text 1:1–5

> [1] Paul, an apostle (not sent from men nor through the agency of man, but through Jesus Christ and God the Father, who raised Him from the dead), [2] and all the brethren who are with me, to the churches of Galatia:
> [3] Grace to you and peace from God our Father and the Lord Jesus Christ, [4] who gave Himself for our sins so that He might rescue us from this present evil age, according to the will of our God and Father, [5] to whom be the glory forevermore. Amen. (NASB)

Commentary

Letters at that time usually began with the name of the sender, the recipient, and a greeting. As he states that he is the sender, Paul also asserts that his apostleship was not an appointment made by the Christian leadership but by God – a theme he emphasizes later too.

Paul's greeting here (and in Romans where it is identical) is 'grace and peace'. Maybe Paul had in mind the Hebrew text (not the LXX) of the lovely prayer: YHWH *bless you and keep you.* YHWH *make His face shine upon you and be gracious to you.* YHWH *lift up His countenance upon you and give you peace* (Numbers 6:24–26). Paul prefaces the usual Hebrew greeting 'peace' (*shalom*), by the idea of grace – real peace comes from experiencing the grace of God. The usual Greek word for 'greeting' (*chairein*, see James 1:1) sounds like the one Paul uses here for grace (*charis*) but means cheerfulness or joy. So Paul's greeting sounds like it is conventional but in fact is God-centred.

Text 1:6–10

> [6] I am astonished that you are so quickly deserting the one who called you in the grace of Christ and are turning to a different gospel — [7] not that there is another gospel, but there are some who are confusing you and want to pervert the gospel of Christ. [8] But

even if we or an angel [or *messenger*] from heaven should proclaim to you a gospel contrary to what we proclaimed to you, let that one be accursed! ⁹ As we have said before, so now I repeat, if anyone proclaims to you a gospel contrary to what you received, let that one be accursed! ¹⁰ Am I now seeking human approval, or God's approval? Or am I trying to please people? If I were still pleasing people, I would not be a servant [or *slave*] of Christ. (NRSVA)

Commentary

Hardly has he got out the greeting than his frustration erupts. He is not looking for the 'quiet life' by compromising on core issues of the gospel (though of course he is willing to be tolerant on unimportant issues as he would later write in Romans 14). These are strong words! In the end it is Messiah (Christ) he serves, he is not courting human popularity. This is a good example to follow, though we have to be sure that it really *is* God we are listening to when we feel impelled to be critical of other Christians who see things differently.

Text 1:11–23

¹¹ For I want you to know, brothers and sisters (Greek: *adelphoi*), that the gospel that was proclaimed by me is not of human origin; ¹² for I did not receive it from a human source, nor was I taught it, but I received it through a revelation of Jesus Christ.
¹³ You have heard, no doubt, of my earlier life in Judaism. I was violently persecuting the church of God and was trying to destroy it. ¹⁴ I advanced in Judaism beyond many among my people of the same age, for I was far more zealous for the traditions of my ancestors. ¹⁵ But when God, who had set me apart before I was born and called me through His grace, was pleased ¹⁶ to reveal His Son to me, so that I might proclaim Him among the Gentiles, I did not confer with any human being, ¹⁷ nor did I go up to Jerusalem to those who were already apostles before me, but I went away at once into Arabia, and afterwards I returned to Damascus.
¹⁸ Then after three years I did go up to Jerusalem to visit Cephas and stayed with him for fifteen days; ¹⁹ but I did not see any other apostle except James the Lord's brother. ²⁰ In what I am writing to you, before God, I do not lie! ²¹ Then I went into the regions of

Syria and Cilicia, [22] and I was still unknown by sight to the churches of Judea that are in Christ; [23] they only heard it said, 'The one who formerly was persecuting us is now proclaiming the faith he once tried to destroy.' [24] And they glorified God because of me. (NRSVA)

Commentary

The Greek term *adelphoi* means 'brothers' but as used by Paul the term is often not intended to be gender specific, so the modern versions that render it 'brothers and sisters' (CEB, NRSVA, NIV and many others) are linguistically correct and not just politically correct! Unfortunately the NRSVA translates it 'brothers and sisters' in Galatians 1:11, 3:15, 5:13 and 6:18, but translates the same word as 'friends' in Galatians 4:12, 4:28, 4:31, 5:11 and 6:1 for no apparent reason. We would have preferred a consistent 'brothers and sisters'.

At the start of Galatians Paul recounts the story of his conversion, and that he received his commission to preach directly from God and not on the authority of the apostles. After a brief period of presumably intense prayer and contemplation in Arabia, Paul returned to preach in Damascus, having three years later to be smuggled out of the city to avoid arrest (Acts 9:25). He went up to Jerusalem and spent fifteen days with Peter (Galatians 1:18), not to seek authority but to 'get to know' him. In Galatians Paul uses the Greek 'Peter' and Aramaic 'Cephas' interchangeably – both mean a rock, and 'Rocky' was the nickname Jesus had given his disciple Simon Barjona (or Simon 'Johnson' – Matthew 16:17) .

Text 2:1–10

[1] Then after fourteen years I went up again to Jerusalem with Barnabas, taking Titus along with me. [2] I went up in response to a revelation. Then I laid before them (though only in a private meeting with the acknowledged leaders) the gospel that I proclaim among the Gentiles, in order to make sure that I was not running, or had not run, in vain. [3] But even Titus, who was with me, was not compelled to be circumcised, though he was a Greek. [4] But because of false believers [Lit: *false brothers*] secretly brought in, who slipped in to spy on the freedom we have in Christ Jesus, so that they might enslave us— [5] we did not submit to them even for a moment, so that the truth of the gospel might always remain with you. [6] And from those who were supposed to be acknowledged leaders (what they actually were makes no difference

to me; God shows no partiality)—those leaders contributed nothing to me. [7] On the contrary, when they saw that I had been entrusted with the gospel for the uncircumcised, just as Peter had been entrusted with the gospel for the circumcised [8] (for He who worked through Peter making him an apostle to the circumcised also worked through me in sending me to the Gentiles), [9] and when James and Cephas and John, who were acknowledged pillars, recognized the grace that had been given to me, they gave to Barnabas and me the right hand of fellowship, agreeing that we should go to the Gentiles and they to the circumcised. [10] They asked only one thing, that we remember the poor, which was actually what I was eager to do. (NRSVA)

Commentary

Fourteen years later he made a second visit to Peter and the other leaders in Jerusalem, just to check that he had been on the right track. He is careful to assert that he did not *need* any endorsement from the Jerusalem church leaders (James, Peter and John) but that he and Barnabas received it anyway. Paul is emphasizing that he was acting in agreement with the apostles and not in any conflict with them. This was before his first great missionary journey. Cornelius had been accepted by Peter and baptised while still a Gentile, but maybe the issue of how much of Jewish custom and ritual Christian Gentiles had to accept had not yet become a big issue. Paul and Barnabas had partly gone up with a donation collected to relieve hardship in Jerusalem, so he was effectively asked to keep up this good work for the poor!

Text 2:11–14

[11] But when Cephas came to Antioch, I opposed him to his face, because he stood self-condemned; [12] for until certain people came from James, he used to eat with the Gentiles. But after they came, he drew back and kept himself separate for fear of the circumcision faction. [13] And the other Jews joined him in this hypocrisy, so that even Barnabas was led astray by their hypocrisy. [14] But when I saw that they were not acting consistently with the truth of the gospel, I said to Cephas before them all, 'If you, though a Jew, live like a Gentile and not like a Jew, how can you compel the Gentiles to live like Jews?' (NRSVA)

Commentary

Back in Antioch after his first great missionary journey with Barnabas, Paul fell out with Peter. Even Barnabas, always one to mediate, was carried away with the compromise Peter had accepted. Paul, however, saw that it was a key issue for the future of the Church. We should note carefully what this was about:

– They were not saying it was necessary to become fully Jewish in order to get forgiveness from God and become Christians.

– It seems that they wanted separate table fellowship for those 'following Jewish customs', ie for the Jewish Christians (effectively) to have a separate church. This would be as though Messianic Jews today formed a separate church (generally they don't by the way).

– To join socially this elite holiness group, Gentiles would have to follow at least some of the basic Jewish customs like circumcision and probably then Sabbaths and diet.

– In theory this might have been presented as separate *but equal* churches, but in any segregation-type system this idea seldom holds in reality.

F.F. Bruce puts it that this social separation:

> . . . in effect amounted to saying to Gentile Christians 'Unless you conform to the Jewish way of life we cannot have social relations with you.' This was practically compelling them to Judaize. (*The Epistle to the Galatians*, p.133)

The circumcision was not being advocated to obtain God's forgiveness (or an individual ticket to a spiritual heaven), but to enter fully into God's salvation plan through Israel.

Peter and Barnabas were going along with this not with any conviction but from 'play acting' (Greek: *hypokrisei*) to placate Jewish sensibilities. The issue of sharing together with Gentiles was the very one Peter had been told about in Acts 10, and of course 'eating together' at that time for Christians included what we call the Lord's Supper or Holy Communion, which was a picture of being one household of God.

When Paul says that Peter 'lives like a Gentile' (Galatians 2:14) it seems highly unlikely that Peter had stopped following Torah. It means that he had no longer been living the kind of separation he said was normal for Jews in Acts 10:28, who regarded it as 'unlawful' to associate with Gentiles. Now he was going along with those who wanted Gentiles to assume Jewish customs (ie the Torah) and separate from their fellow Gentile Christians who had not adopted such customs if they were going to join the Jewish Christian group.

Questions for Thought and Discussion

- How should we deal with disagreements between Christian leaders?
- Why was Paul so adamant on what was apparently just a good compromise?
- How can we decide what really are crucial issues to insist on in church life?

Text 2:15–17

¹⁵ We who are Jews by birth and not 'sinners of the Gentiles', and who know that a person is not justified by works of the Law but by the faithfulness of Jesus Christ, even we had faith in Christ Jesus that we might be justified on the basis of the faithfulness of Christ and not on the basis of works of the law. ¹⁶ Because on the basis of works of the law shall no one be justified. ¹⁷ But if, while we are seeking to be justified by [Greek: *en*] Christ, we are found to be sinners, does this mean that Christ is a minister of sin? Absolutely not! (Longenecker's translation).

Discussion Topic: 'Faithfulness of' or 'Faith in'

Here we have given Longenecker's translation, but in reality the word 'Christ' just means Messiah. 'Christ' was never used as a name and this is clearly indicated by both 'Christ Jesus' and 'Jesus Christ' appearing in the same verse (v15) with reversal of order of the words *Christos* and *Iēsou* in the Greek.

We are justified *in* Messiah, as well as *by* him. We also quite like the Isaac Stern's *Complete Jewish Bible* rendering of this:

> [15] We are Jews by birth, not so-called *'Goyishe* sinners'; [16] even so, we have come to realize that a person is not declared righteous by God on the ground of his legalistic observance of Torah commands, but through the Messiah Yeshua's trusting faithfulness. Therefore, we too have put our trust in Messiah Yeshua and become faithful to Him, in order that we might be declared righteous on the ground of the Messiah's trusting faithfulness and not on the ground of our legalistic observance of Torah commands. For on the ground of legalistic observance of Torah commands, no one will be declared righteous.
>
> [17] But if, in seeking to be declared righteous by God through our union with the Messiah, we ourselves are indeed found to be sinners, then is the Messiah an aider and abettor of sin? Heaven forbid!

Longenecker's translation differs from most translations, because it renders *pisteōs Iēsou Christou* as the 'faithfulness of Jesus Christ'. The CEB, the NIV margin and in a sense the CJB, as shown above, also have the 'faithfulness of Christ'. The Greek phrase is a genitive and so 'faith/faithfulness *of*' would be its natural meaning, but other translations (for example the NIV, NKJV, NASB and NRSV) suggest that it is a so-called objective genitive and that it means 'faith *in* Christ'.

So which is it: 'faithfulness *of* Messiah' or 'faith *in* Messiah'? If the 'objective genitive' were correct, then verse 16 would say:

> '. . . knowing that a man is not justified by works of the Law but though <u>faith in Jesus Messiah</u>, even we have had <u>faith in Messiah Jesus</u>, that we may be justified by <u>faith in Messiah</u> and not by works of the Law.'

If Paul really meant 'faith *in* Messiah' in all three phrases then this would mean that his sentence would be absurdly repetitive, and the argument some have made that this is 'just for emphasis' is unconvincing. It is *what Messiah has done* that is the basis of our justification, not what we have done. Paul *does* say in his middle clause here 'we had faith *in* Messiah Jesus', and in Galatians 3:26 again uses the phrase 'faith *in* Messiah Jesus' (*pisteōs en Christō Iēsou*). So Paul did not need to use a genitive if 'faith in' were really his meaning in the other two clauses either side in 2:15. Many modern commentators (for example Longenecker and N.T. Wright) now accept this, and we have absolutely no doubt that the correct meaning is as shown in Longenecker's translation above – the phrase definitely means 'faithfulness *of* Jesus the Messiah'.

Further comment on this can be found on pages 131–5 in the section on Romans 3:22, where a similar phrase is used.

Discussion Topic: Jewish 'Works' and Righteousness

One of the problems in discussing what first century Jews thought on works and righteousness is that Jewish rabbis were as diverse then as Christian theologians today, and even more prone to hyperbole and exaggeration! So by selecting some particular rabbinical saying (usually from the much later Mishnah) rabbinical thinking can be characterised by commentators in conflicting ways. The classic (especially Lutheran) understanding was that the Jews thought that by doing 'good works' they could earn God's forgiveness, avoid hell and earn a ticket to heaven. This understanding has had enormous and continuing influence, but is greatly misleading on several counts.

One key issue is that to be 'justified' does *not* refer to the initial obtaining of forgiveness to avoid hell, but being *shown to be* in rightstanding with God. Something that *demonstrates* God's acceptance is very different from something that *gains* God's acceptance. This, though, is crucial to understanding how the Pharisees saw their works of the law, and why Paul was so critical of them and asserted 'justification by faith'.

Associated with this, has been a change in the way first century Pharisaic/rabbinic religion is perceived. Two seminal books exploring this were *Paul, Apostle of Liberty* by Richard Longenecker and *Paul and Palestinian Judaism* by E.P. Sanders. Longenecker accepts that there were some Pharisees who were legalists (trying to become holy through works of the law), but there were also what he called 'nomistic' Pharisees (from the Greek word *nomos* = law):

> . . . the religion of a nomistic Pharisee was truly spiritual and noble. While he insisted that faith was wholehearted trust in God and fidelity to His instruction, his emphasis, as opposed to the legalist, was upon God and trust in Him. He agreed that 'God demands obedience,' but likewise insisted that such was 'only as proof and expressions of something else, the intimate personal attitude of trust and love.' (*Paul, Apostle of Liberty*, p.76)

Sanders developed the idea further, characterising rabbinical Judaism as 'covenantal nomism'. Pharisees were just trying, he claimed, through law-keeping to live out being part of the covenant God had freely given them.

So what are the 'works of the law' (a phrase used only in Romans 2:15, 3:20, 3:28, 9:32, Galatians 2:16 (×3), 3:2 and 3:10)? Dunn identified these as meaning the 'social markers' of being Jewish, particularly circumcision, Sabbaths and diet. The phrase does *not* mean good works in general. Rather, it was how you told (in those days) that someone was a Jew – and to them that was the same as the social markers of being part of the people of God. In N.T. Wright's words the 'works of the Law' were '*badges*' of being the people of God, not *means* to earn His forgiveness and acceptance. Longenecker does not fully accept the view of Dunn (and Wright) on this. He accepts that other Jewish believers may have thought of the term as a kind of 'badge' of membership, but then he wants also to revert to some concept of 'winning God's favour by merit-amassing observance of Torah' (Longenecker *Galatians,* p.86). One reason he gives for this is that in Romans 3:20 Paul meant to summarise his teaching in 1:18–3:19 that, although in theory someone could keep all the law, 'in practice no one is able to obey the law well enough so as to gain righteousness before God and so be accepted by him' (*Galatians,* p.349 – repeated in *The Epistle to the Romans*, p.369).

We greatly admire Longenecker, who is one of the greatest of modern New Testament scholars, but on this we believe he is mistaken and Dunn is right. As we will explain in our Romans commentary (see pages 107-18), Romans 1:16–3:19 is *not* about hypothetical non-existent ethically perfect people, but about two streams of humanity – the righteous and the sinners. Romans 3:10–18 is *not* a mass of misquoted Old Testament verses to 'prove' everyone is a sinner, but verses quoted in context to show that the nation of Israel (who *had* the social markers of circumcision, diets and Sabbaths) were castigated as a nation as much by the prophets as were the Gentiles (see pages 125–130). In that context Paul asserts in Romans 3:19 that, to those under the law, it speaks to make everyone accountable, and in Romans 3:20 Paul is saying that the social markers by which Jews set such store are not the signs that someone is right before God. This is perfectly consistent with Dunn's understanding, which we believe is fundamentally correct. In his later book, *The Epistle to the Romans*, Longenecker cites words in fragment 4QMMT of the Dead Sea Scrolls, that 'by doing works of the law you will be doing righteousness' as supposed evidence that to Jews the phrase meant deeds of the Law 'that were viewed in legalistic manner as gaining righteousness before God and so acceptance by Him' (p.368). This is unconvincing. Isaiah 56:1 speaks of 'doing righteousness' and going on to speak of Sabbath keeping without implying that Isaiah believed in 'works-righteousness'. In any case it would be a big jump to conclude from an isolated reference that the phrase was commonplace and was adopted by Paul in the same sense.

Of course Pharisees plainly could slide into legalism both in the sense of becoming bogged down in legalistic detail and in the sense of seeing detailed Torah-keeping as meritorious. But 'social markers' need not always imply some idea of 'merit' in a sense of clocking up credit points.

It is interesting to think about what 'social markers' different people see as indicating who are the 'people of God' we now call Christians. What would you look for in a 'good church' if moving to another area? As a church leadership what would you look for as the social marker of a 'good' church member? For some these markers are external. A 'good' church might be one with a particular creed, for example the Westminster Confession. A 'good' member in some churches might be one who tithes, attends regularly, is teetotal, abhors night clubs, dresses soberly and keeps Sunday Special (as a kind of Sabbath). In theory, of course, none of this is to amass 'merit', though we have been in churches where someone has got up to thank God they are not like the 'other men' outside church! Jesus, though, gave very different social markers of good Christian disciples:

> By this everyone will know that you are My disciples,
> if you have love for one another. (John 13:35)

Again this was not about 'merit', but about what was to show they were the people of God. To Jesus a good Christian is one showing love, and a good church is one on fire with the love of God overflowing into acts of compassion and service. Both these flow out of a close love relationship with God through Jesus.

This is at the core of the dispute between Jesus/Paul and the bulk of the Pharisees. To the Pharisees the key marker of a 'good' Jew (ie a good member of the people of God) was a strict adherence to the Torah as interpreted by the tradition of the elders. To Jesus and Paul it was faith working by love, and in the Christian era demonstrated by the fruit of the Spirit, not by external ritual and law keeping.

In summary, it is not all about how the individual can avoid hell and 'get right with God'. It is about what are the key social markers of the people of God – are they ritual 'works of the law' (in particular circumcision, diet and Sabbath keeping), or faith working by love (Galatians 5:6) and producing fruit of the Spirit?

Commentary

In the Discussion Topic above we explain why Longenecker's translation here is better than for example those of the NKJV or NASB which have 'faith *in* Jesus Christ' instead of 'faithfulness *of* Jesus Christ'. We are justified on the basis of what the Messiah has done, not on anything we have done, though as Christians we do appropriate this through faith *in* Him.

The 'we' in verse 15 continues from Paul's address to Peter in 2:14, and clearly means himself and Peter. Paul and Peter are Jews by birth, not 'sinners of the Gentiles'. It was a common (though not universal) assumption of Jews that Gentiles were automatically counted as 'sinners;' because they did not keep Torah (and usually came from idolatrous families) so they were not living in a way approved by God. Jews thought themselves 'justified' by works of the Law (*ergon nomou*), but for two reasons this does *not* imply that they thought that they *earned* the forgiveness of God through good works.

The first is that 'justification' does *not* mean *obtaining* forgiveness but being *shown to be* in a rightstanding with God and to be one of His people.

The second is that the 'works of the Law' that Jews thought showed they were God's people were not good works in general, but the specific markers of being Jewish, in particular circumcision, diet and Sabbaths. Dunn and N.T. Wright clearly bring out this meaning of the term. It is about the social markers of being God's people. It is not about merit (even if those social markers did often give Jews a feeling of superiority!), but about what shows that someone is a 'person of God.' So the key issue is whether this is demonstrated by these ceremonial 'works of the law' or by faith working in love.

So Paul says that he and Peter know that they are shown to be the people of God not by external rites but by faith *in* Messiah and the faithfulness *of* Messiah in His death and resurrection.

On justification, Dunn in *Jesus, Paul and the Law*, rightly remarks:

> In talking of 'being justified' here Paul is not thinking of a distinctively initiatory act of God. God's justification is not His act in first *making* His covenant with Israel, or in initially accepting someone into the covenant people. God's justification is rather acknowledgement that someone is in the covenant – whether that is as initial acknowledgement or a repeated action of God (God's saving acts), or His final vindication of His people. So in Galatians 2:16 we are not surprised when the second reference to being justified has a future implication ('by works of the law no flesh shall be justified . . .') and the third reference is in the future tense ('by works of the Law no flesh shall be justified'). (p.190)

Also, 'we are seeking to be justified' is in the present tense. Jesus the Messiah was 'delivered up for our sins and raised for our justification' (Romans 4:25). Through His faithfulness in doing this, those who have faith in Him are justified – shown to be in right relationship with God. But, of course, if it is by (or 'in') Messiah that they seek to be justified, this implies their acceptance that Gentiles are also 'in Christ'. Peter and Paul can no longer 'live like Jews' (at least according to the Judaisers who insist on separate eating and communion) – they have to associate closely with Christian Gentiles, and in the eyes of the strict Judaisers this makes them 'sinners', living unholy lifestyles.

In some Jewish eyes, then, it would mean that Messiah (and having faith in Him) has led them into a sinful lifestyle! But of course this is not so, as Paul goes on to explain.

Text 2:18–21

[18] For if what I have once destroyed I again build, I prove myself to be a transgressor. [19] For I through Law to Law died, that to God I may live. [20] With Messiah I have been crucified; and it is no longer I who live, but Messiah in me; and that which I now live in flesh I live by the faithfulness of the Son of God, who loved me and gave Himself over on behalf of me. [21] I do not set aside the grace of God, for if righteousness comes through Law, then Messiah died for nothing. (Our own translation)

Commentary

We have translated this passage quite literally here. The word 'for' (*gar*) at the start of both verses 18 and 19 links the verses to the denial that Messiah is a minister of sin, but the meaning in verse 18 is unclear. F.F. Bruce says, it could mean one of three things:

1. Speaking in the person of Peter trying to rebuild the 'social partition between Jews and Gentiles he had earlier broken down.'

2. Paul is 'now preaching the gospel he had once tried to eradicate.'

3. A rumour that Paul was still preaching circumcision.

We tend to think it is the first – a change of mind would mean that one way or another the person is shown to be a transgressor. Anyway, then Paul gives the real point. He is not saying 'abandon the guidance of Torah and live the life of a libertine'. He died to the Law by being identified in the crucifixion of Messiah, but this was *so that* he could live 'to God'. It is Messiah who lives in him, and the faithfulness which led Messiah to the cross will therefore be reflected in Paul's own behaviour. Paul does not 'set aside' the grace of God to live as libertine, rather he is living out the Messiah *in him*, and that Messiah is faithful and righteous. The Messiah is certainly not leading Christians into sin.

The genitive *'faith of the Son of God'*, like the genitives in 2:15–16 should surely be a subjective genitive: 'faithfulness *of* the Son of God'. The CEB correctly renders it 'faithfulness of God's Son, who loved me and gave Himself for me' (similarly in the ISV, JUB, NET, VOICE and KJV which has 'faith of the Son of God'). Why so few other versions take the genitive in this way (in its most natural meaning) is a mystery, because in this verse Paul even goes on to state in what this faithfulness consisted, ie that the Messiah loved him and gave Himself for him. Paul *is*, of course, living by his faith *in* Messiah (as well as by the faithfulness *of* Messiah), but that is not what it says in this verse.

Messiah died so that He could not only bring forgiveness but could live out life through us. If regulations could achieve the same end then His death was pointless.

Text 3:1–5

> [1] O You foolish Galatians, who has bewitched you, before whose eyes Jesus Christ was publicly portrayed as crucified? [2] This is the only thing I want to find out from you: did you receive the Spirit by the works of the Law, or by hearing with faith? [3] Are you so foolish? Having begun by the Spirit, are you now being perfected by the flesh? [4] Did you suffer so many things in vain—if indeed it was in vain? [5] So then, does He who provides you with the Spirit and works miracles among you, do it by the works of the Law, or by hearing with faith? (NASB)

Commentary

Paul appeals to their own Christian experience. The receiving of the Holy Spirit is a central part of the New Covenant, and they received it by faith and not by complying with circumcision, diet and Sabbaths. How, then, can they imagine that a legalistic way is the best way to go on to increased holiness? This is about being 'perfected' or 'completed', of course, not about 'getting right with God' (which they all accepted was through faith). So the Spirit is there to bring them to completeness and holiness, and how did they receive the Spirit? The Spirit is received by faith and, as Paul will later point out, bears fruit – it is not a matter of legalism and detailed regulations.

Questions for Thought and Discussion

- How often do we find that Christian leaders who founded a church movement are later supplanted by others who claim that the 'way forward' is a different way?

- How often is it that those who claim to be leading into 'deeper things' are actually contradicting the gospel first received?

- How can Christian leaders and missionaries try to avoid this?

Text 3:6–9

⁶ Even so Abraham believed God, and it was reckoned to him as righteousness. ⁷ Therefore, be sure that it is those who are of faith who are sons of Abraham. ⁸ The Scripture, foreseeing that God would justify the Gentiles [Lit. nations] by faith, preached the gospel beforehand to Abraham, saying, 'All the nations will be blessed in you.' ⁹ So then those who are of faith are blessed with Abraham, the believer. (NASB)

Commentary

Paul goes on to illustrate this in several other ways. First, in 3:6 he points out that Abraham had faith in God and it was counted to him, or reckoned to him, as rightstanding. Note again, this was *not* Abraham's conversion – by this time he had been walking in faith with God for at least a decade. So when it was wanted for him to show that he was in such a standing it was not through works of the law, but by faith. At this stage he had not even yet been circumcised. So those (whether circumcised or not) who have faith are blessed with Abraham, and are his true spiritual sons (both male and female believers, Jews and Gentiles, slave and free, have the status of 'sons').

Text 3:10–18

[10] For all who rely on the works of the law are under a curse; for it is written, 'Cursed is everyone who does not observe and obey all the things written in the book of the law.' [11] Now it is evident that no one is justified before God by the law; for 'The one who is righteous will live by faith.' [12] But the law does not rest on faith; on the contrary, 'Whoever does the works of the law will live by them.' [13] Christ redeemed us from the curse of the law by becoming a curse for us—for it is written, 'Cursed is everyone who hangs on a tree'— [14] in order that in Christ Jesus the blessing of Abraham might come to the Gentiles, so that we might receive the promise of the Spirit through faith.

[15] Brothers and sisters, I give an example from daily life: once a person's will has been ratified, no one adds to it or annuls it. [16] Now the promises were made to Abraham and to his offspring; it does not say, 'And to offsprings', as of many; but it says, 'And to your offspring', that is, to one person, who is Christ. [17] My point is this: the law, which came four hundred and thirty years later, does not annul a covenant previously ratified by God, so as to nullify the promise. [18] For if the inheritance comes from the law, it no longer comes from the promise; but God granted it to Abraham through the promise. (NRSVA)

Commentary

Verses 10–14, N.T. Wright rightly says, 'are notoriously difficult' (*Paul and the Faithfulness of God*, p.863) and they need detailed examination. One thing on which commentators like N.T. Wright, Dunn and others agree is that this is *not* about doing good works to earn salvation, it is very specifically about works of the Torah and the situation of Jews. The actual quotation in verse 10 seems to be loosely from Deuteronomy 27:26 and a similar curse is pronounced in Deuteronomy 28:15. Maybe, as Longenecker emphasises, the Judaisers were quoting these to encourage the Gentiles to keep Torah. But how exactly is Paul using them in his counter argument?

The most common understanding of the verse is that complete fulfilment of the Torah would be impossible. However, there is no intimation anywhere in this whole section of Deuteronomy that compliance with what God is asking will be impossible to achieve. The whole context is that Moses is urging them to turn to God and choose life; if it were impossible then either Moses was deluded or he was misleading them. Paul seems here to be contrasting those who are 'of faith' and those who are 'of the works of the law'. Those 'of faith' are sons of Abraham and share his blessing. If, on the other hand, someone is 'of the works of the law', then it can only bring a curse. So does this mean those who are relying on meticulous Torah keeping to develop and demonstrate holiness?

Certainly this was never intended to be the basis of relating to God in the Old Testament, even for those who had Torah. So in Galatians 3:11 Paul quotes (as in Romans) the key verse from Habakkuk 2:4,

> Behold the proud, his soul is not upright in him; but the just (righteous) shall live by his faith.

The Hebrew clearly means that this is how the righteous person should live, but is ambiguous as to whether the word *'ĕmûnâ* means faith or faithfulness. The LXX in different versions takes it either way – ie to live by his own faith or live by God's faithfulness. Paul uses neither the LXX nor the Hebrew, and omits the word 'his' to say literally: 'the righteous by faith shall live'. So did he mean: 'the righteous shall live by faith' (as NRSV, CEB, NIV, ESV, NKJV, NASB), or did he mean to change the meaning and say: 'He who through faith is righteous shall live' (RSV)? Well the original context in Habakkuk is not about how someone should *become* righteous, but about why the righteous are suffering and oppressed and the wicked seem to prosper. God's answer is that the righteous shall live by his faith/God's faithfulness even through the difficulties. In Hebrews 10:38 the same verse from Habakkuk is quoted identically, and the context in Hebrews is endurance through living by faith, just as in Habakkuk. We do not believe that Paul is totally twisting its meaning here in Galatians (nor when he cites the same verse in Romans 1:17). Rather he is making the point that the righteous person is said to be living not by 'works of the Law' but by faith. The modern confusion maybe comes because commentators wrongly thought 'justified' meant 'made righteous'. But, as we discussed above, it means to be shown to be living in right relationship, and so Paul takes it that a person is known to be righteous because he is the one living by faith. The works of the Law do not show this.

In the context, moreover, Habakkuk cannot be speaking purely prophetically of the era post-Messiah. The future tense of 'shall live by' relates to the point that this will continue when the fearsome Chaldeans invade.

Habakkuk has been complaining (1:4, 13) about the fate of the righteous in his own day, so a promise that some centuries later it will be all right after the Messiah comes would be totally inadequate. Habakkuk (in 3:19) himself rejoices that *'The Lord God is my strength, He will make my feet like deer's feet . . .'*

So, the righteous person lives by his faith, but in Galatians 3 is also shown to be righteous ('justified') through or 'out of' faith:

– those who are 'out of' (*ek*) faith are sons of Abraham (v7)

– those who are 'out of' (*ek*) faith are blessed like the having-faith Abraham (v9)

– the Old Testament righteous like Habakkuk shall live 'out of' (*ek*) faith (v11)

– in contrast the Law is not 'out of' (*ek*) faith

– those who are 'out of' (*ek*) 'works of the law' are under the curse it pronounces (v10).

Habakkuk was not told the righteous shall live *ek* works of the Torah, but *ek* faith. Abraham was not shown to be righteous *ek* works of the Torah but by faith. But if someone's reliance is on works of the Law then all this can really do is to bring upon people the curses that are in it – unless of course the recognition of their sin that it brings helps them to cast themselves on God in faith.

Old Testament Jews who were righteous were living by faith. Plainly, though, they were not sinless. Indeed the Torah made it clear to them that they were not. There were sacrifices for sin, but it is notable that when David for example is in the extremity of his guilt in Psalm 51 he does not rush off to do some works of the Law (though we presume he did keep Torah) but cries in anguish 'purge me . . . cleanse me . . .' He, in faith, casts himself on the mercy of God. Works of the law (in particular those demarcating his Jewish distinctiveness) did not bring him life nor form the centre of his spiritual life. Like Habakkuk (and Abraham) what did this was faith.

Paul, as a Pharisee, had an intense awareness of guilt from his inner covetousness (Romans 7). Righteous Old Testament Jews had the awareness of the curse pronounced in the Law, even if they also had the sense of forgiveness given them out of their faith. But now the Messiah has redeemed them from this. He took all the curses pronounced by the Law on Himself in dying on the cross (crucifixion was described as hanging on a tree and a curse on it was pronounced in Deuteronomy 21:23). The 'us' in verse 13 is 'us Jews' but then Paul extends it. In Messiah Jesus, the blessing of Abraham extends to the Gentiles and we all (Jews and Gentiles in Christ) have received the promised Holy Spirit through faith.

It is not exactly clear to which of God's promises to Abraham Paul refers in verse 16. The most obvious Old Testament reference where 'seed' is intended to be singular is in Genesis 22:

> [17] Indeed I will greatly bless you, and I will greatly multiply your seed as the stars of the heavens and as the sand which is on the seashore; and your seed shall possess the gate of [Lit. his] their enemies. [18] In your seed all the nations of the earth shall be blessed, because you have obeyed My voice. (NASB)

Many other promises to Abraham's 'seed' or 'offspring' (Genesis 12:7, 13:15, 15:18, 17:8, 24:7 etc) specifically refer to 'the land'. Galatians does not actually mention 'the land'. Romans 4:13 makes the promise to Abraham and his seed to inherit *the world* but that is not here in Galatians either. Hebrews 11:16 implies that Abraham (and other Old Testament faithful) were looking for a 'heavenly city'. This does not preclude it from also having immediate meaning about the literal country of Israel being given to the Jews. Likewise, for example in Hebrews 4, the writer speaks of the ultimate fulfilment of a promise that God's people would enter 'His rest' – but it also had an immediate reference to the Israelites.

However, in addition Abraham was promised:

> And in you all the families of the earth shall be blessed. (Genesis 12:3)

> Abraham will surely become a great and mighty nation, and in him all the nations of the earth will be blessed. (Genesis 18:18–19)

Is Galatians 3:14 saying that the promise of Abraham came to the Gentiles (or 'nations' – which is the same word as 'Gentiles') 'by' or 'in' Messiah? Galatians 3:16 seems to be saying that the promise to 'the seed' or 'the offspring' ultimately meant to the *one* seed, the Messiah – though of course *in* the Messiah are *both* Jews *and* Gentiles.

The Mosaic Law (Torah) came some 430 years later, and is not part of the means by which this blessing will come to Israel, nor to the nations – the blessing is through the Messiah not through the spread of Torah.

So the Gentiles are to be blessed because they receive the Spirit in faith, not because the Jews bring them Torah. The blessing is through the faithful death of Messiah, not through the Torah. This really contrasts with many Jewish attitudes at the time. Many Jews 'made their boast in the Torah' (Romans 2:23). Longenecker makes the point that contemporary Jewish writings as diverse as Philo, Josephus, Wisdom and Jubilees use phrases like 'the imperishable light of the Torah'. As Paul explored in Romans, many thought that it was the Torah that made them the light to the Gentiles. No wonder they thought that, having turned to God and been forgiven, the Gentiles would best adopt the works of the Law to express all this.

Text 3:19–25

[19] Why then the law? It was added because of transgressions until the Seed for whom the promise was made should come. And it was ordained by (through) angels by means of a mediator. [20] A mediator, however, does not represent just one party; but God is one!
[21] Is the Law, then, opposed to the promises of God? By no means! For if a law had been given that could give life, then righteousness would certainly have been on the basis of law. [22] But the Scripture confined everyone without distinction under sin, so that the promise that is based on the faithfulness of Jesus Messiah might be given to those who have faith. [23] Before this faith came, we were kept in custody under the law, being confined until this coming faith should be revealed. [24] The law, therefore, was our supervisory guardian (*paidagōgos*) until Messiah came, in order that we might be justified by faith. [25] But now that this faith has come, we are no longer under a supervisory guardian. (Longenecker's translation)

Discussion Topic: The *paidagōgos*

The *paidogōgos* was not exactly a tutor, but a respected slave appointed to keep a rich young man in order, and conduct him to lessons etc. Longenecker and others analyse this in depth. For those who were Jewish and became Christians the Torah was a *paidogōgos* to lead them to the Christian faith. Interestingly the picture is not of someone lost in sin and bound for hell until Christian conversion. The subject is an heir, a child of the family, given to the *paidagōgos* to lead him in the right way towards Messiah.

Paul is not explicit about the function of the Torah to, for example, David or Habakkuk – or Zechariah and Elizabeth, Simeon and Anna who almost certainly all died before Jesus' death and the coming of the Holy Spirit in power at Pentecost. They all seem to have experienced the Spirit, and clearly had a faith-life before the coming of *the faith*. Was the Torah a *paidagōgos* to lead them to the kind of Davidic Psalm-51-like plea: 'purge me, cleanse me . . .'? Can that *paidagōgos* role continue until that point in the resurrection when they see and recognise that it is in the Messiah that they are finally justified? (remember that in the biblical sense, justified means shown to be in rightstanding). Paul does not say either way because he is not addressing issues like these. Here in Galatians he is speaking to Jews who *have* become Christians.

In Romans, however, we have a much more general treatment of God's strategy in human history. In Romans, Paul is setting out his whole understanding of God's actions and ways, not firefighting to stop Christian converts sliding into legalism. So more of these general issues can be addressed in Romans.

Commentary

So why did God give the Law? An obvious question!

According to some Christian commentators the sole purpose of God giving the Torah was to show more clearly through the Jews the sinfulness of all people, and only when Christian faith arrived would anyone be all right. But this is not what Paul says.

The Law was a temporary measure until the arrival of the Messiah (3:19). It was added not to enhance the promise, but because of transgression. Abraham and the Patriarchs had a direct relationship with God and didn't need it. In a situation where not everyone had a vibrant relationship with God something would be needed to regulate society.

There is no certainty as to what exactly Paul is getting at regarding the angels in verses 19b–20, but here is our best guess! In the first century it seems to have been a Jewish view that angels were present at the giving of the Law (see also Acts 7:53, Hebrews 2:2 and Josephus, *Antiquities* 15:136). One suggestion is that some rabbis sought thereby to enhance its importance – some rabbis saw Psalm 68:17 as saying that myriads of angels were present enhancing the giving of the Law. So some commentators suggest maybe Paul is turning this against them by seeing it as *lowering* its glory (for details see the commentaries by Bruce and Longenecker). The 'mediator' is Moses, and of course he is a go-between for the two parties (Israel and God) – Israel do not have direct experience of God. In contrast the promise was given directly to Abraham by the One God without a mediator.

How could the Torah in itself give life? All it does is show our imperfections. Note that Paul does not say that Jews should not keep Torah. What he is saying is that:

1. The basis of being shown to be in rightstanding is the faithfulness of Messiah.

2. It is our faith not our rituals that demonstrates that we Christians are part of this.

The promise is given, through Messiah's faithfulness, to those who have faith. Dunn points out that the definite article in verses 23 and 25 means more specifically *this* (Christian) faith. This was not the coming of 'faith' because Abraham had faith and so did a whole list of others in Hebrews 11. There have always been those who had faith. But those to whom Paul is now writing are Jews who have accepted *this* (Christian) faith.

The *paidagōgos* was a respected slave appointed to keep a rich young man in order, and conduct him to lessons etc. For Paul, and the Jewish Christians to whom he writes, he sees this role as being done by Torah. Yet while they were under such a *paidagōgos* they would (as 4:1 indicates) be heirs and children of the master – even if not yet with full sonship privileges.

Questions for Thought and Discussion

- Do we sometimes still need 'rules' to bring us to Christ in our Christian lives?

- How can we balance this with the dynamics of a Spirit-led and Spirit-filled life?

Text 3:26–29

26 For you are all sons of God through faith in Christ Jesus. 27 For all of you who were baptized into Christ have clothed yourselves with Christ. 28 There is neither Jew nor Greek, there is neither slave nor free man, there is neither male nor female; for you are all one in Christ Jesus. 29 And if you belong to Christ, then you are Abraham's descendants, heirs according to promise. (NASB)

Commentary

In verse 26 it really *does* say 'the faith *in* Christ Jesus' (*tēs pisteōs en Christō Iēsou*) rather than 'faithfulness of Christ Jesus'. In saying 'you all' Paul now switches to *all* the Christians, Jew and Gentile. Now, as Christians, they are all sons – with the privileges of sons. We then get this amazing statement – no Jew nor Greek, slave nor free, male nor female. The Church does quite well with the Jew and Gentile bit today, but too often pretty poorly on the other two! How easy it is to make distinctions and give spiritual position to people based on their social ranking. How sad that some churches still stop women from doing any responsible job. Of course, yes, *all* the apostles chosen by Jesus were without exception Jewish, free and male – but this is not how it was meant to stay! Let us apply it consistently in our churches, not just on the Jew-Gentile issue.

So *all* Christians are Abraham's spiritual descendants and heirs according to the promise. Also remember, of course, that 'Christ' really means 'Messiah'. The concept of Jesus as the Jewish Messiah is central in all Paul's thinking – Christians are all in Messiah Jesus.

Text 4:1–7

[1] Now I say, as long as the heir is a child, he does not differ at all from a slave although he is owner of everything, [2] but he is under guardians and managers until the date set by the father. [3] So also we, while we were children, were held in bondage under the elemental things [Greek: *stoicheia*] of the world. [4] But when the fullness of the time came, God sent forth His Son, born of a woman, born under the Law, [5] so that He might redeem those who were under the Law, that we might receive the adoption as sons. [6] Because you are sons, God has sent forth the Spirit of His Son into our hearts, crying, 'Abba! Father!' [7] Therefore you are no longer a slave, but a son; and if a son, then an heir through God. (NASB)

Commentary

The 'elemental things' in 4:3, and also in 4:9, is the Greek word *stoicheia*. The term literally means first principles or elements, and the NASB margin has '*rudimentary teachings* or *principles*'. In *Grace in Galatia*, Ben Witherington well analyses its meaning in this context, and gives three possible interpretations:

1. **Heavenly bodies or some kind of spirits/angels:** This meaning however, has no linguistic support until over a century after Paul was writing. Moreover, Paul seems to apply the term in Galatians to the rules both of Jews and Gentiles. If the meaning is 'angels' in the good sense then this could apply to the Jewish law (Galatians 3:19) but could it really mean that (good) angels gave the Gentiles their regulations? On the other hand if the angelic beings are *demonic* then it would surely be unthinkable for Paul to (effectively) ascribe to ordinances of the Torah some kind of *demonic* association.

2. **The elements of earth, air, fire and water:** This meaning was in use at the time, and 2 Peter 3:12–16 uses the term three times in some such sense, but it would make no sense here.

3. **Elementary rules of conduct:** More commonly *stoicheia* is used by such as Plato, Aristotle, Xenophon and Philo to mean elementary principles. Hebrews 5:12 also uses the term for elementary teachings, not bad in themselves, but things for Christians to move beyond.

Witherington points out that Colossians 2:8 links *stoicheia* to philosophy and human traditions, and Colossians 2:21–22 makes it clear it means basic rules and regulations. So he rightly concludes:

> There are elementary teachings that are found throughout the world, and one form of these elementary teachings is the Mosaic Law. Jews were under one form of these elementary teachings, while Gentiles were under another, but both shared a common condition of being enslaved and under subjection because of these teachings. (*Grace in Galatia,* p.286)

The Torah had been given by God, but of course had been added to by the human 'traditions of the elders'. All rule-based systems were not wrong, but the Son of God Himself came to redeem people from them and move people beyond them. The term 'adoption' in English is a bit misleading. The Greek that is translated as 'adoption' means 'son-placing', coming into the full privileges of sons (a process which happened in Roman rather than Jewish law). In some senses this happened in the New Covenant, but in Romans 8:23 Paul pictures Christians as waiting for the final fulfilment of this at the end of the age.

In this new position of son-privilege, Christians have received the Spirit who makes them cry 'Abba Father' and is the guarantee of their inheritance or future adoption which has begun now (see also 2 Corinthians 5:5, Ephesians 1:14; Romans 8:23).

Text 4:8–11

> [8] However at that time, when you did not know God, you were slaves to those which by nature are no gods. [9] But now that you have come to know God, or rather to be known by God, how is it that you turn back again to the weak and worthless elemental things [Greek: *stoicheia*], to which you desire to be enslaved all over again? [10] You observe days and months and seasons and years. [11] I fear for you, that perhaps I have laboured over you in vain. (NASB)

Commentary

This is now to 'you' Gentiles who once *served those which are not really gods* – Paul no longer says 'we' as for the Jews. Their Gentile religion consisted of various ritual acts, sacrifices, and keeping various ritual rules. But now they have come through faith to know the true God and receive His Holy Spirit.

Yet, as Paul sees it, they are turning back to a set of elementary rules – Jewish ones not pagan, but in the end still slavery! It seems to us unlikely, as already indicated, that by the *stoicheia* he means some kind of spiritual forces. He is simply personifying the idea of elementary rules as used in legalism.

As Christians these Gentiles have 'known' God, as Longenecker notes: 'in the biblical sense of "to experience" . . . Galatian Christians had come to experience God in the intimacy of a family relationship.' (*Galatians*, p.180). How odd then to return to legalism of any kind.

Text 4:12–20

> [12] Friends [Lit. *brothers*], I beg you, become as I am, for I also have become as you are. You have done me no wrong. [13] You know that it was because of a physical infirmity that I first announced the gospel to you; [14] though my condition put you to the test, you did not scorn or despise me, but welcomed me as an angel of God, as Christ Jesus. [15] What has become of the goodwill you felt? For I testify that, had it been possible, you would have torn out your eyes and given them to me. [16] Have I now become your enemy by telling you the truth? [17] They make much of you, but for no good purpose; they want to exclude you, so that you may make much of them. [18] It is good to be made much of for a good purpose at all times, and not only when I am present with you. [19] My little children, for whom I am again in the pain of childbirth until Christ is formed in you, [20] I wish I were present with you now and could change my tone, for I am perplexed about you. (NRSVA)

Commentary

The 'brothers' (*adelphoi*) certainly now includes the Gentiles, but presumably here refers to the Galatian Christians in general. Witherington (though he sometimes seems to exaggerate) usefully points out how Paul uses different approaches recognised in formal Greek rhetoric in developing his various arguments. Here Paul tries personal pleas to his 'little children' for them to see sense.

Text 4:21–31

> [21] Tell me, you who desire to be subject to the law, will you not listen to the law? [22] For it is written that Abraham had two sons, one by a

slave woman and the other by a free woman. [23] One, the child of the slave, was born according to the flesh; the other, the child of the free woman, was born through the promise. [24] Now this is an allegory: these women are two covenants. One woman, in fact, is Hagar, from Mount Sinai, bearing children for slavery. [25] Now Hagar is Mount Sinai in Arabia and corresponds to the present Jerusalem, for she is in slavery with her children. [26] But the other woman corresponds to the Jerusalem above; she is free, and she is our mother. [27] For it is written,

> 'Rejoice, you childless one, you who bear no children,
> burst into song and shout, you who endure no birth pangs;
> for the children of the desolate woman are more numerous
> than the children of the one who is married.'

[28] Now you, my friends [Lit: *brothers*], are children of the promise, like Isaac. [29] But just as at that time the child who was born according to the flesh persecuted the child who was born according to the Spirit, so it is now also. [30] But what does the scripture say? 'Drive out the slave and her child; for the child of the slave will not share the inheritance with the child of the free woman.' [31] So then, friends, [Lit: *brothers*] we are children, not of the slave but of the free woman. (NRSVA)

Commentary

To Jews the term 'the Law' or 'Torah' could mean the set of rules and regulations, but could also mean what we call the Pentateuch or first five books of the Bible. Paul uses its double sense here, and takes the core story of Abraham in the book of Genesis and allegorises it. Ishmael represents Abraham's own fleshly effort to fulfil God's promise. Isaac is the genuine miracle son of the promise born by the power of the Spirit of God, and it is Isaac who is chosen as the line of promise. As we note in *God's Strategy in Human History*, none of this is to do with the personal eternal destiny of Isaac and Ishmael. God was with Ishmael as he grew up (Genesis 21:20) and he retained a son's duties at his father's burial (Genesis 25:9). But in the allegory, ironically, the flesh-effort birth is represented by the Jewish leaders in Jerusalem, while the child of promise by those (including Gentiles) who have faith like Abraham's! Sinai is outside the land of promise, and this is where the Torah was given. In Paul's day those who were Christians resting purely on the promise of God were persecuted by those who emphasized fleshly effort and legalism, just as Ishmael scoffed at Isaac (Genesis 21:9). So, the allegory shows the true heirs of Abraham are the Christians who have renounced any fleshly efforts.

Text 5:1–12

[1] For freedom Christ has set us free. Stand firm, therefore, and do not submit again to a yoke of slavery. [2] Listen! I, Paul, am telling you that if you let yourselves be circumcised, Christ will be of no benefit to you. [3] Once again I testify to every man who lets himself be circumcised that he is obliged to obey the entire law. [4] You who want to be justified by the law have cut yourselves off from Christ; you have fallen away from grace. [5] For through the Spirit, by faith, we eagerly wait for the hope of righteousness. [6] For in Christ Jesus neither circumcision nor uncircumcision counts for anything; the only thing that counts is faith working [or made effective] through love.

[7] You were running well; who prevented you from obeying the truth? [8] Such persuasion does not come from the one who calls you. [9] A little yeast leavens the whole batch of dough. [10] I am confident about you in the Lord that you will not think otherwise. But whoever it is that is confusing you will pay the penalty. [11] But my friends [Lit: *brothers*], why am I still being persecuted if I am still preaching circumcision? In that case the offence of the cross has been removed. [12] I wish those who unsettle you would castrate themselves! (NRSVA)

Discussion Topic: Jews and Torah Observance

Is Paul saying here that Jewish families should no longer circumcise their infants and can now eat bacon butties? No, this is not the context. The context is whether Gentile Christians need to be circumcised in order to go on further in holiness. When Paul later revisited the churches in South Galatia he found Timothy who was the son of a Jewish Christian woman (Acts

16:1). His father was Greek and he had never been circumcised, but as the son of a Jewish woman he would be considered Jewish. So Paul had him circumcised. Those like Titus and Trophimus, however, were *not* circumcised even though they went to Jerusalem (Galatians 2:3, Acts 21:29). Circumcision could be a sign of being Jewish, but it was faith and not circumcision that marked people off as being in Messiah. So we should not take Paul's words out of context. There is no indication that he believed that circumcising Timothy would make 'Christ 'of no benefit to him' (as Galatians 5:2).

In Acts 21 when Paul went to Jerusalem the Christian leaders there welcomed him and said:

> [20] You see, brother, how many thousands of believers there are among the Jews, and they are all zealous for the law. [21] They have been told about you that you teach all the Jews living among the Gentiles to forsake Moses, and that you tell them not to circumcise their children or observe the customs. (NRSVA)

The implication in their words was that Paul was not in fact saying that Jews should stop circumcising and keeping Torah. He *was* saying that *Gentiles* need not do this and that it was not a badge of being in rightstanding with God, but was *not* saying that the Jews should stop observing it.

Longenecker states this so well:

> Paul is not opposed to Jewish Christians living out their lives as circumcised individuals and in a nomistic fashion (cf 1 Cr 7:17–24; see also my *Paul, Apostle of Liberty.* 245–67). What he strenuously opposes is the imposition of circumcision and a nomistic lifestyle on Gentile believers as being necessary for living out their Christian faith in a proper fashion, for that takes us right back to the basic issue of righteousness (both forensic and ethical) as being based on either 'works

of the law' or faith in 'the faithfulness of Jesus Christ'
. . . For Gentiles to revert to the prescriptions of
Jewish law as a necessary form of Christian lifestyle
is, in effect, to make Christianity legalistic rather than
Christocentric, and so not to have Christ's guidance in
one's life. (*Galatians*, p.226)

Surely Jewish Christians today can circumcise their sons, and
keep Passover and Purim as part of their national heritage, just
as the British keep Remembrance Sunday. But when Brits keep
Remembrance Sunday they don't (or at least should not) imagine
that it somehow marks them out as special to God, or that Britain
has a special place in the future of Christianity (rather than, say,
South Korea). At a recent remembrance service the church of one
of the present writers also had a German helping lead the music,
the service was not nationalistic.

Discussion Topic: National Israel as the Chosen People

If Jews can continue to keep Torah, does the nation of Israel have
some special place in God's future plans separate from the Church?

This point is not addressed in Galatians, and we see no
evidence for it in either Galatians or Romans. The people of
God are now identified as the Christians, Jews and Gentiles
in the body of Messiah, and the distinguishing mark of them
is faith, irrespective of whether or not they keep works of the
law. These rituals served their purpose in bringing people to
Messiah, but why should they have any function beyond this?

Moreover, if national Israel (presumably some future Christian national Israel) has some future special part to play then would not some Gentile Christians want to opt in to that special part by becoming Jewish? Paul's whole theology is that the promise to Abraham that in his seed all nations would be blessed concerned the one Seed, Jesus the Messiah, and that national Israel would bless the world through him.

Some suggest that, for example Hosea 3:4–5 or Ezekiel 20:34 or Isaiah 11:11–12 prophesy that Jews will retake the land area of Israel. Well, they have already retaken the land area, and did it *without* national repentance and turning to Messiah, yet such returns are usually conditional on repentance and turning back to God. In Isaiah 11 it seems to be in context of the New Heaven and Earth where the wolf dwells with the lamb. Prophecies (such as the prophecy of Jonah that Nineveh will be destroyed) are often conditional, and not easy to be sure of in meaning.

Discussion Topic: The Value of Torah

Sometimes commentators claim that Paul's attitude towards Torah is more negative in Galatians, whereas in Romans 8 he can speak of the 'Torah of the Spirit of Life'. This is misleading. The Torah in Galatians has the positive function of leading to Christ – but while Jews were still under this they were children of God's household though not having the privileges of Sons. Where Paul sees Torah negatively is specifically when it is presented to Gentile Christians as a way into greater holiness. Like all other moral/ritual codes (or *stoicheia*) it cannot give life or make holy, it can only guide people towards the God with whom relationship gives rightstanding.

Commentary

Here Paul is extending his earlier comments. How about just getting circumcised and not doing all the Law? Well he sees this as pointless. If you are in Messiah (in Christ) what is the point of circumcision?

Again we reemphasize, none of this is about earning an individual ticket to a spiritual heaven. This may have been Luther's Reformation preoccupation but it is just not how first century Jewish people thought. The 'Judaisers' did not deny that the Gentile Christians had been accepted by God and received the Spirit through faith and *without* circumcision. The issue was how to *live out* being part of God's covenant people. This did not mean a sinless life. James Dunn in his commentary on Galatians rightly states:

> No Jew that we know of thought of the Jewish way of life as a *perfect* life, that is, without any sin or failure. Rather, it was a *total* way of life which, through the cult, its sacrifices and atonement, provided a means of dealing with sin and failure. (*The Epistle to the Galatians,* p.266)

Circumcision, Dunn claims, was naturally seen by most Jews as a step in an adoption of a fully Jewish lifestyle. This (they believed) was how to *live out* being God's people. Again we repeat (because a mistaken view of the term is so deep-seated in many people's thinking) the word 'justified' does *not* mean being *made* right with God, but being *shown to be* in a rightstanding with God. They were thinking that in order to be shown or demonstrated to be in such a rightstanding Gentiles needed to adopt the Torah practises. The 'hope' is not a vague 'hope for the best' of course, but an assured expectation. The 'hope of righteousness' is an ongoing thing, dynamic but with a culmination. The Spirit is the guarantee of our inheritance (Ephesians 1:14), and the love we experience through the Spirit is associated with our hope (Romans 5:5). Dunn says:

> Clearly expressed here is the 'future tense' of justification – to be justified/counted acceptable to God, not simply as an initial act (conversion) but as a sustained relationship with God culminating in the favourable verdict of the final judgement. (p.269, see also F.F. Bruce *The Epistle to the Galatians,* p.231)

In Jesus the Messiah circumcision is irrelevant. The key to living out being the people of God is 'faith working through love'. Faith is not just a set of beliefs but something dynamic, working out in practice through love (Galatians

5:6). In Galatians 5:14 Paul will make it clear that if the faith that works by love really is operating then the real meaning of the Torah and its moral centre (though not its literal rituals) will be fulfilled. Moreover, he will go on to say that if it really is such a faith then there will be fruit of the Spirit.

Those commentators who have wrongly thought 'justification' meant being made right with God at conversion have therefore sometimes mistakenly seen James and Paul as in tension. Actually, as repeatedly noted, being 'justified' means to be *shown to be* in rightstanding with God. Throughout someone's life they show this by living in a faith that works by love. But how are we to recognise such a faith? James 2:18 says that such a faith is demonstrated by acts of Christ-like compassion (not of course by ritual 'works of the Law' like circumcision, diet and Sabbaths). How do we know if someone really has the Holy Spirit living in them? Later in this chapter Paul will say that we should see some fruit of the Spirit in them. So there is no tension between James and Paul.

The one who calls (or names) them is God, and it is not from God that this obsession with legalism comes.

Questions for Thought and Discussion

- How easy is it for holiness movements to slide into legalism?

- Do people who are legalistically 'holy' have attractive personalities?

- How can we avoid legalism without becoming sloppy and libertine?

Text 5:13–15

> [13] For you were called to freedom, brothers and sisters; only do not use your freedom as an opportunity for self-indulgence [Lit: the flesh], but through love become slaves to one another. [14] For the whole law is

summed up in a single commandment, 'You shall love your neighbour as yourself.' [15] If, however, you bite and devour one another, take care that you are not consumed by one another. (NRSVA)

Commentary

In their Christian faith they have liberty. But this certainly does *not* mean that Paul is saying that as long as they believe then their lifestyle is unimportant. The 'imputation of righteousness' is a central Lutheran idea. This is that the righteousness of Christ is imputed to Christians, or as some have put it, when God looks at us he sees only the righteousness of Christ. Another way to put it is that the ethical perfection of Jesus is ascribed to us. Any such idea is foreign to Paul's thinking as we look at in the commentary on Romans 4:1–8 on pages 137–143). This is not now talking about Messiah fulfilling the Law for them, it is *they* who will fulfil the Law – though not the ritual 'works of the Law' but its true meaning: circumcision of the heart not the body, separation by holiness not by diet, and resting in God through being bound in relationship not by observing Sabbath. In verse 13, the NRSV phrase 'become slaves to one another' is not an improvement on the RSV (and others) 'serve one another'. If you love your neighbour as yourself you do have to love yourself first, and becoming a slave to self-centred Christians is not doing this. Serving each other in love is, however, at the very heart of it.

Sadly, often those within the church who have become legalistic and effectively self-righteous (though they may 'thank God that they are not like other men' as the Pharisee did in Luke 18:11!), they do bite and devour one another. (Probably this is also what Paul means by the 'Law of Christ' in 6:2 – it is all about mutual love.)

Text 5:16–26

[16] But I say, walk by the Spirit, and you will not carry out the desire of the flesh. [17] For the flesh [Lit: lusts against] sets its desire against the Spirit, and the Spirit against the flesh; for these are in opposition to one another, so that you may not do the things that you [Lit: wish] please. [18] But if you are led by the Spirit, you are not under the Law. [19] Now the deeds of the flesh are evident, which are: [sexual] immorality, impurity, sensuality, [20] idolatry, sorcery, enmities, strife, jealousy, outbursts of anger, disputes, dissensions, factions, [21] envying, drunkenness, carousing, and things like these, of which

I forewarn you, just as I have forewarned you, that those who practice such things will not inherit the kingdom of God. [22] But the fruit of the Spirit is love, joy, peace, patience, kindness, goodness, faithfulness, [23] gentleness, self-control; against such things there is no law. [24] Now those who belong to Christ Jesus [Lit: *are of Christ Jesus*] have crucified the flesh with its passions and desires. [25] If we live by the Spirit, let us also walk by the Spirit. [26] Let us not become boastful, challenging one another, envying one another. (NASB)

Commentary

Paul here in Galatians 5:16 uses a favourite metaphor – *walk* by the Spirit. The 'flesh' in these verses represents focusing on the purely human – whether in self-indulgence or in self-effort and legalism. The 'works of the flesh' are all kinds of bad things. But if we really have the Spirit then it produces the famous fruit (singular) of love, joy, peace, etc. We have a choice how to walk, and 6:7 will give a warning about the consequences of our choice.

Commentaries give detailed analysis of the Greek words for each of these 'deeds of the flesh', but we can pick them up well enough even in translation. We all know that things like adultery and lewdness are fleshly things, but also contention, jealousies, selfish ambition, and dissension – which are all too common in churches. The fruit of the Spirit is good in all social situations: home, church and work. It is interesting to read through the Ten Commandments (Exodus 20:3–17 or Deuteronomy 5:7–21) – arguably, someone could actually fulfil *all* of these without exhibiting *any* of the fruit of the spirit! Paul has said (Galatians 5:14) that all the law is fulfilled through the one command 'love your neighbour as yourself' and Jesus picked out both this and 'love God with everything' as core. But the fruit of the spirit is all to do with outworking this in sweetness of character, and gentleness of spirit.

Against this fruit 'there is no law'. If someone is really walking in and by the Spirit they do not need detailed regulations, but their characters and actions indicate whether they are walking in the right way. The Spirit can lead us in actions specific to a given situation in a way that even the most detailed regulations could not.

In verse 25, the Greek text does not actually say 'walk by the spirit' but 'be in line with (*stoichomen*) the Spirit' so Paul is accepting a kind of *stoichaea,* or 'elementary principle' (see pages 47–8), but only insofar as it is bound up with a Spirit-related walk.

Questions for Thought and Discussion

- Is it a good thing to make the Ten Commandments prominent for Christians?
- You may be keeping all of them, but how are you doing on the fruit of the Spirit?

Text 6:1–5

[1] Brethren, even if anyone is caught in any trespass, you who are spiritual, restore such a one in a spirit of gentleness; each one looking to yourself, so that you too will not be tempted. [2] Bear one another's burdens, and thereby fulfil the law of Christ. [3] For if anyone thinks he is something when he is nothing, he deceives himself. [4] But each one must examine his own work, and then he will have reason for boasting in regard to himself alone, and not in regard to another. [5] For each one will bear his own load. [6] The one who is taught the word is to share all good things with the one who teaches him. (NASB)

Commentary

This just repeats and emphasizes Paul's point. If someone is in error then any correction should be in a spirit of gentleness. Gentleness is important in the fruit of the Spirit – but how often is indignation and anger apparent rather than gentleness. All too often in churches, correction or disagreement can be in a spirit of self-righteous indignation! Church life should be a sharing of burdens. In this way we do fulfil a kind of 'law' but it is the law of Messiah. Spiritual arrogance and a belief that one has a hot-line to God can be a real danger in church life. Paul is not saying that we simply ignore it if a brother or sister is in a moral lifestyle error, but that our attitude should always be gentleness and concern and not self-righteousness or spiritual pride.

Text 6:7–10

> [7] Do not be deceived, God is not mocked; for whatever a man sows, this he will also reap. [8] For the one who sows to his own flesh will from the flesh reap corruption, but the one who sows to the Spirit will from the Spirit reap eternal life. [9] Let us not lose heart in doing good, for in due time we will reap if we do not grow weary. [10] So then, while we have opportunity, let us do good to all people, and especially to those who are of the household of the faith. (NASB)

Discussion Topic: Legalism, Libertinism and Liberty

In Christian faith it is clear that forgiveness for sin is based on Christ's atoning death, and we can do nothing to earn it. The 'traditional' understanding of 'salvation by works' is that by doing good deeds a person can earn God's forgiveness and acceptance. In the UK this is often a kind of do-it-yourself folk religion – *I've not lived a bad life so hopefully God will accept me*. Traditionally Christians have seen the religion of the Pharisees as a kind of extreme version of this. This, of course, safely removes it from any of our bible-believing churches! But in reality the Pharisees' mistakes were far nearer to home.

In the history of the Judeo-Christian faith there have been two opposite extremes. On the one hand there have been those who effectively believe that as long as you fulfil certain conditions (either particular rites, or assent to a correct set of theological beliefs), a moral lifestyle is non-essential. In Christian expressions of this, either through 'going to confession' or from belief that Jesus died for us, the ticket to heaven is available irrespective of lifestyle.

On the other hand, Christian holiness movements have reacted against this – just as Paul did in both Galatians 6 and Romans 6, where the 'wages of sin is death' and you 'reap what you sow' are both addressed to Christian believers. Such holiness movements have been spearheaded, for example by Pelagius, the Anabaptists, John Wesley, Phoebe Palmer, the Brethren movement and Charles Finney, as well as various others throughout Christian history. The problem is that such movements always have the danger of degenerating into legalism. This is not a view that by keeping certain rules a Christian can earn God's forgiveness, but rather that a good Christian lifestyle consists in keeping a long list of rules. These might include Old Testament rules such as tithing and keeping the Sabbath (sometimes renamed the 'Lord's Day'), but also a list of **don'ts,** like dancing, wearing makeup, drinking any alcohol, wearing jewellery, etc. These sometimes become considered to be 'markers' of being in good standing in the Christian community.

The Pharisees were the heirs of a heroic holiness movement. Many of their Messianic hopes and aspirations were good – and Paul still identifies himself with this in Acts 23:6. Unfortunately they too often lapsed into a legalistic emphasis on meticulous keeping of the Law, particularly the ceremonial Laws, as elaborated in their 'traditions of the elders'. So in the gospels we read of them criticising Jesus' disciples: *For the Pharisees and all the Jews do not eat unless they wash their hands in a special way, holding the tradition of the elders* (Mark 7:5), and finally deciding to kill Jesus because he rejected their uncaring interpretation of the Sabbath laws (Mark 3:6). Jesus savagely criticises them in Matthew 23:

> [23] 'Woe to you, scribes and Pharisees, hypocrites! For you tithe mint, dill, and cummin, and have neglected the weightier matters of the law: justice and mercy and faith. It is these you ought to have practised without neglecting the others. [24] You blind guides! You strain out a gnat but swallow a camel!

²⁵ 'Woe to you, scribes and Pharisees, hypocrites! For you clean the outside of the cup and of the plate, but inside they are full of greed and self-indulgence. ²⁶ You blind Pharisee! First clean the inside of the cup, so that the outside also may become clean. (NRSVA)

Meticulous keeping of the rules as elaborated in their traditions was considered to be the key marker in recognising someone as a godly person. Love, mercy and compassion coming from the heart were too often absent. This being so, their religion was 'play acting' – the meaning of the Greek *hypokritai*.

Jesus said that his followers' righteousness had to exceed this (Matthew 5:20) to get into the Kingdom! Not that they had to keep the rules more assiduously, but that they had to exhibit the more fundamental things which show that the love of God is in them (or Paul might have said the fruit of the Spirit).

So the Jesus/Paul answer is neither Libertinism nor Legalism but Christian Liberty. A vibrant faith-relationship with God, and in the New Covenant the indwelling Spirit, results in fruit of the Spirit in a person's life. That fruit is Christ-likeness because Christ is in them. This does not mean ethical perfection, but consistently the New Testament says: *Let no one deceive you. He who practices righteousness is righteous, just as He is righteous* (1 John 3:7). The marker of this, as John also says, is that the love of God in them is reflected in their demonstrated love for others (1 John 3:17 etc).

Commentary

Note that this warning in Galatians 6:7 about reaping what you sow is said to Christians, though it does apply more generally. But those Christians who walk in the flesh (either fleshly self-effort or fleshly self-indulgence) will reap failure and corruption, those who sow by walking in the Spirit reap everlasting life. This is a quality of life, not a ticket to a spiritual heaven.

This noticeably mirrors Deuteronomy 30:

> [19] I call heaven and earth to witness against you today that I have set before you life and death, blessings and curses. Choose life so that you and your descendants may live, [20] loving the Lord your God, obeying Him, and holding fast to Him; for that means life to you and length of days, so that you may live in the land that the Lord swore to give to your ancestors, to Abraham, to Isaac, and to Jacob. (NRSVA)

Love God, hold fast to or cling to him – that is the secret of life. In the New Covenant this means choosing to walk in the spirit, but it is always a human choice. Let us not weary in doing good – Christians are to do 'good works' if you like, but these are not 'works of the Law', nor works of self-effort. They are good works flowing from love relationship with God and His indwelling Spirit.

We are to do good to everyone, but especially to Christians. We share with them a household, we are family. In Ephesians 2:19 Paul refers to the 'household of God'. We are part of God's faith-family.

Questions for Thought and Discussion

- Does the gospel of grace mean that our lifestyle is unimportant?

- How is the repeated warning that judgement is based on lifestyle to be balanced with the forgiveness and life we find in Jesus the Messiah?

Text 6:11–18

[11] See what large letters I make when I am writing in my own hand!
[12] It is those who want to make a good showing in the flesh that

try to compel you to be circumcised—only that they may not be persecuted for the cross of Christ. [13] Even the circumcised do not themselves obey the law, but they want you to be circumcised so that they may boast about your flesh. [14] May I never boast of anything except the cross of our Lord Jesus Christ, by which the world has been crucified to me, and I to the world. [15] For [other ancient authorities add *in Christ Jesus*] neither circumcision nor uncircumcision is anything; but a new creation is everything! [16] As for those who will follow this rule—peace be upon them, and mercy, and [Greek: *kai*] upon the Israel of God.

[17] From now on, let no one make trouble for me; for I carry the marks of Jesus branded on my body.

[18] May the grace of our Lord Jesus Christ be with your spirit, brothers and sisters. Amen. (NRSVA)

Commentary

Jews often tended to 'boast in the Law' (Romans 2:23). The Jewish Christians ('those who are circumcised') did not even keep all the Law, at least as it was understood in contemporary traditions. But Paul wants only to boast in the cross of Messiah.

No ritual or symbol counts for anything in Christ, just a new creation. These are wonderful words.

Paul has spoken of a physical Jerusalem and a spiritual Jerusalem. Now he speaks of an 'Israel of God'. This is the only time he uses the word 'Israel' in Galatians. The Jews in Galatians are Christian Jews, and, unlike in Romans, Paul has not dealt at all with the situation of national Israel. Plainly here, then, the 'Israel of God' does not mean national Israel as this would be totally out of context.

So it could mean one of three other things:

1. All those who have been and are in right relationship with God (before and after Christ).

2. All Jews who do and will believe in their Messiah.

3. All those who are in Messiah (Jews and Gentiles).

Apart from possibly Romans 11:26 (see below on page 245) 'Israel' is never applied to the Church, so could it be option 2, ie just the Jewish Christians? Well, Longenecker in *Galatians* rightly notes that the whole Galatian context is that circumcision avails nothing, so it would be odd to single out believing Jews as 'Israel of God' rather than all Christians. The immediate past context in verse 15 was precisely that 'in Christ Jesus' circumcision makes no difference. The *kai* in verse 16 could mean (as it often does) 'even' rather than 'and' so it could read 'even upon the Israel of God'. The Israel of God would then be those who 'walk according to the rule' that 'in Messiah Jesus neither circumcision nor uncircumcision count for anything but a new creation'. This probably means that all those in the Messiah and who accept that circumcision makes no difference, ie option 3 of these alternatives. It could just possibly be option 1, if we assume that ultimately all those justified through faith in God will be placed 'in Christ'.

So Paul finishes his letter as he began, with grace and peace. But the peace is specifically on those who follow the rule of faith working by love, rather than seeking holiness through ceremonial works of the Law. These are the true Israel of God.

The Letter to the Romans

Introduction to Romans

Commentaries

CEB Cranfield and James Dunn have each produced two-volume analytical or 'critical' commentaries that look in detail at the text, though neither is easy to read without some knowledge of New Testament Greek. Cranfield often lists succinctly all the alternatives suggested for points of controversy, but unfortunately we too often found that he then picks one that does not make the most sense of the context. Dunn's *Word Biblical Commentary* is the critical commentary which in our view remains generally the best and makes the most sense of the text. *Paul's Letter to the Romans* by Hultgren is a large single-volume critical commentary which gives some historical insights. Another one-volume commentary is by Robert Jewett, and the earlier one by Jospeh Fitzmyer gives a modern Catholic perspective. Leon Morris and Colin Kruse each offer fairly traditional large one-volume commentaries for those without any New Testament Greek, though at many points we don't believe that their traditional accounts fit the text. Glen Davies (now Archbishop of Sydney, with a reputation as a theological conservative) in *Faith and Obedience in Romans* brings out well that Romans1:18 and following verses is *not* about 'universal sinfulness', which would fit neither the text nor the Old Testament verses cited.

N.T. Wright's larger 2002 commentary, and of course his many books on Paul, have some good points of insistence, for example on the 'faithfulness of Jesus the Messiah'. We cannot, however, follow his insistence that God's righteousness is virtually exclusively to do with his specific covenants, or his apparent implication that saving faith came only with Christian faith (if this isn't what Wright means in *Paul and the Faithfulness of God* he does not make this clear). In some ways N.T. Wright is radical but in others seems simply to follow tradition. Wright's 2015 *Paul and his Recent Interpreters* outlines in context major changes in Pauline scholarship over the twentieth century. Some of the many crazy versions of Paul are also exploded in his volume 1 of *Paul and the Faithfulness of God*.

Abasciano's two commentaries are useful detailed critical commentaries that can be recommended. They cover Romans 9:1–9 (2005) and 9:10–18 (2011) and another volume is coming on verses 19–24. They particularly look at the Old Testament contexts from which Paul quotes.

The Epistle to the Romans by Richard Longenecker (2016) is a massive (1140 page) single-volume critical commentary. It is highly technical in its linguistic analysis, and thorough in its presentation of diverse viewpoints. On some issues (for example 'the faithfulness of Jesus the Messiah') Longenecker strongly supports and expands positions we have long held. On others (such as the meaning of 'works of the Law', the meaning of 'all Israel will come in', and the unexplained change from God's wrath being against 'those who suppress the truth' to being against 'humanity') we find his rationale unconvincing. Much detail is valuable, though it is hard in reading the work to retain sight of the wood for the trees in the flow of Romans.

Throughout the ages, various commentaries (for example Luther, Calvin, Hodge, Haldane, Kruse, Lloyd-Jones, Murray, Moo, Sproule and Schreiner) take what can loosely be called a Reformed line and arrive at an Augustinian/Calvinistic God, who frankly we could not follow. Some older commentaries, like Beet and Sanday & Headlam have a good spirit, though of course lack some of the later scholarship. Barth often seems to ignore the cultural context, though the Barthian Brunner actually does look at what the text really says. The Lutheran Kasemann takes a different view of God's righteousness as God's saving activity which we don't find convincing, although neither do we agree with Wright and Talbert that it is virtually exclusively covenant faithfulness.

We have read many other and smaller commentaries which are listed in the bibliography, some of which make some valid points, but we are not going to cite or quote them. Most of the actual citations and quotations we make will be from Cranfield, Dunn or Longenecker, but of course some of the ideas we look at (and often dismiss!) come from various others.

There are many other books on Paul, such as those by J.C. Beker, Ben Witherington III and Jakob Van Bruggen, which contain insights, but again we will not be citing them much in this work.

Quite a number of the points and reasoning we sketch here are contained in much greater depth in our previous works: *Reason, Science and Faith* (2000) and *God's Strategy in Human History* (2 vols, 2014), and these will also be cited.

The Background of the Letter to the Romans

The Church in Rome

The church in Rome was not founded by Paul, and up to this point he had not been there. In Romans 1:15 and 15:24, 28, however, he shows how he thought it a strategic centre for world evangelism. We don't know who started the church in Rome, but it probably happened soon after Pentecost in Acts 2, as there must surely have been Jewish people there who came from Rome and became Christian converts. In Acts 18 (c50 AD) we find that Aquila and Priscilla had left Rome because the Emperor Claudius had expelled all Jews from there. The later Roman historian Suetonius says this was because of riots instigated there by 'Chrestus' (ie Christ), and this is placed at 49 AD. Paul lived and worked with Aquila and Priscilla, and greets them in Romans 16:3, so by that time they had evidently returned. He was then, probably quite well informed about the Roman church context. It may be that from 49–54 AD when Claudius died and Nero allowed Jews to return, there was a purely Gentile church left in Rome. Yet when Paul eventually arrives there in (we believe) around Spring 58 AD, he calls together what seem to be non-Christian Jewish leaders to preach to them (Acts 28:17). Maybe the church had not yet made a great impact on the returned Jewish community. In *The Mystery of Romans*, Mark Nanos argues that Paul never gave up the two-step approach 'to the Jew first and also to the Gentile' (Romans 1:16), and saw the natural root for evangelism to come through the restored Jewish community – even if in practice the Jewish reaction was always mixed.

Anyway, when Paul wrote, the Rome church was a mixed Jew/Gentile community, but the Gentiles predominated (1:5–7; 1:12–14; 4:1,16; 11:13; 11:28–31; 15:16). Romans 7:1, however, makes it clear that they are people who know the Jewish Law, the Torah, and Paul makes it a basis for a theological point there.

The Jewish community in Rome at this time was quite large, maybe 40–50,000 (many of them Roman citizens like Paul) and they had special privileges under Roman law. The Church at this time was generally considered in terms of a small Jewish sect. When Paul reached Rome (Acts 28:17) he almost immediately called the Jewish leaders to come to hear him speak, as throughout Acts he always saw the Jewish community as the natural place to begin with the gospel – again 'to the Jew first and also to the Gentile'. The

Jewish leaders' reaction shows that until this time there had been no particular friction between the Christian church and the Jewish community there. They had heard of 'this sect' and wanted to hear more. Their reactions, as always, were divided, and so Paul declared that the salvation gospel would go to the Gentiles who would listen (28:28).

Date and Occasion

By the time of his letter to the Romans, Paul had been a missionary for twenty years. He was originally sent out from the very Jewish church in Antioch (Acts 13:1–3) but had moved into Europe (Acts 16:10) where in Macedonia his key convert was a Gentile businesswoman named Lydia whose home became his first European Christian hub. His activities then ranged from Ephesus back in Asia across to Macedonia, Athens and Corinth.

The letter to the Romans was most likely written from Corinth. Acts 20:2–4 places Paul in Greece for three months, and he had a 'Gaius from Derbe' and Timothy among others with him. The Gaius may have been the one baptised in 1 Corinthians 1:14 and his 'host' when he wrote the Romans letter (16:23). Paul also sends Timothy's greetings (16:21) as well as greetings from Erastus, who was a City Treasurer and in 2 Timothy 4:20 is said to be still in Corinth. The letter to Rome is carried by Phoebe, a lady who was a Minister in a church in the Corinthian port of Cenchrea (16:1). All this points to the letter being written in Corinth, while Paul was staying there for those three months. At that time he hoped to visit Rome with a view to going on to Spain in his evangelistic programme (1:1, 13, 15; 15:20–22, 24, 28). He had completed a collection for the Jerusalem Christians as part of a plan to further cement together the Jewish and Gentile elements in the church (15:25) and wanted the prayers of the Christians in Rome. This is all that Paul himself indicates about his motives for writing, though Morris and Hultgren for example both go through a dozen different views of scholars on this! The date of writing is in Winter/early Spring either of 55–56 or 56–57 (and for this see also Cranfield, *A Critical and Exegetical Commentary on The Epistle to the Romans*).

The letter is not a complete and systematic theology. For example, it contains nothing about the communion service (as in Corinthians) and nothing about marriage (as in Corinthians and Ephesians). Nevertheless it is a deliberately structured treatise dealing with God's salvation strategy in human history and some major practical implications of this in personal and church life. The Jewish-Gentile issues and the standing of the Jewish nation must have been heavy in his mind as he prepared for his crucial Jerusalem visit and was probably uncertain of his reception there.

The date of Paul's letter to the Galatians is uncertain, but as explained in the Introduction, it seems to us that most likely it was written to churches in Southern Galatia and around 50 AD just before the council of Jerusalem in 51 AD. At that Council of Jerusalem some Pharisee Christians were arguing that the Gentiles needed to be circumcised in order to be saved (Acts 15:5). The church leaders ruled that the Gentile Christians needed only to abstain from food offered to idols, from blood and from fornication (15:29). But there were rumours and misrepresentations of what Paul was teaching. One absurd one was that people should do evil that good may come (Romans 3:8). Another was that Paul was teaching Jews 'to forsake Moses, not to circumcise their children or observe the customs' (Acts 21:21). Maybe there were also rumours that he was now teaching that it was all right to eat meat offered to idols in contradiction of the Jerusalem council letter. On this latter issue the Corinthian church had apparently asked him and when he wrote to them around 53–54 AD he seemed to imply it was unimportant (1 Corinthians 8). This part of the Council of Jerusalem letter was repeated in Acts 21:23 when James and the Jerusalem elders (in spite perhaps of Paul's fears) welcomed him warmly and advised him how to quash the rumours about him.

These issues colour the background of the Romans letter. In it Paul covers the Jew-Gentile issues: the meaning of the choice of Israel, the purpose of the Torah and the basis of salvation. These concerns also come through when he deals with the practical level. In Romans 13:9–10 he reiterates the Ten Commandments (though omits the one about the Sabbath which was specifically to the Jews), but points out that basically they are all implied by love. In chapter 14 he looks for a way to keep Jews with their practices (Sabbaths and dietary laws) in the church alongside Gentiles: mutual toleration on issues of symbolism. Paul did know some people (Jews and Gentiles) in Rome as chapter 16 shows, but in view of the general issues in his mind at the time we do not need to suppose that they had told him that any of the matters he would raise were particular problems at Rome – this is nothing like the situation with the Corinthian or Galatians letters which were to deal with issues very specific to those churches. If his comments on civil authority in chapter 13 had particular significance in Rome, nevertheless they were issues common throughout the empire.

Paul, uncertain of his reception in Jerusalem, is setting out systematically his gospel and teachings. Why write to the Roman Christians in particular about this? As already mentioned, he was planning a mission to Spain, and irrespective of what support he received from Jerusalem he wanted their prayers and practical support in this further mission.

Context of the Letter

Paul was dictating a letter to be publically read aloud to the various churches. They knew basics of the Torah, like the marriage Laws (7:1) which incidentally still form the background to Paul's advice on divorce in 1 Corinthians 7. However, some of the jumps in reasoning commentators have argued that Paul expected his hearers to make seem highly improbable. The suggestion, for example, that in Romans 7 Paul *really* is talking not about himself but of Adam seems a ridiculous jump to expect hearers to make when the text gives no indication of this, and he gives no indication of such an idea in any other letter. He may, of course, have had the Adam story as a background to his own experience of a first sin, but this is a different suggestion.

On the other hand we should also remember that by this time Paul had written to the Galatians and Corinthians. He had spent 18 months living with Aquila and Priscilla in Corinth, and they went with him to Ephesus where at some stage he wrote back to Corinth including their greetings (1 Corinthians 16:19). They were both expert enough in Jewish-Christian theology to be able to train the converted Hellenistic Jewish Rabbi Apollos (Acts 18:24–6). They will have been familiar with Paul's thinking as expressed in his earlier letters, and on hand to explain some things in Romans which earlier letters had given in more depth. Aquila and Priscilla and others who knew the Old Testament Scriptures seem to have shared their knowledge with the church in general (see also Romans 7:1).

These kinds of consideration are especially important where commentators suggest that Paul is effectively contradicting the Old Testament. Many Christians in Rome had heard the narrative stories and Psalms in the Old Testament and found repeated contrasts between 'righteous' and 'sinners'; if Paul really intended to begin his whole letter (as many commentators suppose) by arguing that *everyone* is unrighteous and under condemnation, then he had better make it really clear or none of his hearers will get it. In actual fact he does nothing of the sort, and Romans 1:18 and following verses is nothing to do with any supposed 'universal condemnation', nor would his hearers have imagined that it was. As we shall see, it is about a contrast between the righteous and sinners.

Genuine points of cultural background, especially in regard to first century Judaism, are really helpful to understanding Paul's message. Unhelpful are over fanciful impositions of abstract schematic themes that are neither indicated in the text nor found in any other literature, nor found in earlier Pauline letters.

Concerns in the Letter

The historical-cultural background, then, can cast much light for us on the concerns in the letter. We must reject any interpretation of Paul that has him contradicting his own core beliefs or supposes him to be answering questions that no one was asking in his time and culture. Unfortunately there are many such unlikely interpretations in various commentaries.

When he was a (non-Christian) Jewish Pharisee Paul firmly believed:

1. That the Old Testament was inspired, and that the prophets in it spoke God's truth.

2. That the way to serve God was meticulous adherence to the Torah Law.

His conversion brought a radical reorientation. From his letters we can see that the first belief above remained unaltered, and as shown in Acts 28:17–20 he regarded his new faith as a fulfilment of the hope of Israel. The second belief, however, changed radically in the following ways:

– He came to believe that the way to be in a right relationship with God and justified (ie shown to be) had *always* been through faith even when this was lived out through Torah.

– A set of rules, in themselves, could neither give a way for sins to be forgiven, nor provide spiritual power for a truly holy life. Both of these things could be achieved only through a Messiah who died a sacrificial death for sin and rose again to bring spiritual power.

– Now that the Messiah had come and had died and risen again, the truths to which Torah ritual had pointed were here in reality rather than in 'shadows', and were optional in the New Covenant.

Christianity was certainly radical! It had no specialised priesthood, no human high priest, no sacrifices and no sacred places. But any interpretation of Paul has to be wrong if it has him reject not only rabbinical Pharisaism but the core teaching of the Old Testament prophets. And frankly, there are more than a few such versions of Paul – even amongst those recognised as biblical scholars.

Thus for example, one of the major themes in the Old Testament is the division of mankind into the righteous and the unrighteous or 'sinners'. Noah is 'righteous' (Genesis 7:1). Job claims to be righteous (12:4, 32:1) and God said he had spoken rightly (42:7). Abraham asks whether God would 'destroy the righteous with the wicked' (Genesis 18:23), and he is not speaking about those inside and outside any specific covenant but the people of Sodom. The contrast of righteous and wicked is in Psalm 1:5–6, 7:9; 11:5–7 and 58:10 among many others, as well as in Proverbs 12:5 etc. Prophets as in Hosea 14:9 make the contrast. Habakkuk makes as a central point in his revelation the fact that the righteous are living by faith while the wicked person is just puffed up and empty (2:4).

None of this righteous/wicked split relates only to some prophetic future time after the Messiah comes; it relates to the times of Noah, Abraham and Job, and throughout Israel's history.

If, then, Paul were really saying either that literally *no one* except Jesus is 'righteous', or that no one other than a Christian can be 'righteous', he would be fundamentally rejecting the Law, the Psalms and the Prophets. Yet various commentators have ascribed both of these views to Paul.

We need, of course, to understand the words Paul used in terms of how they were understood at the time. Being 'righteous' in this context meant being in a rightstanding before God, it is essentially a legal rather than ethical term (though of course a legal standing could depend on lifestyle choice). No one believed that to become righteous meant someone could live a life without ever sinning. This idea was simply not around. Paul did not have to 'prove' that everyone had sinned because none of his Jewish opponents would have denied it; Jesus made his challenge in John 8:7 knowing that they all knew full well they had sinned.

So it is mistaken to suppose that in the early part of Romans Paul is 'proving' that everyone has sinned, because he didn't need to, and to suppose that he is 'proving' that everyone is 'unrighteous' is wrong because this would have contradicted much of the Old Testament.

So what *were* his concerns? What, for a start, were his Jewish opponents and critics arguing? In Galatians, the critics he had in mind were a Jewish Christian faction in the church. Here in Romans he seems to have more in mind his Jewish anti-Christian critics who had dogged all his missionary activities.

It is difficult to know exactly what first century rabbis taught because they often disagreed and their words were written down long after. The much later Babylonian Tractate 90a xi says 'All Israel have a portion in the world to come, for it is written, your people are all righteous; they shall inherit the land for ever' – though then it lists exceptions! Jesus was criticised for eating with people like tax-collectors and prostitutes who were Jewish but thought to be 'sinners' rather than righteous (see also Mark 2:13–17); but it was probably a common assumption that most Jews would be all right. Later Rabbis differed over whether righteous *Gentiles* might have a place in this new age. Paul's own experience, however, seems to have been that what drove his Jewish opponents to fury was not his experience of the risen Jesus nor his identification of Jesus as the Messiah, but that Paul believed he had been sent to the Gentiles (see Acts 22:21). There was a real feeling of national superiority; the Jewish nation was to be a 'light to the Gentiles' as Isaiah had prophesied (see also Romans 2:17 and following verses).

So as far as the Jews were concerned, Paul had to show the following seven things:

1. Taken overall the nation of Israel as God's Servant had *not* acted as a light to the Gentiles (as in Isaiah 42:6; 49:6). As a whole it had been little better morally than the Gentiles who therefore blaspheme rather than turn to God when they look at the Jews (Romans 2:20).

2. The *Messiah* rather than the *nation* has become the faithful Servant of God and is that light of the world.

3. The mark of a 'righteous' life (ie a life in right relationship with God) is not the 'works of the Law' (particularly the symbols of Sabbath, circumcision and diet). Rather it is, and indeed always

has been, faith. The Torah Law approached in the flesh leads to death, approached in faith and in the Spirit it leads to life (Romans 8:1–4).

4. It is now revealed that the way in which God could forgive sin was through the faithfulness of Jesus the Messiah in dying for the sins of the world. This applied both to sins forgiven in the past and to those done by believers after Jesus died and rose again. Ceremonial 'works of the Law' (even the sacrifices ordained by God) could not in themselves bring atonement; they were efficacious only if they were done in faith that God would provide a way to forgive. Now that the reality to which they point has appeared (ie the sacrificial death of the Messiah) they are no longer relevant. We don't need the 'shadows' when we have the reality (Hebrews 10:1).

5. The unfaithfulness of Israel as a whole (both historically and in Paul's own lifetime) is not God's fault but theirs. In the first century, as in the days of Elijah (or the Psalmist or Habakkuk), there is a faithful *remnant* who relate to God through faith and are accepted by grace.

6. What is new is that this faithful remnant of Jews are now combined with faithful Gentiles to form the body of Christ, the light of the world and the light to the nations.

7. All 'Israel' will indeed be saved from judgement and have a part in the world to come, but 'Israel' is now defined in a spiritual sense not in terms of physical genetics (Romans 9:6; 11:25–26).

All these are taken up in Romans, but of course Paul also has to answer some general questions for both Jewish and Gentile Christians. In particular he addresses:

– On what basis are their sins forgiven and they declared to be in a right relationship with God (as point 4 above)?

– How can they be released from the power of Sin in their lives, and live increasingly Christ-like lives of love for God and others?

– What destiny does God have in store for them?

These are issues Paul covers as he develops the first eleven chapters of this careful and systematic treatise in his letter to the Romans. Then, in the last five chapters, he applies this to the individual in relation to God, church, society and civil life under Roman rule.

The letters Paul wrote for example to Corinth and Galatia were dealing with questions and issues specific to those churches. In this letter he does not have to 'firefight' on urgent issues in the Roman church – it is a more general treatise. Maybe this is why some early manuscripts of it circulated without the personal greetings in chapter 16 because these were later considered unnecessary to the general treatise.

Summary of the Letter to the Romans

Explanation

Various Bible versions and commentaries commonly impose on Romans an interpretive structure that its actual words just do not indicate. So, for example the NIV entitles Romans 1:18 and the following verses as 'God's wrath against mankind' when actually it speaks of His wrath against the unrighteous. As we will see, interpretations like this from the NIV (and many commentaries) require a substantial 'reading in' of ideas not present in the text. This is not based on any first century cultural context, but reflects the later preoccupations and theologies of such people as Augustine and the Reformers.

What we ask is that the reader suspend ideas from commentaries or headings inserted in their Bibles (whatever version they use), and just look with us at what the text actually says in the light of the cultural and linguistic background. We usually quote the NRSVA or NASB which are generally accurate, and explain at any point where we have to give a more strict translation.

It is actually very hard to split Romans into sections, apart maybe from chapters 1–11 and 12–16. The idea of two streams of humanity (righteous and unrighteous), flows into noting that Jews have no national superiority, and that the righteous are credited with rightstanding with God through faith. The gospel as the power unto salvation is continued from chapter 1 into chapters 5–8. The Jewish issues are in 9–11, yet already approached in chapters 2–3.

In this book we have divided Romans up into three main parts:

1. God's Scheme for Humanity 1:1–8:39
2. God's Faithfulness and His dealings with the Jews 9:1–11:36
3. Theology worked out in Christian Lifestyle 12:1–16:27

Here below we give a schema of how we have divided up the text within those three main parts, and give a summary of each passage.

Part 1. God's Scheme for Humanity 1:1–8:39

Chapters 1–3: Introduction, the Two Streams of Humanity and God's Way of Faith

1:1–13 It was normal in a first century letter to begin with the name of the writer, identification of those to whom it was sent, and a greeting. Paul does this, but includes in this identification part of the themes of his letter.

1:16–32 Paul moves smoothly into a major theme of the contrast between the righteous and the unrighteous. To those (Jews or Gentiles) who have a faith in God, the Christian gospel brings power to transform them (salvation). To those who suppress the truth in unrighteousness the wrath of God is being revealed in the consequences of spiritual death worked out in their lifestyles.

2:1–11 We all have moral standards and know we fail them. Those who have no knowledge of Torah or the Bible should know through nature that God intends to lead them to repentance. But there is a contrast between those who 'seek for glory and honour and incorruption' (2:7) who will receive eternal life, and those who have stubborn and unrepentant hearts (2:5) who suppress the truth in unrighteousness and now face (1:18), and will face (2:5), wrath.

2:12–29 The 'righteous' person is the one living out what the Law means to teach, ie a faith relationship with God. Just knowing the Law is not the point, and sometimes Gentiles are actually living it without even knowing about it. The Jewish attitude that Israel was the light of the Gentiles was not borne out in practice because of the unholy lifestyles of many of the people.

3:1–8 If both Jews and Gentiles throughout history could be righteous or unrighteous, what is the advantage of being a Jew? Well obviously it was an advantage to have 'the words (*logia*) of God', and it was not God's fault if some Jews throughout history did not have faith (v3).

3:9–18 So overall has Israel as a nation actually been any better than the Gentiles? Paul produces a string of quotes, *not* to prove that *no one* before Jesus has ever been righteous (which would have seemed absurd to a man like Paul who took the Old Testament as inspired), but that actually throughout history the nation of Israel has contained as much overall unrighteousness as other nations. They have the Law, but this is no reason for the kind of national pride and feelings of superiority that they often show. It just means they have greater guilt and less excuse.

3:19–20 Whatever the Torah says to those who are 'under the Law' it says simply to make them conscious of sin and so accountable to God. The 'works of the law' mark them off as Jews, but this does *not* show that they are in rightstanding with God, because (as Paul has just shown) on the whole the Jewish nation is castigated by the prophets as often as the Gentiles.

3:21–26 BUT NOW the real basis by which God gives rightstanding (righteousness) has finally been made known. It is through the faithfulness of Jesus the Messiah. There is no difference between Jews (like Abraham and David and Habakkuk) who had faith, and non-Jews (like Noah and Job). Since all have sinned and so fall short of the glory of God, they all need the redemptive work accomplished by the faithful Messiah. This, it is now clear, is the basis on which God forgave sins in the past, and it is the basis of receiving forgiveness in the New Covenant too.

3:27–31 So the Jewish national pride and feelings of superiority are unfounded. A person is declared in rightstanding with God through faith, irrespective of whatever rituals he observes. However this is not to nullify the Torah Law but to uphold it.

Chapter 4: Faith Not Works Has Always Been the Way

4:1–21   This principle of rightstanding through faith is illustrated in Abraham, whose story is in the Torah. First, it was his faith that was credited to him for rightstanding. Not that his faith 'earned' that rightstanding, but that God in His grace so credited it. Moreover it was *before* Abraham was even circumcised, so it was not because he kept the Law. He is the physical father of the circumcised, but in the spiritual sense the father of only those throughout Jewish history who have walked in his way of faith. Moreover, in a sense, anyone who has had real faith in God and walked in Abraham's ways is a child of Abraham.

Chapters 4:23–6: Christians and the Freedom from Sin's Power

4:23–25   The words 'credited to him for rightstanding' are also for us, who believe in Him who raised Jesus our Lord from the dead. Here for the first time since launching into 1:16 etc, Paul refers specifically to *Christian* faith rather than faith in God (bearing in mind the common mistranslation of the genitive in Romans 3:22 and 26, of which more later).

5:1–5   As Christians we have been declared righteous through faith, so let us have shalom/peace with God through our Lord Jesus the Messiah. We also rejoice in the hope of the glory of God in the coming kingdom, and this helps us to get through our present trials and sufferings. The Holy Spirit has been given us as God pours His love into us.

5:6–11   God showed His love in sending Jesus to die for us, and if we are declared in rightstanding by His blood we will the more be saved from God's wrath both now (as in 1:18) and in the coming judgment.

5:12–20   The first human sin brought spiritual death into humanity. Of course, most humans between the man in Genesis 2–3 and the time of Moses had no specific divine commands to break. But the fact that they experienced spiritual death shows that (as Paul earlier argued) they were aware of moral standards. Through the first human sin came spiritual death, and it has spread to everyone because everyone has sinned. But the righteous act of Jesus the Messiah brought a counter flow, and through Him grace is offered to all. Through opting in to sin many were constituted sinners, but through opting in to faith the grace of God through His Messiah constituted them righteous.

6:1–14   So shall we continue in the power of sin so that we can keep getting forgiven? Certainly not. Baptism shows how we have died to sin and been raised again to life in the Messiah. So we have the freedom not to let sin reign in us.

6:15–23   All right, but even if we are free to choose, why not carry on sinning and enjoying it and getting forgiven? Because if we choose sin we choose spiritual death, both as a present ongoing experience and, if we persist, as a culmination.

Chapters 7–8: Working Out Our Spiritual Freedom and Working With God

7:1–6   Our righteous lives are not lived simply by human effort (flesh) to keep the Torah. As baptism shows (6:3) we died to the power of sin which controls people who just try in self-effort to keep the Law.

7:7–25   Paul found in his own life that self-effort based on Law did not work. His knowledge of God's high standards actually brought him spiritual death because he found that he could not keep them. He realised that (as Jesus also taught) sin is not just what we do but what we long for. Paul presumably did not steal, but covetousness (v7) was something he could not control. He gives a cry of anguish 'who can save me from this body of death' (v24) and he cannot help himself (as he dictates to his scribe Tertius) exclaiming an answer (v25a). However, v25b sums up his dilemma as a Pharisee without faith (and indeed an experience into which Christians can also slide back).

8:1–13   His release came in realising that he had been set free from sin and the Law through what the Messiah did. The Torah which had been a 'Law' of sin and death, is now a 'Law' of spirit and life. Our purely human flesh is too weak to keep the Law, but in the Messiah that flesh was condemned so that we can now keep its requirements by the power of the Spirit. So we have to set our minds on the Spirit, and not on human effort. It is no longer 'flesh' that controls us but God's Spirit.

8:14–21   It is difficult really to divide up Romans 8 because 8:13 leads smoothly into 14, the inner experience of the Spirit which assures us we are God's heirs. As heirs we are not waiting for some spiritual heaven floating on clouds, but to be God's agents to redeem creation.

8:22–28   The creation groans, but so do we as we await our 'son-placing' (adoption) – our revealing as sons. So in prayer we cooperate with the Spirit in us, not knowing what to pray for but in the Spirit uttering inexpressible words. This cooperation with God is further expressed as working together with Him to bring good into any situation however bad it is (see the correct translation of verse 28 in the NRSV or NIV margin).

8:29–30   For God foreknew He would have a people to whom He would give a destiny ('predestination' means giving a horizon) to be conformed to the image of His Servant Son. Those given that destiny have been named (*hagaios* or holy ones, see 1:7), have been declared righteous and have been glorified.

8:31–39   God has declared us to be His chosen (as Messiah was the 'chosen one' and Paul in Ephesians notes that as His body we are 'chosen in the Messiah'). No one, then, can accuse us because God has declared us righteous, ie having rightstanding before Him. Nothing can separate us from God's love, whatever human hardships we may go through.

Part 2. God's Faithfulness and His dealings with the Jews 9:1–11:36

Chapters 9–11: Israel and God's Historical Strategy

After Paul's ringing confidence in the Love of God, one can imagine a critic saying: 'Well hang on a minute. God once promised everlasting Love for His people the Jews, and now you claim that He has abandoned them. If He is that fickle how can you trust Him so much?' So this section contains a complex intertwining of three basic themes:

1. The choice or 'election' of Israel was purely in the strategy of God, not anything to do with them or any moral superiority.

2. The choice of Isaac over Ishmael has a symbolic significance in that faith and not works is the basis of being the 'true Israel', ie in rightstanding with God.

3. The present Christian Jews are the faithful remnant in the nation, and there has always been only a remnant of them with faith.

9:1–5   Paul first declares that he still identifies as being a Jew. They indeed really did receive the covenants, the Torah, the Temple worship and the promises, and from that nation came the Messiah.

9:1–9   Their present widespread lack of faith is not because God's promises have failed. Physical descent from Jacob does not make a person a true part of 'Israel'. The basis of true Israel is indicated in the story of Isaac and Ishmael (as Paul expounds in full in Galatians 4). The child of the promise is chosen as the line to the Messiah because Isaac represents faith-grace rather than works.

9:10–18   God's choice of Jacob not Esau was purely decided by His strategy. Jacob did not earn a place in God's plan. God also raised up Pharaoh to make a public demonstration of His power and get His name proclaimed. God assigns places in His plans both to the Israelites and to Pharaoh. He shows mercy (in the sense of special favour) and strengthens opposition according to His plans, not according to what we decide.

9:19–23   Is God treating Israel unjustly then? Should He not assign places based on meritocracy? In Jeremiah God is pictured as a potter, and the potter has the right to make of the clay what he wishes. This is not a passive picture (and no Jew could take it that it was), because what Jeremiah is explicitly saying is actually that God can change His mind depending on whether or not humans change their ways. As the clay reacts well or badly the potter can change his mind about what kind of pot to make. But now God is using the one lump of Israel to make *two* pots. One is to demonstrate His riches, and the other His wrath. He is no longer treating the nation as one lump as He did previously.

9:24–26   Israel was formerly called His special people. But now Gentiles too are to be publically identified as God's people – His servants and representatives in the world.

9:27–29   In Israel it was *always* recognised that only a remnant were faithful.

9:30–10:4 Some Gentiles who were not obsessed with rightstanding with God actually achieved it, but many Jews who were obsessed with it went about it in the wrong way and didn't get it. It is through Messiah that righteousness comes to everyone who has faith.

10:5–13   When Moses gave them the Law he said that through doing it they would get righteousness. But he also implied that this was not through some superhuman efforts on their part, but that the word was near them and in their hearts. It is this same word of faith which Christians now teach. The word today is that Jesus is Lord and God raised Him, and that anyone, Jew or Gentile, who calls on the name of the Lord will be saved (Joel 2:32) and Gentiles as well as Jews now call on that name of Jesus.

10:14–21 All this is now part of the prophecies of the days of Messiah and is also referred to by Moses himself. Gentiles can enter in, and many Jews will not do so.

11:1–10   So God did not reject His people Israel. Rather, there has always been a remnant saved on the basis of faith-grace. But those who refuse to repent are given a spirit of stupor. The Old Testament prophets obviously refer to a suffering Messiah like Jesus, but when the non-believing Jews read the prophets a veil is over their eyes which is removed only if they repent (see 2 Corinthians 3:14–16).

11:11–24   Gentiles should not crow over this sad situation. If any of them abandon faith then they too will cease to be a part of the olive tree that represents God's servant-people on earth. On the other hand, if Jews repent and turn to their Messiah they will the more naturally be grafted back into God's people. Gentiles should be showing the blessing of relationship with God to the Jewish people so that they realise what they are missing and become Christians.

11:25–32   The physical Israel has experienced a hardening in part at this time. But when the full number of Gentiles come in then all the spiritual Israel – Gentiles and Jews – will be saved, Israel still has a special place because of their history. That special place – the patriarchs, the prophets, receiving the promises of the Messiah – which was part of their 'election' – is still there.

11:33–36   Doxology.

Part 3. Theology worked out in Christian Lifestyle 12:1–16:27

Chapters 12–15: The Practical Implications for Christian Lifestyle

12:1–2   Understanding all this theology, the Christian response is to realise that the kind of sacrificial priestly service God really wants is for us to give Him our whole selves and bodies. We are not to be simply formed by the culture around us, but transformed in our minds by God in an ongoing process.

12:3–13   In the Church the core attitude should be love, service, hospitality etc.

12:14–21   To the world in general we love our enemies (showing this practically) and as far as possible live in harmony with everyone.

13:1–6   God uses civil government to preserve law and order in society, so unless we are told to do something morally wrong we should be good obedient citizens.

13:8–14   A real love of others should lead a Christian to spontaneously fulfil all the moral commands in the Torah.

14:1–23   Symbolic issues of diet and Sabbath keeping were central to Jewish identity, but they are peripheral to Christians. If you have personal convictions that you should keep a Sabbath each week, or not eat certain foods, then follow those convictions. But don't try to force them on others. Equally, if you don't keep a Sabbath or diet restrictions, don't try to force another person whose faith is weaker to break rules which would be going against their conscience.

15:1–13   So mutual acceptance in peripheral matters of symbolism should be the rule. The strong should help the weak rather than forcing them to go against their consciences.

15:14–32 Paul relates his own call to proclaim the gospel to Gentiles. He hopes to be able to come to Rome to continue this and asks for their prayers.

Chapter 16: Personal Greetings and Final Words

16:1–16   A female minister, Phoebe, brings the letter, and Paul asks them to receive her in a way worthy of the 'holy ones' which is what they have been named by God. There follows a series of greetings to and from various people, men and women, Jews and Gentiles. The prominence in these of women is noteworthy.

16:17–27 Further greetings, warning to beware of those who sow divisions, and a final prayer.

Commentary on Romans
Part 1: God's Scheme for Humanity 1:1–8:39

Romans 1:1–3:31 | Introduction, Two Streams of Humanity and God's Way of Faith

Text 1:1–7

> [1] Paul, a bond-servant of Christ Jesus, called as an apostle, set apart for the gospel of God, [2] which He promised beforehand through His prophets in the holy Scriptures, [3] concerning His Son, who was born of a descendant of David according to the flesh, [4] who was declared the Son of God with power by the resurrection from the dead, according to the Spirit of holiness, Jesus Christ our Lord, [5] through whom we have received grace and apostleship to bring about the obedience of faith among all the Gentiles [Lit: nations] for His name's sake, [6] among whom you also are the called of Jesus Christ; [7] to all who are beloved of God in Rome, called as saints: Grace to you and peace from God our Father and the Lord Jesus Christ. (NASB)

Commentary

Greek letters usually began with the names of the sender and recipient(s) and then a greeting. Paul does this here, including clear designations of his and their roles, and also claims of continuity with the Jewish hope (of a Messiah) but with his own slant on who are now the 'holy ones'.

Paul begins that he is 'a slave of Messiah Jesus, a called/named apostle'. In the Old Testament Israel is spoken of as the servant of God (Jeremiah 46:27; Ezekiel 28:25; Isaiah 41:8). The term is also applied to Job, Moses, Joshua, David, and the prophets (eg Job 1:8; Joshua 14:7; 24:29, Deuteronomy 34:5; Judges 2:8; Psalm 89:3; Isaiah 20:3, 37:35; Ezra 9:11). Isaiah refers both to individuals and to the nation as the 'servant of God', but later, by chapter 53, seems to narrow the suffering servant to be a Messiah figure. The concept, then, is a very Hebrew one. Paul is claiming continuity with figures God named to His service in Israel's history, but refocuses it as slavery to Messiah. At the same time, of course, he actually sees all Christians as slaves to Messiah (1 Corinthians 7:22ff; Ephesians 6:6; Romans 12:11, 14:18 etc). Later, though, Paul says (Romans 8:15) that we have not received a spirit of slavery but one of sonship, but still he makes himself as a 'slave of God' in love.

Some versions have 'called to be' in verses 1 and 7, but the words 'to be' are not strictly there in the Greek. Paul is 'named' an apostle (which means a messenger or missionary), and *they* are 'named' holy ones (*hagiaos*) or 'saints'. To be 'named' as something by God is also, of course, a kind of call to live, to 'walk', in a way worthy of the name they have been given (Ephesians 4:1). Longenecker rightly emphasizes that this idea of calling or naming

> . . . always includes the concept of God as the agent in 'calling' people to some purpose or responsibility. (Longenecker, *The Epistle to the Romans* p.86)

The implication is always too that someone can fail to live up to their calling, as seen supremely in Judas who was one of the twelve apostles. This is why Peter tells Christians to *'be even more diligent to make your call and election sure, for if you do these things you will never stumble'* (2 Peter 1:10).

Paul saw his apostleship as parallel to the twelve, as an apostle to the Gentiles (Romans 11:13, Galatians 2:8, 1 Corinthians 15:9) as he had seen the risen Lord and received a direct commission. However, the use of 'we' in verse 5 seems to indicate that he also sees apostleship (or missionary calling) as a more general calling shared by companions – as for example in Romans 16:7 (a female missionary) or 1 Corinthians 4:9. There were other missionaries to the Gentiles and he himself had not founded the Roman church.

This Messiah of whom Paul is servant and messenger is definitely the Jewish one: a physical descendant of David and prophesied in the Jewish Scriptures. However, *they* (the Church) are 'named' as 'saints' or 'holy ones, the 'named/called of Jesus the Messiah'. In the Old Testament the 'holy ones' are the whole nation of Israel (eg Leviticus 19:2 'You shall be called holy for I am holy') or a remnant of them (Isaiah 4:3), and the 'saints of the most high' (Daniel 7:18) will possess the coming kingdom. These 'saints' or 'holy ones' to Paul are now the Church – Jews and Gentiles.

At the very beginning, then, Paul states how their respective roles have been assigned by God. Verses 1–6 contain the kernel of his message. The good news of the kingdom concerned God's only Son who came as the promised Jewish Messiah. He was physically Jewish, but it was through His resurrection that He was appointed 'Son of God in Power'. The word 'declared' is misleading because in all its other uses (seven in the New Testament) it means defined or appointed, rather than simply a declaration of what already is. Jesus was declared as God's son, at His birth and at the transfiguration, but designated as the 'Son-of-God-*in-power*' from the time of the resurrection. The resurrected Messiah sits in the heavenly places at the right hand of the Father (on this see also Cranfield's commentary).

Verses 3–4 may be taken from some kind of confession of faith already circulating because they are not in typical Pauline language (for example the 'Spirit of holiness'). The words probably refer back to 2 Samuel 7:8–17 (or 1 Chronicles 17:7–15):

> [12] I will raise up your descendant after you, who will come forth from you, and I will establish his kingdom. [13] He shall build a house for my name, and I will establish the throne of his kingdom forever. [14] I will be a father to him and he will be a son to me . . . (NASB)

This verse is the only place where the idea of Davidic descendant (seed) and sonship are associated in a Messianic context. The promise to 'raise' this descendant as a Son may even be taken to refer to the resurrection.

None of this Old Testament connection, however, should make us miss the wonderful allusion to the fantastic glory of a God who enters into our humanity in order to enter into our death and mortality, and in defeating death shares with us His own eternal life. We should never imagine that Jesus was a kind of space visitor disguised as a human. In the incarnation, God entered a human form for the first time, experiencing from the inside what it was like to be human (Hebrews 4:15).

In verse 5, the phrase 'of faith' is a genitive, and is probably a subjective genitive which would mean 'obedience that comes out of faith'. The NASB is better here than the NKJV. The same phrase appears in Romans 16:26 where the obedience of faith again comes out of making known God's gospel to the nations. The Greek word for 'nations' is also the word for 'Gentiles' but in this context 'nations' is probably correct (the NASB actually uses 'nations' for the same phrase in 16:26!)

In verse 7, his greeting is 'grace and peace', just like the one to the Galatians (see page 23).

Text 1:8–15

[8] First, I thank my God through Jesus Christ for all of you, because your faith is proclaimed throughout the world. [9] For God, whom I serve with my spirit by announcing the gospel of His Son, is my witness that without ceasing I remember you always in my prayers, [10] asking that by God's will I may somehow at last succeed in coming to you. [11] For I am longing to see you so that I may share with you some spiritual gift to strengthen you— [12] or rather so that we may be mutually encouraged by each other's faith, both yours and mine. [13] I want you to know, brothers and sisters, that I have often intended to come to you (but thus far have been prevented), in order that I may reap some harvest among you as I have among the rest of the Gentiles. [14] I am a debtor both to Greeks and to barbarians, both to the wise and to the foolish [15] —hence my eagerness to proclaim the gospel to you also who are in Rome. (NRSVA)

Commentary

Greek letters often followed the initial greeting with some kind of prayer to the gods for health and wealth. Paul begins his prayer instead with a prayer of *thanks* for the Roman church – hopefully when we pray for people today we do the same thing. *Then* he prays for their *spiritual* wellbeing, wanting for a spiritual gift to be imparted to establish them. Paul assures them of his great concern for this church at the centre of the Roman world at that time, but that their faith is well spoken of. He is not writing to firefight any particular problems there, nor to seek to revise their foundations.

In verse 12, we find that Paul wants to find *mutual* benefit (repeated in 15:32 as mutual refreshment). Even an apostle needs spiritual support and ministry, so much more then is there such a need today for support for missionaries and pastors. We all need encouragement in our faith, so let us ensure that our own church is providing it, rather than the strife which churches often seem to have.

Sometimes the term 'Greeks' is contrasted with 'Jews' and means non-Jews. Here he parallels it with 'barbarians', a term with an undertone of contempt used by those of a Greek culture (which could include Romans) towards those whose languages sound like 'bababa', and by implication this meant uncultured persons. Paul is in Greece, writing to Rome but as an apostle sent specifically to the Gentiles he has an obligation to all kinds and all nationalities of Gentiles to minister to them as God has called him (including, as he intended, Spain). We should all seek to exercise whatever ministry God has given us to all kinds and classes of people: cultured and uncultured, wise and not-so-smart.

Text 1:16–18

[16] For I am not ashamed of the gospel; it is the power of God for salvation to everyone who has faith, to the Jew first and also to the Greek. [17] For in it the righteousness of God is revealed through faith for faith; as it is written, 'The one who is righteous will live by faith.'

[18] For the wrath of God is revealed from heaven against all ungodliness and wickedness of those who by their wickedness suppress the truth . . . (NRSVA)

Discussion Topic: Universal Condemnation?

Most commentaries and some Bible translations make verse 18 start a new section and entitle it something like 'Universal Condemnation' or 'The Guilt of Humankind' (NRSVA) or 'God's Wrath Against Mankind' (NIV). The whole of the rest of the first chapter is then portrayed as a universal condemnation of all humanity, concluding from 3:19ff that literally 'No-one is Righteous' (NIV). The passage is taken to show that (apart from Jesus) there is not a single righteous human being.

There are some basic mistakes in this.

1. The cultural and biblical context is that throughout the Old Testament it is assumed that there are the righteous and the unrighteous (as noted). If Paul is dissenting from this, then from 1:18 onwards he is fundamentally contradicting Genesis, the Psalms, Proverbs, and the prophets.

2. If Romans 3:9–12 really meant that literally not a single human is righteous then Paul would be quoting all the verses against their Old Testament context where there is always a contrast between these wicked and 'My people' (Psalm 14:4) and 'all who take refuge in You' (Psalm 5:11).

3. The immediate context is that Paul has quoted Habakkuk 2:4: 'The one who is righteous shall live by faith.' The whole message in Habakkuk is the contrast between the righteous person who lives by faith and the wicked who is empty and puffed up. The future tense of 'the righteous shall live by faith' is not because it is looking forward to the Messianic age centuries later, but in the context Habakkuk looks forward to the prophesied invasion by the Chaldeans. Like many prophecies it had an ultimate fulfilment in the messianic age, but it was also a message for Habakkuk and his people in their own age – as the prophet implies in Habakkuk 3:9. And it is fundamentally a *contrast* between righteous and unrighteous, *not* a complaint that literally no one is righteous. Habakkuk 1:4, 13 show that the wicked were both inside and outside Israel – something shown later by Paul in his quotations of the Psalms in Romans 3:10–18.

4. The linguistic evidence is that Paul does not intend to start a radically new section. The structure is that he is not ashamed of the gospel:

    FOR: it is the power of God for salvation for everyone who has faith, to the Jew first and also to the Greek.

    FOR: in it the righteousness of God is revealed from faith to faith, as it is written the one who is righteous shall live by faith

    FOR: the wrath of God is revealed from heaven against all ungodliness of those who by their wickedness suppress the truth (literally: *'all ungodliness and unrighteousness of those who suppress the truth in unrighteounsess')*.

This is a reprise and expansion of Habakkuk. The *righteous* live by faith while the *unrighteous* suppress the truth and experience divine wrath worked out in their psyches and bodies.

But it does *not* say that literally everyone is unrighteous, which would contradict Habakkuk and much of the Old Testament. Even less does it say (as some commentators want to make it say) that everyone *would be* unrighteous *except* for the grace of God and the sacrifice of Christ. This is true, of course, as a hypothetical idea, but it is just not what the text of the passage says. The text has no 'would be' in it and it is not the point Paul is making.

The passage 1:18–32 is about 'those who suppress the truth in unrighteousness', it does not say everyone does this and manifestly they do not because the righteous are living by faith.

Davies in *Faith and Obedience in Romans* rightly says:

> When Paul, therefore, begins to describe the revelation of the wrath of God in Romans 1:18 (introduced

by the connective γαρ), we suggest he is doing so within the framework of the prophet's message which identifies a division between the righteous and the wicked. In 1.18ff Paul is not describing a universal condemnation of all mankind. Rather he is describing 'all ungodliness and wickedness of men who by their wickedness suppress the truth'. (p.44)

In *Early Patristic Readings of Romans* Gaca & Wellbord also argue that the idea of it referring to universal sinfulness is not indicated by the text and is 'tenuous on historical grounds' (p.8). The Early Church Fathers tended to identify the target in Romans 1:18ff as the Greeks, though differed about how far there were exceptions.

The meaning of Paul is clear, and it is not about 'universal human sinfulness', but commentators seem almost mesmerised by the idea. So Longenecker (one of the very greatest and learned of modern commentators) well renders 1:18 as:

The wrath of God is being revealed from heaven against all the godlessness and wickedness of those who suppress the truth by their wickedness. (p.189)

He notes how this relates to denunciations of the wicked from Old Testament sources, Jewish sources, John the Baptist and Jesus (p.195) – not one of whom universalised it. So Longenecker accepts it is specifically about 'those who suppress the truth in unrighteouness'. But then suddenly we find him saying:

In the five verses that follow the theme statement of 1:18, Paul presents two reasons why God's wrath is now being expressed against humanity. (p.205)

Paul's indictment of all humanity, Gentiles and Jews alike, runs from 1:18–3:20. (p.237)

No explanation is given of this sudden jump from 'those who supress the truth', to humanity as a whole, nor how it could possibly fit into the teaching of the Old Testament writers, John and Jesus, none of whom assert that literally everyone is unrighteous nor that God is angry with all humanity. It leads, of course, to what Longenecker then calls 'a major theological problem' (p.241) for him with the passage, because if most of it really *were* about 'universal condemnation' it would be very strange that Paul could go on to speak of those seeking glory and honour and incorruption who will receive eternal life. Longenecker continually refers to the 'deep puzzles' in the section, which of course there would be if Paul were really talking about 'universal condemnation' rather than contrasting wrath against the unrighteous who suppress the truth, with blessings for any who turn to God in faith based on what they know. To defend the conventional interpretation of 3:1–10 which would mean Paul is quoting all the verses out of context, Longenecker has to invent some earlier Jewish writer (p.336) who brought the verses together to 'prove' that literally 'no one is righteous before God', in order for us to be able to blame someone other than Paul for the verses being misquoted (even though there is not a shred of evidence for any such person). All this difficulty and confusion comes from presenting the whole section as about 'universal condemnation' rather than as developing the Habakkuk contrast between righteous and unrighteous humanity, which is what Paul's language plainly implies.

Commentary

The word gospel means 'good news'. In what sense is it good news? There have always been those like Enoch, Noah, Job and Abraham who had faith and so were declared by God to be His. So it cannot mean that until Paul's day no one was right with God but now they can be. It cannot mean that only Christians are right with God or that faith only arrived with Christianity because the Old Testament is full of references to the 'righteous' and Hebrews 11 lists off many people who had real (and presumably saving) faith in God but never heard of Jesus.

So what does Paul mean by the gospel being 'the power of God unto salvation'? Well by grace we *have been* saved (Ephesians 2:8) and there is a future wrath from which we *will be* saved (Romans 5:9). But we may note that it is also a present process, and elsewhere Paul tells Christians to *'work out your own salvation with fear and trembling; for it is God who works in you both to will and to do for His good pleasure'* (Philippians 2:12–13). So salvation is also a salvaging process going on in us now, which will reach its culmination at the second coming of the Messiah Jesus. The gospel brings a power of the indwelling Holy Spirit to achieve this present salvation, and an assurance of salvation at that judgement day when we will be finally saved from our present mortal bodies and transformed into bodies like His (Philippians 3:20–21). So Paul is proclaiming that the gospel is the *power* of God for 'salvation'. Some of the Jews who heard the Christian gospel, of course, would already be living in faith (like later versions of Zechariah, Simeon and Anna in Luke 1–2), and to them the gospel brought the *power* of the Holy Spirit (see also Acts 19:1–7). It is the power of God to salvation for those who have faith. Paul must have heard how this applied just as much to a Gentile like Cornelius. Cornelius had *not* entered the Jewish covenant, yet Acts 10:2 calls him *a devout man and one who feared God with all his household, who gave alms generously to the people, and prayed to God always.* God accepted his 'prayers and alms' and told him to send for Peter. Peter concluded in surprise that *'God shows no partiality. But in every nation whoever fears Him and works righteousness is accepted by Him'* (v34–35). This does not refer to Gentile Christians because as yet there weren't any. Peter did not tell Cornelius to repent – he had already repented and was living a faith-life with God. What the gospel brought him was *the power of God* – immediately manifest in the same experience as the Jewish believers at Pentecost had in fulfilment of Jesus' promise of 'power from on high' (Luke 24:49).

In 1:17 the phrase 'righteousness of God' is a genitive just as in 3:5, and it seems a mystery why some commentators have tried hard to give it a different meaning than righteousness as a divine characteristic. It was a technical term in late Jewish apocalyptic writings for God's saving justice and faithfulness (for example, 1QS 10:25f; 11:12; 1QM 4:6; Test. Daniel 9:7; Enoch 7:14; 99:10). As Paul will later say in 3:25, the gospel shows how God can indeed be righteous but also justify people because of the faithfulness of Jesus the Messiah (3:22) in His righteous act (5:18) of sacrificial death (3:25). In Habakkuk's day, the prophet questioned how the righteous could so suffer if God were righteous, and the response was that the righteous person lived by faith even through difficulty.

So God's righteous dealing on both counts is shown through the gospel. Of course it is true that our rightstanding *is* given us by God, but we don't know of anywhere in which the phrase 'the righteousness of God' definitely means a righteousness that is bestowed by God. In his *Romans* commentary Longenecker (p.170) seems to identify Augustine as the source of this idea, based on his Latin Bible. Longenecker himself cites 2 Corinthians 5:21 and Philippians 3:9 as clear instances of righteousness bestowed by God, but this is doubtful. In Corinthians we *become* the righteousness of God in Christ. Philippians 3:9 is not a simple genitive but reads:

> Not having my own righteousness out of (*ek*) the Law, but the righteousness through (*dia*) the faithfulness of Messiah, the righteousness out of (*ek*) God based upon (*epi*) faith.

The Hebrew of Habakkuk 2:4 which Paul quotes here in Romans could be taken either as 'the righteous lives by his faith', or 'the righteous lives by God's faithfulness' – the Hebrew word *'ĕmûnâ* could mean either, and in different versions of the LXX Greek translation the Jewish translators take it either way. Maybe in saying 'from faith(fulness) to faith' Paul wants to link both meanings: God's faithfulness is there to those who live in faith. Longenecker says:

> Paul can be seen here as setting out in rather cryptic and somewhat perplexing brevity, both of the primary factors involved in God's salvation and reconciliation of humanity: (1) *divine faithfulness*, which is the source and basis for all that the gospel proclaims, and (2) *human faith*, which is necessary for its reception. (p.178)

Paul then sets out his major theme. The righteous person (the word 'man' given in the NKJV is not there in the Greek) lives *by faith* not by some kind of ritual works. In contrast, the unrighteous person, who suppresses the truth, experiences divine wrath (which can also be called spiritual death) as an ongoing process.

Text 1:18–32

[18] For the wrath of God is revealed from heaven against all ungodliness and unrighteousness of men who suppress the truth in unrighteousness, [19] because that which is known about God is evident within them; for God made it evident to them. [20] For since the creation of the world His invisible attributes, His eternal power and divine nature, have been clearly seen, being understood through what has been made, so that they are without excuse. [21] For even though they knew God, they did not honour Him as God or give thanks, but they became futile in their speculations, and their foolish heart was darkened. [22] Professing to be wise, they became fools, [23] and exchanged the glory of the incorruptible God for an image in the form of corruptible man and of birds and four-footed animals and crawling creatures. [24] Therefore God gave them over in the lusts of their hearts to impurity, so that their bodies would be dishonoured among them. [25] For they exchanged the truth of God for a lie, and worshiped and served the creature rather than the Creator, who is blessed forever. Amen. [26] For this reason God gave them over to degrading passions; for their women exchanged the natural function for that which is unnatural, [27] and in the same way also the men abandoned the natural function of the woman and burned in their desire toward one another, men with men committing indecent acts and receiving in their own persons the due penalty of their error. [28] And just as they did not see fit to acknowledge God any longer, God gave them over to a depraved mind, to do those things which are not proper, [29] being filled with all unrighteousness, wickedness, greed, evil; full of envy, murder, strife, deceit, malice; they are gossips, [30] slanderers, haters of God, insolent, arrogant, boastful, inventors of evil, disobedient to parents, [31] without understanding, untrustworthy, unloving, unmerciful; [32] and although they know the ordinance of God, that those who practice such things are worthy of death, they not only do the same, but also give hearty approval to those who practice them. (NASB)

Discussion Topic: Gay Relationships

In modern western and European culture 'gay marriage' is not only accepted, but anyone who disagrees with it is likely to be pilloried, pronounced 'sexist' or 'homophobic' or accused of 'denying gay people their human rights'. They may even lose their jobs, or be expelled from an academic course, for example in social work. Several issues need to be clarified:

1. To say that gay relationships are morally wrong is not to say either that they should be illegal or that there should be any prejudice against someone in a gay lifestyle in employment or social contexts. Christians believe that idolatry is morally wrong, but a Hindu who worships Ganesh should not find him or herself a subject of discrimination. Neither should such a one be excluded from the love and friendship of Christians.

2. Any form of homophobic bullying, name calling, or anything short of the love that Jesus told us to show to all people, even our enemies (and people in gay relationships are not our enemies), is abhorrent and evil.

3. The English word 'homosexual' means a person sexually attracted to their own gender. There is no word for this in Hebrew or Greek; the Greek word *arsenokoitas* means a man 'going to bed with a man', and refers to the (same) sex act, not the inclination. It is this that Paul lists with other sins in 1 Corinthians 6:9 where the NASB translation 'homosexuals' is therefore misleading (better as for example, the NIV 'men who have sex with men' or ESV 'men who practice homosexuality'). Here also in Romans 1 it is

the acts and lifestyles, and not any inbuilt inclination, that Paul condemns. Inclination is not 'lust' unless the person is dwelling on it and drooling for the forbidden (whether hetero- or homosexual sex). In this sense there can be no objection to a 'homosexual' (ie a person exclusively with gay inclination) holding any office in full fellowship in the church. Such a person, however, would not be in a gay sexual relationship (permanent or otherwise), but would be celibate and following what Jesus said in Matthew 19 as noted in point 5 below.

4. The gay sex activity is listed in 1 Corinthians 6:9 with idolatry and adultery – it is not some special kind of sin. Here in Romans 1 Paul also speaks of a long list of sinful traits. Sometimes Christians, alas, may also commit such sins. But the issue is that they should not be choosing them as a lifestyle.

5. Jesus, in Matthew 19, also implies that sexual activity is right only within a committed monogamous heterosexual relationship. Jesus deliberately introduces the 'male and female' from Genesis 1 into the 'leaving and bonding' of marriage in Genesis 2. This is how Jesus defines marriage as God intended. A bisexually orientated person may be able to choose to enter a permanent heterosexual marriage, a person exclusively homosexually orientated is likely to find this difficult or feel it impossible. Jesus goes on to say that if someone cannot enter a heterosexual relationship with one partner, intending it to be permanent, then they should choose celibacy for the sake of the Kingdom of Heaven. Such a celibate life is open to any heterosexual or homosexual who finds Jesus' marriage alternative impossible. But however

society chooses to define 'marriage', and whatever other religious groups conclude, sex for Christians should surely take place only within marriage as Jesus says God intended: monogamous, heterosexual, and intending permanency.

6. Empirical studies show that some people have bisexual inclinations, some may be really heterosexual but try to experiment, but there are some who are inherently homosexually orientated. For them this is not some kind of choice. Moreover 'therapy' to change orientation may work for some, but for many, perhaps even most, it does not. People should be free to try 'therapy' to try to change orientation if this is their choice, but not be bullied into it nor misled about its effectiveness. Of course not all kinds of therapy offered to gay people are to try to change their orientation, some focus on helping them live with and come to terms with it, and we know gay-orientated Christian friends who have found this helpful.

Some people have claimed that Paul is talking here only about a particular *kind* of gay sex and is not referring to loving gay sex in a permanent relationship. So (they say) maybe Paul would disapprove of promiscuous gay sex today or the increasing trend for young people to experiment bisexually, but not of permanent loving gay partnerships. But this is really not plausible. Of course it is true that Paul does not see gay sex as some kind of 'special' sin (indeed here he lists all kinds of things as wrong). But, as noted, *arsenokoitas*, simply means the (male) homosexual act, not (as sometimes claimed) activity only in a cultic context. There is no indication from Paul that sexual acts in some kind of permanent loving gay relationship are OK. Much of the gay sex in the first century was indeed exploitative, for example older men expecting sex from pupils – but loving gay relationships were also known. Paul and his contemporaries must surely also have known some people for whom their inclination was wholly homosexual. So if it really were right for gay people to fulfil their natural inclinations in any kind of gay lifestyle (loving or otherwise), it would surely have to be accepted that Paul was simply wrong or misguided.

Is it just a matter of culture? Of course Paul is well aware that some things are purely 'cultural' on which, for example in Romans 14 he urges mutual tolerance. But these are issues of symbolism, not of sexual morality.

Jesus, in his advocacy of committed monogamous heterosexual marriage in Matthew 19, plainly referred to the creation narratives (and specifically refers to male and female in marriage in 19:4). It seems very likely that Paul here had in mind a similar framework. Hultgren suggests (*Paul's Letter to the Romans*, p.102) that by 'unnatural': 'in Paul's day the concept would primarily have to do with anatomical differences'. He therefore suggests that if today we find that physiological or genetic factors are looked at, then what we see as 'natural' may change. But this seems basically mistaken. Surely, to Paul 'natural' meant what God intended? To deduce morality from nature would have seemed to be to worship and serve the creation rather than the Creator. We may find genetic or physiological factors for all kinds of behavioural tendencies, but in deciding which of them is 'right' we have to look to something beyond simply the fact that some humans have them.

Finally, some people argue that homosexual relationships are in the same category as slavery or gender equality or remarriage after divorce. 'So,' they say, 'the church is now more enlightened on all these issues, so why not gay marriage?' These arguments, and all the other issues, are looked at in detail in Paul Marston's book *Gay Partnerships and the Jesus-Centred Church*. However, in brief, slavery is never condoned in the New Testament. Paul advises slaves to be people of integrity and make the best of their bad situation, and seek freedom if they can, but does not condone the institution (Ephesians 6:5, Colossians 3:22). Moreover, Paul's instruction to masters to treat slaves as God has treated them (Ephesians 6:9) should have sounded a death knell for slavery in any society influenced by Christianity. Chrysostom, indeed, hinted as much, but the Augustinian Catholicism and later Reformed thinking (for example in America) did not recognise it. Our own theological tradition – Wesley, Finney, etc – always regarded slavery as an abomination in any society, especially in one claiming to be Christian. We also fully accept Paul's and Jesus' position on women in leadership, and on remarriage after divorce, as explored in Paul Marston's books *Women in Church Leadership and in the Family* and *Christians, Divorce and Remarriage,* and Faith & Roger Forster's book *Women and the Kingdom*. Both the apostle Paul and Jesus have been woefully misrepresented on these issues, but this is not their fault.

All human exegesis is fallible, and we are aware that there are those who would vehemently disagree with us on all this, but we cannot avoid presenting how we understand it and why, because this passage is in Romans.

Commentary

Paul's denunciation of godlessness amongst Gentiles reflects contemporary Jewish views, and has parallels with the book of *Wisdom* which is found in the LXX though not considered by Protestants to be part of Scripture. *Wisdom* 15:3 also states: 'To know you is the whole of righteousness, and to acknowledge your power the root of immortality.' *Wisdom* 11:23 states: 'But you are merciful to all men because you can do all things; you do overlook the sins of men to bring them to repentance . . .' The parallels may help us to remember that Paul's words are in a Jewish context.

Dunn points out that the 'wrath of God' is not just about end times because 'God's final judgement is simply the end of a process already in train (see also particularly 1 Enoch 84:4, 91:1–7)' (*Romans*, p.54). Both the divine righteousness and the divine wrath are being revealed now. And so the effects of suppressing the truth are spelt out.

In this section Paul is obviously thinking of Gentile societies because there is no mention of the Jewish Torah or Law. The core issue is 'idolatry' which to Paul means putting anything else in the place of God. The most obvious way in which this happened may have been the literal construction of idols. However there are other ways in which people may elevate the physical creation rather than the One who created it. Scientific knowledge of nature is a good thing, largely pioneered by practising Christians, but it is not good when from this people attempt to derive moral principles. Empirical research seems to show that for some people homosexual inclinations are inherent (though not exclusively genetic). Possibly one day we will know more exactly the physical causes of this. But surely from this to derive the belief that gay relationships must be good seems to be to worship the creation rather than the Creator. There are many other inherent inclinations in some human beings which we decide definitely are wrong to follow. For Paul the conscience (as we will see) can be a guide, but ultimately the truth about what God intended is in God's revelation to us.

Verse 32 contains a sting in the tail. It is not just *doing* such things but approving them that he condemns. In our present Western societies we are all but at the point where disapproval of gay sex acts is seen as reprehensible.

Questions for Thought and Discussion

- What are the problems in applying what Paul says to our own society today?
- How can we discuss these passages in ways that are relevant to a modern listener?
- The words 'professing to be wise they became fools' is biting, but where can it be applied to our society today?

Text 2:1–3

¹ Therefore you have no excuse, whoever you are, when you judge others; for in passing judgement on another you condemn yourself, because you, the judge, are doing the very same things. ² You say, 'We know that God's judgement on those who do such things is in accordance with truth.' ³ Do you imagine, whoever you are, that when you judge those who do such things and yet do them yourself, you will escape the judgement of God? (NRSVA)

Commentary

Paul has just spoken of those who claim in their 'wisdom' that debauchery or greed or strife are 'natural' and so excusable. But what of those in society who *do* accept that such things are wrong? Often people have in theory a high standard but in practice live lifestyles which do not keep to it. Paul is not speaking here of some kind of mythical ethical perfection – this was not a concept in first century Judaism or Paganism. He speaks rather of a lifestyle that is not in a repentant relationship with God. To 'do (practice) such things' speaks of the lifestyle of someone that Jewish people (including Jesus) would call a 'sinner' as compared to a righteous person.

Text 2:4–16

⁴ Or do you think lightly of the riches of His kindness and tolerance and patience, not knowing that the kindness of God leads you to repentance? ⁵ But because of your stubbornness and unrepentant heart you are storing up wrath for yourself in the day of wrath and revelation of the righteous judgment of God, ⁶ who will render to each person according to his deeds: ⁷ to those who by perseverance in doing good seek for glory and honour and immortality, eternal life; ⁸ but to those who are selfishly ambitious and do not obey the truth, but obey unrighteousness, wrath and indignation. ⁹ There will be tribulation and distress for every soul of man who does evil, of the Jew first and also of the Greek, ¹⁰ but glory and honour and peace to everyone who does good, to the Jew first and also to the Greek. ¹¹ For there is no partiality with God. (NASB)

¹² All who have sinned apart from the law will also perish apart from the law, and all who have sinned under the law will be judged by the law. ¹³ For it is not the hearers of the law who are righteous in

God's sight, but the doers of the law who will be justified. [14] When Gentiles, who do not possess the law, do instinctively what the law requires, these, though not having the law, are a law to themselves. [15] They show that what the law requires is written on their hearts, to which their own conscience also bears witness; and their conflicting thoughts will accuse or perhaps excuse them [16] on the day when, according to my gospel, God, through Jesus Christ, will judge the secret thoughts of all. (NRSVA)

Discussion Topic: Who are these People who 'Do Good'?

Paul contrasts those who despise God's goodness and stubbornly stay impenitent with a group he describes as follows:

- Those who by perseverance in doing good seek for glory and honour and incorruption (2:7)
- Everyone who 'does good' (literally: 'works what is good') (2:10)
- Gentiles who have not the Torah Law, but instinctively (literally 'by nature') do those things in the law, show 'the work of the law' (which the NRSVA renders 'what the law requires') written in their hearts (2:14–15)
- Those whose conscience also bears witness and their conflicting thoughts accusing or perhaps excusing them on that (judgement) day (2:16)
- Those who are uncircumcised but 'keep the Law' – the 'true Jews' who have circumcision of the heart (2:26–29)

Who are these good people?

Some commentators (like Kasemann, Fitzmyer and Dunn)

see the earlier and later verses as referring to different groups, but this would be a lot to expect Paul's hearers to grasp.

Plainly, they are Gentiles not Jews. They 'have not the Torah' so presumably are *not* like the Christian Gentiles in Rome who *are* familiar with the Torah (Romans 7:9) so 'have the Torah'. They seem to rely on their consciences and 'nature' leading them to God, rather than any kind of specific revelation – whether we speak of the revelation of the Torah or the revelation of the words of Jesus.

In *The New Interpreters Bible*, N. T. Wright identifies three possibilities as to who they are (p.441). We can summarise these three alternatives as:

a) 'This is a purely hypothetical category. Paul is indicating that, when God judges the secrets of all hearts, if there should be any who succeeded in doing good, they would indeed reap the appropriate reward; but he is holding up a mirage that will disappear when the argument is complete. There may, in other words, be Gentiles who fulfil part of the Law, but this will count for nothing.'

b) 'Others have . . . seen 2:1 as evidence that Paul does not hold, after all that all humans are sinners. He is aware, they say, that in both the Jewish and pagan world there are some humans who really do that which God intends, who avoid vice and practice virtue, and who will be suitably rewarded at the end.'

c) 'The people in question are Christian Gentiles.'

The first option a), seems absurd though it was basically the approach of Augustine and Luther (and Schreiner (*Romans*, p.114) supports it and gives a list of supporters). Why talk about hypothetical non-existent people? Who would it convince anyway? What weight would a hypothetical non-existent Gentile carry with the Jews in 2:17 to whom Paul talks about such Gentiles? Why does Paul not make it clearly suppositional: '*If there were* any Gentiles who kept the whole of the Torah and lived perfect lives then God *would* accept them'?

The second, b), is ambiguous and Wright does not really clarify what he means. As we have noted, both the Old and New Testaments consistently contrast the 'righteous' and the 'sinners'. If Wright means 'sinners' in the *biblical* sense then plainly not all humans are sinners. But how then can Wright go on to claim that this option 'falls foul of Paul's emphasis on the universality of human sin'? Paul (like everyone else) knows that everyone has sinned, but nowhere says that all humans are 'sinners' in the biblical sense of this term. In *Romans for Everyone* (p. 41) Wright seems to identify this option b) as 'any Gentile who happens to make a special moral effort'. However Scripture never suggests that what it calls a 'righteous' person is to be defined as someone 'who makes a special moral effort' – faith is *always* the basis of being righteous. In summary, therefore, if b) means people who have never sinned it is the same as a), and is absurd. If it means Gentiles who 'make a special moral effort' there is no indication anywhere in Scripture that this could be a basis of being in right relationship with God. In either case, b) cannot be what Paul means.

Wright himself goes for his option c) (as do Cranfield, Jewett, and others). In chapter 2 of our book *Reconsidering Key Biblical Ideas* we look in detail at this and explain why it is very unlikely on both contextual and linguistic grounds. Here we will just mention the two major problems with it:

1. First, why would Gentile Christians have to rely on nature and conscience etc to know what is right? They have access not only to the Old Testament Jewish Scriptures but also to the sayings of Jesus

conveyed to them by his followers. The prophecy in Jeremiah 31:33, about the New Covenant, promises that Christians (Jews and Gentiles) will have *the law* (the Torah) written on their hearts, but there is no implication that they don't know what the Torah is. In *Paul's Letter to the Romans* Witherington rightly notes: 'Paul does not speak here of the Law written on pagan's hearts, but rather the effects of the Law written on their hearts' (p.83). The Christians in Rome, Jews and Gentiles, know what the Torah says (Romans 7:1). The people mentioned here in Romans 2 don't have *the Law* written on their hearts, they have the *work of the Law* (or 'what the Law really requires') – but it is explicit that they do not have or know the Torah-Law itself. So it is *not* Gentile Christians, who do have the Torah itself.

2. Secondly, these people in Romans 2 lack the Christian certainty of God's forgiveness. Paul characterizes them thus: *their conscience also bearing witness, and between themselves their thoughts accusing (or else excusing them) in the day when God will judge the secrets of men by Jesus Messiah*. This contrasts with the ringing confidence later in the letter with which he assures Gentile Christians that they have been 'declared righteous by faith' (5:1) 'have peace with God through our Lord Jesus the Messiah' (5:1) 'have died with Messiah' and been buried in baptism and risen anew with him (6:2–5) and there is 'now therefore no condemnation for those who are in Jesus the Messiah' (8:1). With all this, are Gentile Christians just to kind of hope that our thoughts might accuse or maybe even excuse

111

us on the day of judgement? Whoever these people are in Romans 2:15–16, surely they cannot be us Gentile Christians. Wright suggests that for Gentile Christians 'being outside the Torah and yet fulfilling it from the heart, leaves them with questions that may produce a moment of panic in even the most settled believer' (p.442). We disagree! We don't know of any Christians to whom not having fulfilled Torah is an issue, and any Christian we know who has died at peace has never had a moment of panic that they have not fulfilled the Jewish Law. It is all just wildly improbable. Paul is not talking here about people who sound anything like Gentile Christians.

These people are none of the three groups that Wright suggests., so *who are they?* **They are Gentiles who have faith in God because His goodness in creation has led them to repentance and to seek glory and honour and incorruption through their faith in Him.** We know that Jesus was the man crowned with glory and honour (Hebrews 2:9) who did not see corruption (Acts 2:31). They didn't realise it but really they were seeking Jesus the Messiah. They are not sinless, but are 'righteous' – like the Gentiles Noah and Job as well as the Jew Habakkuk and many others. The meaning of 'righteous' is looked at in depth in our book *Reconsidering Key Biblical Ideas,* chapter 2. Davies in *Faith and Obedience in Romans* again rightly states that this refers to 'pre-Christian Gentiles who are not only doers of the law but who are also justified before God' (p.60–67).

Epimenides taught the Athenians to sacrifice to the unknown God in the sixth century BC. In Acts 17 Paul says he has found an Athenian altar to the unknown God and,

> [23] Therefore what you worship in ignorance, this I proclaim to you. [24] The God who made the world

and all things in it, since He is Lord of heaven and earth, does not dwell in temples made with hands; [25] nor is He served by human hands, as though He needed anything, since He Himself gives to all people life and breath and all things; [26] and He made from one man every nation of mankind to live on all the face of the earth, having determined their appointed times and the boundaries of their habitation, [27] that they would seek God, if perhaps they might grope for Him and find Him, though He is not far from each one of us; [28] for in Him we live and move and exist, as even some of your own poets have said, 'For we also are His children. (NASB)

This is the same theme as Romans 2, the idea that people who never heard the Jewish/Christian revelation could find God. The quotation 'in Him we live and move and exist', quoted with approval, is from Epimenides, who is also quoted in Titus 1:12.

Then Paul goes on in Acts 17:29–31:

[29] Being then the children of God, we ought not to think that the Divine Nature is like gold or silver or stone, an image formed by the art and thought of man. [30] Therefore having overlooked the times of ignorance, God is now declaring to men that all people everywhere should repent, [31] because He has fixed a day in which He will judge the world in righteousness through a Man whom He has appointed, having furnished proof to all men by raising Him from the dead. (NASB)

God has overlooked a certain amount of ignorance mixed with worship of the true God. Now He calls on everyone to accept His Messiah, the righteous judge, repenting of any former ignorance.

Discussion Topic: The Basis of Judgement

Jesus spoke more than anyone else about a coming Day of Judgement. Consistently He said that this will be based neither on people's ancestry, nor their creed, nor their rituals, but on the kind of life they have lived. So Jesus said:

> The hour is coming when all who are in their graves will hear His {Jesus'} voice [29] and will come out—those who have done good, to the resurrection of life, and those who have done evil, to the resurrection of condemnation. (John 5:32)

In Matthew 7:21 Jesus makes it clear that a Christian profession will not be enough – they escape judgment only if they actually do God's will in their lives. In Matthew 25 (and we look at this in our *God's Path to Victory*) Jesus said clearly that their fate will be based neither on their claiming Him as Lord nor on whether they did great deeds for Him, but on whether their lives reflected His own love and compassion. God judges people according to their work (1 Peter 1:17). John in 1 John 3:7 says that a righteous person is someone who acts righteously. In Revelation 22:12 Jesus says:

> Behold, I am coming quickly, and my reward is with me, to render to every man according to what he has done . . . the dead were judged according to their works, as recorded in the books. (NASB)

Paul himself said in 2 Corinthians 5:10:

> [10] For all of us must appear before the judgement seat of Christ, so that each may receive recompense for what has been done in the body, whether good or evil.

In Romans 2 Paul says:

> [6] For He will repay according to each one's deeds: [7] to those who by patiently doing good seek for glory and honour and immortality, He will give eternal life; [8] while for those who are self-seeking and who obey not the truth

but wickedness, there will be wrath and fury. [9] There will be anguish and distress for everyone who does evil, the Jew first and also the Greek, [10] but glory and honour and peace for everyone who does good, the Jew first and also the Greek. [11] For God shows no partiality. (NRSVA)

Some commentators find all this puzzling? Surely justification and salvation are based on grace alone, not on 'works', and works must mean anything we do? So Paul's words may be explained away as referring to 'purely hypothetical non-existent perfect people', though how the words of Jesus and John can be similarly explained away is never made clear.

Actually there is no contradiction:

1. Justification/salvation are never 'earned' but always a free and undeserved gift from God.

2. God gives these gifts, and forgiveness of sin, based on the faithfulness in sacrificial death of Jesus the Messiah.

3. He gives them by graciously accounting faith as rightstanding.

4. But 'faith' (whether for Old Testament Jews, non-Jews like Enoch or Job, or Christians) is never merely belief, but a dynamic relationship in which love for God overflows into love for others.

5. Anyone whose lifestyle does not reflect this is not righteous (1 John 3:7) has a 'faith' that is dead (James 2:26) and, whatever their profession of Christianity, is bound for judgement (Matthew 7:21–23, Matthew 25).

So judgement according to what someone 'has done' does not mean they have to clock up a set of deeds, and even less does it mean they need to fulfil some meticulous legalistic markers of being religious. It means whether their lifestyle has been lived in a love relationship with God, reflected in their behaviour to others.

Commentary

God's longsuffering and care as revealed in nature are meant to lead people to repentance. If this were impossible for them to do, then these would be empty words – and surely God cannot 'mean' for it to lead to something that can never in fact happen? Actually, repentance leads not to ritual works but to a faith-life. A 'righteous' person, we repeat, is not someone who never sinned but someone living a faith-life with God. Neither Paul nor anyone else thought there could be people who never sinned (apart from Messiah Himself), and inventing hypothetical ones would be silly.

Paul, like the other apostles, is always clear that judgement is based on lifestyle, and that a righteous lifestyle is not indicated by ritual works but by a life lived in faith-relationship with God.

John also makes the distinction between someone who 'sins' as a lifestyle choice, and a faith-life Christian who sometimes falls into sin. John says:

> [7] Make sure no one deceives you; the one who practices righteousness is righteous, just as He is righteous; [8] the one who practices sin is of the devil. (1 John 3:7–8, NASB)

As John makes clear, 'doing what is right' is living a faith-life, so *no one who is born of God sins* (1 John 5:18). Again, in this sense to 'sin' refers not to isolated and then repented acts, but to a chosen sinful lifestyle in rebellion against God. Similarly in Paul, those who 'sin' inside or outside the Jewish Torah Law are contrasted with those who 'work what is good' and this refers to lifestyle choice. Neither John nor Paul are talking about some kind of salvation by works, and on the other hand neither are suggesting that a 'righteous' person is merely someone who somehow claims Jesus' righteousness irrespective of their own lifestyle.

In reality 'those who work what is good' does not refer to hypothetically perfect but in fact non-existent people, or the text would say 'God would give them glory and honour and peace, but in fact there aren't any.' It does not refer exclusively to Christians, for else how would faithful Old Testament Jews receive any glory and honour and peace? Neither does 'work what is good' mean that through works they earn God's forgiveness. To 'work what is good' means a life lived in a faith-relationship with God to whatever limits of knowledge of God a person has.

Paul says that some Gentiles instinctively or 'by nature' do 'the things in the Law'. Of course this does *not* mean that they perform the ceremonials and symbolism in the Law – they do not keep the diet, physical circumcision and Sabbaths. These latter are called by Paul 'works of the Law', and Gentiles do not keep them. But, he says, they have the *real meaning* of them written on their hearts. Diet and Sabbaths are 'shadows' of the realities in Messiah – so believes Paul (Colossians 2:17) and the writer to the Hebrews (Hebrews 8:5). Gentile lifestyles can reflect what these symbols were actually meant to teach, ie a faith-life of right living; the 'works of the law' are in their hearts (see also 2:28).

Many commentators have pointed out that the core passage 2:6–11 has what is technically called a chiastic structure:

> **Ai:** God will judge everyone according to their deeds (2:6)
>
>> **Bi:** Those who seek glory and honour and incorruption and do good will attain eternal life (2:7)
>>
>>> **Ci:** Those who selfishly do unrighteousness will incur wrath and anger (2:8)
>>>
>>> **Cii:** Those who do evil will suffer tribulation and distress (2:9)
>>
>> **Bii:** Those who do good will receive glory and honour and peace (2:10)
>
> **Aii:** God will judge everyone impartially (2:11).

A chiasm is a repetition of similar ideas in the reverse sequence, but to bring out some particular emphasis. Paul here adds 'to the Jew first and also to the Gentile' to both Cii and Bii, to spell out the impartiality theme developed in the second part of the chiasm. Parts Ai, Bi, and Ci, would seem unexceptional to Jews. Throughout the Old Testament God's eye is on the righteous to reward them, but His wrath against the unrighteous. Paul is developing a familiar theme of there being two streams of humanity (which is what this whole section is about – not about 'universal condemnation' which is an un-Jewish invention of later Christian commentators). In the second part of the chiasm (Cii, Bii and Aii) Paul says the principles that the Jews would have accepted must apply to both Jew and Gentiles. It is a shame that commentators have confused this beautiful structure by making one half of the chiasm non-existent imaginary people or exclusively Christians so that through most of history God was indeed partial and accepted only Jews.

Following on from this, Paul wants to develop three fundamental arguments in this part of Romans:

1. God has *always* been 'impartial' – Jews have always been first to receive blessing (they have the oracles of God (3:2)), *but also the first to receive judgement* (hence the last part of the chiasm).

2. The basis of being given rightstanding before God (for Jew or Gentile) has always been faith in God, not rituals or national markers.

3. We now at last realise that the basis on which God can count faith as rightstanding has always been on the faithfulness in sacrificial death of Jesus the Messiah (3:21).

Text 2:17–29

[17] But if you bear the name 'Jew' and rely upon the Law and boast in God, [18] and know His will and approve the things that are essential, being instructed out of the Law, [19] and are confident that you yourself are a guide to the blind, a light to those who are in darkness, [20] a corrector of the foolish, a teacher of the immature, having in the Law the embodiment of knowledge and of the truth, [21] you, therefore, who teach another, do you not teach yourself? You who preach that one shall not steal, do you steal? [22] You who say that one should not commit adultery, do you commit adultery? You who abhor idols, do you rob temples? [23] You who boast in the Law, through your breaking the Law, do you dishonour God? [24] For 'the name of God is blasphemed among the Gentiles because of you', just as it is written. [25] For indeed circumcision is of value if you practice the Law; but if you are a transgressor of the Law, your circumcision has become uncircumcision. [26] So if the uncircumcised man keeps the requirements of the Law, will not his uncircumcision be regarded as circumcision? [27] And he who is physically uncircumcised, if he keeps the Law, will He not judge you who though having the letter of the Law and circumcision are a transgressor of the Law? [28] For he is not a Jew who is one outwardly, nor is circumcision that which is outward in the flesh. [29] But he is a Jew who is one inwardly; and circumcision is that which is of the heart, by the Spirit, not by the letter; and his praise is not from men, but from God. (NASB)

Commentary

Paul here turns to attack the feelings of national pride and superiority that many Jews felt. God had given them the Torah, and this marked their superiority. Actually they might well ascribe their superior position in regard to holiness to God: 'God, *I thank you* that I am not as other men', said the Pharisee in Luke 18:11! It is not so much just the self-reliance but the attitude of moral superiority that Paul attacks.

Obviously not all Jews committed adultery and robbed Temples, so there are two thoughts here:

– First, though the unconverted Saul of Tarsus probably did not steal, he did covet (Romans 7:8). He probably did not commit adultery, but maybe he did lust. Jesus taught that when we really long for and drool over something we should not have, then this is a sin (Matthew 5:28).

– Secondly, in spite of what the commentaries seem to say, Paul is not having to show that *all* Jews were like this. Plainly they were not. Those like Zechariah, Anna and Simeon (not to mention the many righteous Old Testament Jews who lived by faith) did not live that kind of life. But Paul is thinking of the generality of the Jewish nation. The name of God is blasphemed not because every single Jew is wicked, but because people look at the group as a whole. Actually the same could apply to the Church, and all too often does. If people look at the Church and see a lot of greedy, quarrelsome, self-righteous, and judgemental people in it, they may blaspheme the name of our God – even if there are some Christians in it who are none of these things. So before we think too strongly about how the Jews failed to be a 'light to the nations', we might wonder about the Church.

The Gentile could 'by nature' do the things in the Law (2:14), and could 'fulfil the Law' (2:27). Again, of course, this did not mean all the ceremonials of the Law. It is in the sense of Romans 13:8 that all the Law is fulfilled if Love is central. To reiterate, this is not talking about hypothetical but non-existent ethically perfect and sinless people, it is talking about real people walking in faith with God and reflecting this in lifestyle.

Questions for Thought and Discussion

- Today the church is meant to be the 'light of the world' (Matthew 5:14). But in practice how much better at this has it been than the nation of Israel?

- In what ways do Christians behave unlovingly towards those of differing views?

- The Pharisee in Luke 18:11 said 'God, I thank you that I am not like other men . . .' He accepted that it was 'all of grace', so what was it about his attitude that Jesus didn't like?

Text 3:1–8

¹ Then what advantage has the Jew? Or what is the value of circumcision? ² Much, in every way. For in the first place the Jews were entrusted with the oracles of God. ³ What if some were unfaithful? Will their faithlessness nullify the faithfulness of God? ⁴ By no means! Although everyone is a liar, let God be proved true, as it is written,

'So that You may be justified in Your words, and prevail in Your judging.'

⁵ But if our injustice serves to confirm the justice of God, what should we say? That God is unjust to inflict wrath on us? (I speak in a human way.) ⁶ By no means! For then how could God judge the world? ⁷ But if through my falsehood God's truthfulness abounds to His glory, why am I still being condemned as a sinner? ⁸ And why not say (as some people slander us by saying that we say), 'Let us do evil so that good may come'? Their condemnation is deserved! (NRSVA)

Discussion Topic: The Situation of Jews and Gentiles

What were the situations of Jews and Gentiles before the Messiah came? Put starkly, different commentators have advocated the following four alternatives:

1. The 'Law' was impossible to keep, it was given only to show how bad sin was, and so all Jews (as well as Gentiles) before Jesus were damned. *Christian* faith is the only way to be right with God.

2. In the Old Testament there was a 'dispensation' of Law, and people could be saved through keeping the Torah, but in the new dispensation, after Jesus died, only Christians can be saved.

3. Jews who were in the Abrahamic covenant could be saved through faith in Old Testament times (the Mosaic covenant being only to condemn), but Gentiles outside that covenant and without Scripture were all damned.

4. Having the Scriptures was an *advantage* for Jews, but Gentiles who through nature had the meanings of the Torah on their hearts could live a faith-life and be righteous before God, just as could faithful Jews. In both cases this was a remnant, and the Jews and Gentiles as a whole were not righteous.

The first of these, seems absurd as we have already said. Some may argue that in some oblique sense David and Isaiah were 'Christians', but this seems hard to apply to the 7,000 faithful men in Elijah's time (1 Kings 19:18, Romans 11:4). Moreover Hebrews 11 lists many Old Testament people of faith, some of whom like Gideon and Barak, lived before even any clear prophecy about the Messiah had been given. How could they be called 'Christians'?

To spell out the meaning of option 2 consider Barnhouse's comment in his *Romans* commentary:

> . . . there is no hope for any man outside of Christ, whether that man lived beyond the bounds of the gospel call or within its bounds. Only those covered by the grace of God manifested at the cross will be able to enter God's Heaven. This would mean that the company of the saved includes the Old Testament believers and the New Testament believers. This company began with the salvation of righteous Abel who believed God's Word about the blood, and continued through the glorious multitude of those who were blessed in the covenant of Abraham, that vast number of the children of Israel who were saved because God looked upon their faith when the High Priest offered the sacrifice on the day of atonement as being faith in the Lord Jesus. (ii p.69)

The second sentence is undoubtedly true. But Barnhouse's interpretation of this is that those saved in the covenant of Abraham are those who had the Jewish Day of Atonement, ie had the Torah. Full-blown 'Dispensationalists' see seven different eras in which God related differently to humans, and during the time from Moses to Jesus God related through the Mosaic Law. According to Barnhouse, at least during this whole period, only Jews could be saved through their Day of Atonement. Well if this were really correct Paul *should* have said in Romans 3:1 *'What advantage then has the Jew? Total advantage. For some two millennia until the era (or dispensation) of Jesus only Torah-keeping Jews could be saved; all the Gentiles were damned.'*

The third option is no more plausible than 2. Again this view seems odd because when Paul asks: 'What advantage then has the Jew?' (3:1) he should then again have replied: *'Much in every way because up until the time of Messiah only Abrahamic*

Jews could be saved.' His whole point is the level playing field between Jews and Gentiles, but option 3 would imply that (in his day) for all the time since Abraham none but Jews could be saved and only in the last thirty years since Jesus died was it open to Gentiles as well.

The only answer which fits the cultural and textual contexts is 4. It is faith in God that God accounts as rightstanding – whether that faith is faith of Abraham or Job or Epimenides. The Law is just one way in which that faith can be expressed – but Abraham and Job did not have the Law and it would seem odd to imagine that although until the time of Moses God could relate to any individual in any land He chose on an individual basis, after the giving of Torah He restricted Himself to Israel. The Jews had an advantage not because they had the Law but because they had the specific words of God which were an aid to faith. However an 'advantage' does not mean that all those who (like Job) never heard the Torah were damned.

Commentary

So if Jews can be as bad as Gentiles, and Gentiles can come to recognise God through the light of nature, what advantage is there in being Jewish? Paul's answer is not 'because they have Torah' but because they have the 'oracles' or 'words (*logia*) of God'. It was not so much the 'Law' but more generally the 'words' of God. These words are a better way to come to know and understand God than merely the light of nature. So this is an *advantage*, but it is not condemning all Gentiles before Jesus to damnation, and neither is it any grounds for feelings of Jewish moral superiority.

Moreover, if *some* Jews were unfaithful, this was not God's fault. Note that he says *some* here, because of course not *all* Jews were unfaithful. None of this has been about any supposed 'universal condemnation' as so many commentators have invented. Of course there had been righteous Jews as the Old Testament repeatedly makes very clear.

In 3:4 Paul quotes David in Psalm 51:4. Nathan has declared God's judgement, and David has recognised his great sin. David is recognising God to be righteous in pronouncing judgement, even though he is part of the Jewish covenant community and is its appointed king. David does not blame God for his sin, rather God is justified (shown to be righteous) in His judgement on it. Later, in Romans 4:6–8 Paul will cite David's thankfulness in Psalm 32 that his sin is not imputed to him. But the point is that God's faithfulness to His covenant people does not mean that he shows partiality in the matter of judgement. The covenant always contained both blessing and curses, and it is their response that determines which is applied at a given point. None of it is about 'works' but about whether they are truly walking in faith.

In 3:5–8 Paul deals with a quibbling objector. Paul must often have met such a person in his preaching, and these are silly objections which Paul dismisses. The first objection is that if God actually finds a use for our unrighteousness then He is unjust to punish us for it. Well of course God did not cause that unrighteousness unless one assumes that everything that happens is determined directly by Him. If this were true (as was taught by Augustine and his followers down to the modern theologian Paul Helm) then the objector would have a point, but neither Paul nor his Pharisaic opponents believed this. The Essenes *did* believe that everything was preordained by God, but Josephus (himself a Pharisee) insists that the Pharisees had a more balanced view. Alfred Edersheim nicely summarised this long ago:

> Although every event depended upon God, whether a man served God or not was entirely his own choice. As a logical sequence of this, fate had no influence as regarded Israel, since all depended upon prayer, repentance, and good works. Indeed, otherwise that repentance, on which Rabbinism so largely insists, would have no meaning. Moreover, it seems as if it had been intended to convey that, while our evil actions were entirely our own choice, if a man sought to amend his ways, he would be helped of God . . . in the language of the great Akiba: 'Everything is foreseen; free determination is accorded to man; and the world is judged in goodness.' (*The Life and Times of Jesus the Messiah*, pp.318–319)

The second objection is equally silly: 'If God uses everything for His purposes why not do evil because God will find some useful purpose in it?' Paul does not even bother to answer this, he dismisses it contemptuously.

Text 3:9–18

⁹ What then? Are we better than they? Not at all; for we have already charged that both Jews and Greeks are all under sin; ¹⁰ as it is written,

'There is none righteous, not even one;
¹¹ There is none who understands,
  There is none who seeks for God;
¹² All have turned aside, together they have become useless;
  There is none who does good,
  There is not even one.'
¹³ 'Their throat is an open grave,
  With their tongues they keep deceiving,'
  'The poison of asps is under their lips';
¹⁴ 'Whose mouth is full of cursing and bitterness';
¹⁵ 'Their feet are swift to shed blood,
¹⁶ Destruction and misery are in their paths,
¹⁷ And the path of peace they have not known.'
¹⁸ 'There is no fear of God before their eyes.'

¹⁹ Now we know that whatever the Law says, it speaks to those who are under the Law, so that every mouth may be closed and all the world may become accountable to God; ²⁰ because by the works of the Law no flesh will be justified in His sight; for through the Law comes the knowledge of sin. (NASB)

Discussion Topic: Universal Sinfulness and the Old Testament

Leon Morris in *The Epistle to the Romans*, as many others, heads this section 3:1–9 'Universal Sinfulness – Proof from Scripture'. Many commentaries see this as Paul 'proving' from the Old Testament either that everyone has sinned, or that everyone is unrighteous, but neither of these two suggestions makes cultural or contextual sense. Paul did not have to 'prove' that everyone has sinned because no one doubted it, and in any case the Old Testament verses he quotes are not saying this. Nor are any of the passages he quotes saying that literally everyone is unrighteous, because in each of the verses Paul cites there is a comparison between the bulk of people who are acting wickedly and the remnant who *are* righteous.

Many commentaries (for example those by Morris, Dunn, Cranfield and Longenecker) give us the sources of Paul's quotations here, and it is important to note that:

- Ecclesiastes 7:20 comes after a reference to a 'just (righteous) man who perishes in his righteousness' (v15)
- Psalm 14:1–3 contrasts those complained of with 'my people' (v4)
- Psalm 53:1–3 again contrasts those condemned with 'My people' (v4) and 'His people' (v6)
- Psalm 5:9 follows in v11 with 'let all those rejoice who put their trust in You.'
- Psalm 140 (v3) finishes in verese 13 by rejoicing that the 'righteous will give thanks to your name'.
- Psalm 10:7 is in a passage which refers throughout to the 'wicked' who seem to be getting away with it. In verse 14 this is contrasted with the 'helpless' who 'commits himself to You' and in verse 17 God hears the voice of the humble.
- Isaiah 59:7–8 is part of a great lament over national apostasy, yet it follows his earlier laments in 57:1 that 'the righteous perishes and no man takes it to heart.'
- Psalm 36:1 continues with a whole series of references to 'the children of men' who 'put their trust under Your wings' and receive blessing, to 'those who know You' and receive lovingkindness, and to those who are 'upright in heart'.

In *none* of these is the writer saying that *everyone* is guilty or unrighteous. In *every* instance there is reference also to the 'righteous', the 'upright in heart', 'those who trust in God', or 'God's people'. If Paul really were trying to prove 'universal sinfulness' (either in the sense that 'all have sinned' or that 'everyone is unrighteous') he would be grossly misquoting these Old Testament verses. In *Faith and Obedience in Romans* Davies (p.82ff) looks in more detail at the Old Testament quotes and notes:

> None of the texts cited refers to the universal sinfulness of man. Rather they all testify to the sinfulness of the wicked (be they Jew or Gentile) in contrast to the faithfulness of the righteous.

If this were really about supposed 'universal and total depravity' Davies notes 'it makes Paul's choice of Old Testament passages singularly inept' (p.89). Some commentators recognise this but claim that Paul had the authority to misquote. This seems silly because Paul was used to dialoguing in synagogues on such issues (see Acts 18:4; 18:19; 19:8–9; 28:23) and it would have been totally pointless to quote verses out of context based on his 'apostolic authority'. Actually, Paul studied under Gamaliel, who studied in the school of the renowned teacher Hillel. The seventh of Hillel's interpretive rules or *middoth* (the rule *dabar halamed me-'inyano*) argued that a passage must always be interpreted by its context (see Longnecker *Romans,* p.480). Surely Paul would do this? Even if (as Longenecker claims) some earlier (though unknown to us) Jewish writer bunched these quotations together out of context to prove 'universal sinfulness', surely the great apostle would not have done so?

Dunn says that Paul is not 'thinking of everyone as specific individuals. But of Jews and Gentile sin in general, as an ethnic and social solidarity to which the particular 'I' belongs' (p.156). Yet, although Dunn is one of the greatest of modern commentators, so strong is the tradition that it must mean 'universal sinfulness' that on the next page Dunn says that in verse 19 it means that everyone is unrighteous. Somehow, then, when Paul quotes a set of Scriptures in which each of them compares the unrighteous with the wicked, 'when these Scriptures are read without the blinkers of Jewish presumption of privilege' actually 'they mean *no one*'. But this would be a very poor kind of exegesis for Paul to make. If we decode what Dunn implies, then it means that because Paul has previously claimed (as Dunn believes) that everyone is unrighteous, then even though these verses say nothing of the kind they must really mean this. Another commentator suggests that while in each individual verse there is a contrast between righteous and wicked, when we put them all together it implies universal sinfulness. This is a bizarre argument, like saying that if we have ten boxes containing each a mixture of black and white tiles, when we put the boxes together then all the tiles are black.

All of this strange argument is to try to preserve the common commentator fixation with an idea of universal condemnation of all humankind (ie all individuals) which fits neither with the literary background nor with the Old Testament historical cultural context, nor with what Paul actually says.

The real point is that Paul often speaks in general terms of nations – as we do today. We may say 'The Chinese don't care about cricket' or 'The British today are ungodly and materialistic'. But this does not imply that there is *no one* in China who likes cricket (actually there *is* a national Chinese cricket team!), or that there is *no one* in Britain who is god-fearing and living righteously in relationship with God as a faithful Christian. N.T. Wright in *Paul and the Faithfulness of God* says:

> The frequent OT phrase 'all Israel' makes the point (eg Ex. 18.:25; Dt. 1.1; 5.1; 13.11; 29.2; 31.11; 34.12; Josh. 3.7; 1 Sam. 3.20; 7.5; 25.1; 2 Sam. 8.15; 1 Kgs. 8.62; 12.1; 18.19; 1 Chr. 9.1; 18.14; 29.21; 2 Chr.

12.1; 29.24; Dan. 9.11); these regularly refer to the great bulk of the people without at all implying 'every single individual'. (vol 2, p.673)

This is the point. These verses (and Paul's quotation of them) are referring to characteristics of nations as a whole. It is nothing to do with any supposed idea of 'universal human sinfulness'. We are not denying, of course, that all humans *have* sinned, just that this was not Paul's point here. He makes that point in passing later, knowing that no one would deny it. But Paul never says that all humankind are under the wrath of God, because those (Jews and Gentiles) who live by faith are justified and accepted by God, and so are not under wrath. Paul's point is that God's wrath is revealed against *those who suppress the truth in unrighteousness* – and there have been many times when such people predominated in Jewish as well as Gentile societies.

Commentary

There are variant ancient manuscript readings of 3:9 but we take the standard Nestle Greek version as most likely. In Romans 3:1 Paul asked what advantage had the Jew, and answered 'a lot'. He is now going to ask something on which he will be more critical of the Jews, and so includes himself and identifies with the nation: 'What then? Do *we* (Jews) excel?' The exact meaning of this term rendered 'excel' is controversial. The word *proechó* translates as 'to hold before' and here seems to mean to excel or surpass. The NIV makes this question in verse 9 exactly the same question as 3:1, but it would be odd for Paul to ask the same question twice and give opposite answers. Surely also, having an advantage must mean that someone *is* 'better off' and wouldn't this make it the same question? The NKJV and NASB (and various other translations) seem to us correct in taking it, not as 'Are we Jews better off?', but simply as 'Are we Jews any better?' Though Cranfield seems to take the answer as 'Not altogether' most commentators take it to mean 'Not at all'. The Jews have an *advantage* but are they therefore better in practice? No!

Paul then says 'for we have previously charged both Jews and Greeks, all under sin.' Many commentaries take this to refer back to a supposed 'universal sinfulness' of all men in 1:18, but it seems more likely to refer to 2:24, or maybe by the 'we' he means 'we Jews' in the Old Testament quotes which follow. In either case, of course, it is speaking about the nations as a whole, not implying that every individual is unrighteous, as this is plainly not so.

The quotations with which Paul follows this are not saying that every individual in both categories (Jews and Gentiles) is unrighteous (which is clearly *not* the Old Testament teaching), nor that every individual has sinned (which no one denied but is not the point of these verses). Paul's point is that actually the Old Testament prophets castigated the Jewish nation at least as often as they did Gentile ones. Israel in general did *not* use its advantage of having God's words to be a light to the Gentiles; more often than not the nation was deplorable in its unrighteousness, and the name of God was blasphemed because of them (as in 2:24). They did *not* excel.

Having God's direct words, then, was an advantage, but having the Torah did not produce national superiority, and ritual observance was no indicator of a righteous lifestyle.

Text 3:19–20

[19] Now we know that whatever the Law says, it speaks to those who are under the Law, so that every mouth may be closed and all the world may become accountable [Greek: *hupodikos*] to God; [20] because [Greek: *dioti*] by the works of the Law no flesh will be justified in His sight; for through the Law comes the knowledge of sin. (NASB)

Commentary

The NASB (or indeed the NRSVA) translates this much better than for example the NKJV, though we would prefer the punctuation to read: *'Now we know that whatever the Law says to those under the Law, it speaks . . .'* Those who are 'under the law' (or 'in the law') are the Jews. Morris suggests those who 'have their whole being in the Law' (*The Epistle to the Romans* p.170), but where this phrase is used in Galatians it simply seems to mean those who are under the Torah's direction. The stopping of a mouth was symbolised by a defendant putting his hand over his mouth to indicate that he had no more to say. In his commentary, Cranfield says that the word *hupodikos* 'is used in extra-Biblical

Greek to describe someone who is guilty in the sense of having offended against the law and so made himself liable to prosecution and punishment' (p.197). In English translations a few render it as 'guilty', more as 'under judgement' but even more as 'accountable' (including the ESV, AMP, NASB, NIV and NRSVA). Maybe 'answerable' (as Sanday & Headlam and Moffat) is not quite strong enough, but 'guilty' (as, for example KJV and N.T. Wright) is too strong. 'Accountable' is the real meaning, or 'under judgement' not in the sense of already condemned but as being held to account.

It is unfortunate that the obsession of commentators with supposed 'universal condemnation' has distorted understanding of these verses. Paul's point is simple. Increased knowledge brings increased accountability. So not only has the Jewish nation failed to stand out as a light to the Gentiles, but Jews, like Gentiles, stand in the dock awaiting a verdict. What they seek is to be 'justified', ie to be declared righteous by God the judge. But works of the Law (and by this Paul means primarily ritual works like circumcision, diet and Sabbaths) are not in themselves a basis for such a declaration because they cannot atone for sins. They are social markers of being Jewish, and in the verses that Paul has just quoted he has shown that the prophets often castigated the nation of Israel as a whole as being ungodly sinners – in spite of them (unlike Gentiles) having these markers.

Actually, in a strange sense, God is also in the dock; His righteousness needs to vindicated. Throughout history there have been a remnant of both Jews and Gentiles who have been 'righteous', ie declared by God to be in rightstanding. But how could God do this? How could He Himself be a righteous judge and yet accept as righteous those who live by faith although they have sinned? In themselves, neither ceremonial works nor faith could cancel out sin, and the Law simply increases knowledge of sin and so potential guilt.

Text 3:21–26

> But now God's righteousness has been revealed apart from the law – though the law and the prophets bear witness to it: it is God's righteousness through the faithfulness of Jesus the Messiah to those who believe [have faith]. For there is no distinction, for all sinned, and came short of the glory of God, and they are justified freely, by His grace through the redemption which is in the Messiah

Jesus. God put Him forth as a means of atonement, through faithfulness, by means of His blood; this was to demonstrate God's righteousness because in His forbearance He had passed over previous sins. It was to demonstrate His righteousness in the present time – that He himself might be in the right [righteous] and might justify [declare righteous] people by Jesus' faithfulness. (N.T. Wright, *What St Paul Really Said* p.128 – Longenecker's translation in his *Romans* commentary is similar.)

Discussion Topic: God's Righteousness and Faithfulness

It should be remembered here that in Greek the terms 'justification' (*dikaiōsis*) and 'righteousness' (*dikaiosynē*) are closely related, and 'faith' and 'believe in' are also from the same root (*pistis, pisteuō*). Here we have used the N.T. Wright translation with some explanatory square brackets of our own reflecting this word identification. Davies in *Faith and Obedience in Romans* gives a very similar rendering. We do so because most of the translations take the genitive phrase *pisteus Iēsou Christou* to (faith/faithfulness of Jesus Christ) as a so-called 'objective genitive' to mean 'faith *in* Jesus Christ'. As we first noted in 1973, the overwhelming evidence is that it is a normal subjective genitive 'the faithfulness *of* Jesus the Messiah'. N.T. Wright, Longenecker and an increasing number of other commentators now accept this. Much detail of the evidence is given in our *Reconsidering Key Biblical Ideas* chapter 3, and Davies also well summarises it, as does Longenecker (*Romans* p.409f) and translates this passage very similarly to Wright. As a short summary:

– Romans 3:3 already referred to the faithfulness *of* God.

– A similar phrase is used in Romans 3:22; 3:26

and Galatians 2:16; 3:22. In all the occasions on which this phrase is used it is more natural to take it to mean 'faithfulness of Jesus the Messiah'. Remembering that in Greek 'believe in' and 'have faith in' are the same word, if the phrase *pisteus Iēsou Christou* meant 'faith in Jesus Christ' it would become absurdly repetitious in Galatians. The claim that this is just for emphasis is unconvincing.

– There is no other use anywhere in any known literature which uses the genitive of faith in an objective sense. George Howard in *On the Faith of Christ* looks at all the uses of faith in such a genitive in the Apocrypha, Pseudepigrapha, Philo, Josephus.

– 'Faith in Christ' makes nonsense of the context here, because Paul is giving the basis on which God forgave sins of *anyone* who had faith in Him. If this is 'faith *in* Jesus the Messiah' then how could Old Testament saints be forgiven?

– As commentators like Davies and D.W.B. Robinson have pointed out:

> It makes much better sense to say that God's righteousness has been manifested by the character of Christ's work than to say it has been manifested by man's faith in Christ. For how can man's faith be said to have demonstrated God's righteousness? (*Faith and Obedience in Romans* p.108)

– The whole point is that it is not something we have done but something the Messiah has done which is the basis of forgiveness of sin. Paul later refers (5:18) to the one righteous act of Messiah leading to the offer of justification to all people.

Commentary

Aha! The gospel reveals the truth about the 'righteousness of God' from faithfulness to faith (see Romans 1:17). The basis on which God declares people to be in rightstanding with Him (including people of faith in any era before or after the crucifixion) is the faithfulness of Jesus the Messiah in dying for our sins. All of us who have faith have (as no one would dispute) sinned, and so fallen short of the glory of divine perfection. God's declaration that we are in rightstanding with Him is based on what Jesus the Messiah did – His atonement through His sacrificial death. Paul clarifies that it was only through this sacrificial death that God 'passed over' sins committed in Old Testament times. The word for 'passed over' (*páresin*) does not merely mean ignored, but that God did not exact judicial punishment. In the present time it shows how God himself can be righteous yet declare us righteous through the faithfulness of Jesus the Messiah in dying for our sin. Our forgiveness is bought not with our works, nor with our faith, but by the Messiah's faithfulness in dying for us and shedding His blood as an atonement.

Note then, that this applies to anyone who has faith *in God*, not just to those with specifically *Christian* faith. Through this, God justified Noah, Job, Lot, Barak, Elijah, and all those in the Old Testament who had faith in God but never knew about Jesus. Given what Paul has just said about Jews and Gentiles one presumes that there were Gentiles (maybe like Lao Tze and Epimenides) who were likewise justified through the faithfulness of a Messiah of whom they never heard. The suggestion of some commentators that only Jewish sins could be 'passed over' in earlier times is an effective denial of Romans 3:29 for all the time up until Jesus died.

God is vindicated as a righteous judge, because He has had a basis on which to declare people right before Him through faith – it is the faithful atoning death of the Messiah.

In *Faith and Obedience in Romans,* Davies puts it thus:

> Faith in God has always been the path that leads to God's righteousness, for Jew and Gentile alike. The newness of the gospel, however is the demonstration of God's justice (righteousness 3:25) in so reckoning faith as righteousness by the faithfulness of Christ. (p.166)

To Paul the 'aha' moment must have come when he met the risen Messiah on the Damascus road, and realised that in raising Him from the dead God had shown Him really to be the Messiah and Son of God with power. So the death of the Messiah (in some ways a strange idea to swallow) made sense. This was the key event through which God forgave sin and declared people of faith to be righteous before Him.

The phrase 'all have sinned' is actually referring here to all those who have faith (and are justified by the faithfulness of Jesus the Messiah). Longenecker wants 'all have sinned' to refer to all human sin through history and so disguises this by beginning verse 24 as a new paragraph: 'We are justified . . .' The Greek text simply says 'being justified . . .' and Wright is correct to make it refer back to the 'all' who have sinned, so the reference is to believers. Of course we know it *is* true that literally everyone, believer or unbeliever, has sinned, but it is not what Paul is saying here.

All of us may be aware that half of Romans 3:23 is often quoted to unbelievers to 'prove' that they are sinners, often with good effect, but actually in our experience we have not met anyone who claimed never to have committed anything wrong even by their own standards – people don't really need a 'proof text'. Contemporary Jewish people did not need a proof text either, as their reaction to Jesus' challenge in John 8:9 shows. Romans 3:23 is not some triumphant conclusion against those who would deny it, but a casual reference to something no one denied: everyone has sinned including those with faith. Paul's real concern is how, given this fact, God can be both righteous and declare to be righteous people who have sinned. His answer is that it is through the faithfulness in sacrificial death of shed blood of Jesus the Messiah.

The Greek word *hilasterion* in verse 25 is translated 'propitiation' (KJV, NKJV and NASB) or 'expiation' (RSV). 'Propitiation' implies assuaging a person's (in this case God's) anger, 'expiation' is the cancelling of sin – is it important which? Actually the Greek word means a 'mercy seat', used in the New Testament only here and in Hebrews 8–10 where Christ is said to be High Priest, Sacrifice and 'mercy seat' (place of sacrifice). Most modern versions translate it 'sacrifice of atonement' which seems well enough.

Text 3:27–31

> [27] Where then is boasting? It is excluded. By what kind of law? Of works? No, but by a law of faith. [28] For we maintain that a man is justified by faith apart from works of the Law. [29] Or is God the God of Jews only? Is He not the God of Gentiles also? Yes, of Gentiles

also, [30] since indeed God who will justify the circumcised by [Lit: out of] faith and the uncircumcised through faith is one.

[31] Do we then nullify the Law through faith? May it never be! On the contrary, we establish the Law. (NASB)

Commentary

Paul has just given us his key thought. The whole basis on which God forgives sin and declares people righteous is the faithfulness of Jesus the Messiah in dying to atone for human sin. The Jewish boast was in the Torah (Romans 2:23) which they thought made them a light to the Gentiles. But if it is in reality the atoning faithful death of the Messiah which has enabled anyone's justification, then boasting in the Law is foolish. Paul often uses the word 'law' (*nomos*), and this word always means a legal requirement – not an observed 'principle' as it sometimes means in English. In Romans 7 he says that the Torah is good (7:7) but that in Paul himself it can operate in a good or a bad way. Approached in human effort it leads to failure, approached in the Spirit it is a Law of spirit and life. The Law should have brought people to faith, to casting themselves on the undeserved mercy of God and seeking to live in His grace and power. A person is justified by faith 'apart from works of the Law'. However, are the works of the Law the only valid way for such faith to be expressed? Paul says not because this would make God the God of the Jews only. It would make Him a purely tribal God, rather than the Lord of all the earth. Verse 30 may hint at the Jewish *shema* recited daily: 'Hear O Israel, the Lord your God is ONE . . .'

Verse 30 literally reads 'shall justify circumcision out of faith and uncircumcision through the faith'. This could mean 'through that same faith' (NIV) or that 'the faith' now shows a basis for faithful Gentiles to be (and have been) declared righteous.

Note again that to some commentators, for 2000 years of history God was in effect the God of the Jews only – because these commentators assume that only covenant Jews with faith could be saved. 'Only now,' they say, 'Gentiles as well as Jews can be saved as Christians'. However this seems really against the spirit of what Paul is saying. God didn't suddenly become Lord of the whole earth when Jesus died, He was always this. We may see the spiritual equality much more clearly in the Church, but there have always been some amongst both Jews and Gentiles who had faith.

Romans 4:1–22 | Faith Not Works Has Always Been the Way

Text 4:1–8

[1] What then shall we say that Abraham, our forefather according to the flesh, has found? [2] For if Abraham was justified by works, he has something to boast about, but not before God. [3] For what does the Scripture say? 'Abraham believed God, and it was credited to him as righteousness.' [4] Now to the one who works, his wage is not credited as a favour, but as what is due. [5] But to the one who does not work, but believes in Him who justifies the ungodly, his faith is credited as righteousness, [6] just as David also speaks of the blessing on the man to whom God credits righteousness apart from works: [7] 'Blessed are those whose lawless deeds have been forgiven, And whose sins have been covered. [8] Blessed is the man whose sin the Lord will not take into account.' (NASB)

Discussion Topic: Jewish Beliefs on Abraham

It is difficult to know exactly what first century Jews believed about Abraham because rabbis frequently disagreed, and in any case the written records (in the *Mishnah*) were not written down until many decades later. Certainly at least one source (Kidd. 4:14) says that Abraham 'performed the whole Law before it was given' though it is uncertain how widespread amongst rabbis this rather implausible view was. Paul anyway makes the point that Abraham was justified before he was circumcised. Did some Jews believe he had never sinned? Some commentators quote the prayer of Manasseh: 'Thou therefore, O Lord, who are the God of the just, to Abraham, Isaac and Jacob, which have not sinned against You; but You have appointed repentance unto me who am a sinner.' The context, however, is that Manasseh was one of the most idolatrous of kings (2 Kings 21:1–18; 2 Chronicles 33:1–9) who in captivity turned

137

in repentance. He may simply have been saying that the patriarchs lived righteous lives (in the sense that Jesus said He had come to call sinners not the righteous to repentance), *not* that Abraham literally *never* sinned. In Exodus 32:33 God says He will blot out from the book of life all who have sinned against Him – but in the context this does not mean everyone. Those who 'sinned against Him' means they led a lifestyle of sin.

Other commentators suggest that the Jews regarded Abraham's faith as having 'merit'. Cranfield in his commentary suggests that 2 Maccabees 2:52 means this, whereas actually it says:

> [52] Remember how Abraham put his trust in the Lord when he was tested and how the Lord was pleased with him and accepted him. [53] Joseph, in his time of trouble, obeyed God's commands and became ruler over the land of Egypt. [54] Phinehas, our ancestor, because of his burning devotion, was given the promise that his descendants would always be priests.

Phinehas, acted in zeal for God and, like Abraham, had this accounted to him for righteousness (Psalm 106:31). However, 1 Maccabees says nothing about 'merit'. It is hard to avoid thinking that such commentators are reading into these texts a kind of 'merit righteousness' and/or an idea of righteousness as ethical perfection, both of which are simply not present. Davies in *Faith and Obedience in Romans* (p.158) also shows that where Cranfield translates some words in the *Mekilta* (Jewish *Mishnah* comments on Exodus) as 'merit of faith' for Abraham, it more likely simply means 'reward of faith'. Longenecker in his 2016 commentary (p.477) also cites Maccabees, but in a real scraping of the barrel can then only find a fourth century Jewish amora sage from whom to characterise Jewish belief in Abraham's 'merits'.

In summary, there is good reason to be sceptical of any claims that Jewish theologians commonly believed that Abraham clocked up 'merits' to be saved.

Discussion Topic: Justification

Both the present authors were brought up in a tradition which presented 'justification' as the initial act of God declaring the sinner to be righteous and so (effectively) making him so. However as we show in our word study in *Reconsidering Key Biblical Ideas* (and indeed figures like N.T. Wright and Alister McGrath have demonstrated), the word 'justify' does not (as often suggested) mean to 'make righteous' or to forgive, but to declare righteous. God Himself can be 'justified' (Luke 7:29), ie declared to be in the right. Paul says that 'having been' justified by faith let us have peace (*shalom*) with God (Romans 5:1) which speaks of justification in the past tense. But God also *now* justifies the elect (Romans 8:33) and in the day of judgement they will be justified (Romans 2:13). 'Justification' in the sense of being declared or shown to be righteous can occur at any stage in a relationship with God, not just at the beginning of it.

The incident in Abraham's life which Paul refers to here comes in Genesis 15:6, decades after (according to Hebrews 11:8) Abraham first went out in faith in response to God's call. When he believed God in Genesis 15:6, he was not *made righteous* because he was already righteous – he was *declared righteous*. This also explains why James 2:21 says that Abraham was 'justified by works when he offered up Isaac'. Hebrews 11:17 makes it clear that this act expressed Abraham's great faith – a faith that God could even raise Isaac from the dead if need be. The 'works' James refers to were not ritual works, but something which really did show Abraham's faith, and arise from it. They *justify* him in the sense of showing that he really was righteous, ie in a right faith standing with God. If 'justify' had meant to 'make righteous' then James and Paul would contradict both each other and Hebrews 11:8. As it is, there is no contradiction at all.

Discussion Topic: Justifying the Ungodly

Paul says that Abraham 'has faith in him that justifies the ungodly'. The word 'ungodly' (*asebe*) is not used much in the New Testament, but is always a negative term, usually associated with being a 'sinner' in the biblical sense (1 Timothy 1:9; 1 Peter 4:18; Jude 15). In Psalm 1:5–6 we are told: *Therefore the ungodly shall not stand in the judgment, Nor sinners in the congregation of the righteous. For the* LORD *knows the way of the righteous, but the way of the ungodly shall perish.* In a Jewish context, what Paul says is paradoxical and shocking. In general, of course, the ungodly certainly are not and should not be, proclaimed to be in the right. What then does he mean? We suggest that he means that at the point where a sinner repents and asks God for forgiveness God declares him righteous, although until that point the person has indeed been an ungodly sinner. God does not wait until the sinner has lived a righteous lifestyle for a while. In calling unrighteous sinners to repentance God offers to the ungodly a declaration of rightstanding with Him.

Was Abraham, then, 'ungodly' at the time of Genesis 15:6? Some commentators say 'yes' because 'ungodly' meant someone who did not keep the Law and Abraham didn't have it yet. This is implausible for two reasons. First, whatever one or two rabbis may later have said, Paul was clear that Abraham never ever had the Torah (Galatians 3:17). If 'ungodly' meant not keeping Torah then Abraham was 'ungodly' throughout his whole life. That Paul would expect Jewish hearers to pick this up from his brief words here would surely be highly unlikely. Secondly, in Job 16:11, Job complains that '. . . the Lord has delivered me into the hands of unrighteous men, and thrown me upon the ungodly (LXX: *asebesin*).' The Jewish writer who set down the story of Job does not present him as a Torah keeping Jew: Job was probably a near contemporary of Abraham, and God boasts of him as His servant in Job 1:8; 2:3; 42:7. By 'ungodly' Job means someone *not* living in relationship with God, unlike Job who clearly *was* living that way. In 2 Peter 2:5 the writer (who praises Paul's writings in 3:15) contrasts Noah as a preacher of righteousness with the 'ungodly' – but of course Noah no more had the Torah than they did. It seems unlikely, then, that the paradox can be resolved by saying that 'ungodly' just means people who don't try to gain righteousness by keeping Torah.

Abraham's childhood background had, indeed, been polytheistic (Joshua 24:2) so he himself could have previously experienced a transformation from ungodly to righteous. But by Genesis 15:6 he is a righteous man living a godly life. However, his continuing faith was in a God who justifies the ungodly, and his confidence is based not on any ritual works but on God's grace.

So Abraham's faith was in a God who justifies the ungodly, who gives life to the dead and calls into existence the things not seen (4:17). His faith was that God would give him a son – something naturally impossible. It was this faith, in this kind of God, Paul says, that was reckoned as righteousness.

Commentary

Paul here is really addressing the Jews who are physically descended from Abraham, and as in Romans 3:9 he includes himself in the group. Rabbis, inevitably, differed among themselves, but believed that Abraham had faith and obedience. Some even suggested that he had been given the Law and kept it – though plainly he was not sinless as he lied twice about Sarah being only his sister and followed a fleshly suggestion about using Hagar to produce an heir.

The idea of 'boasting' appears in Romans 2:17, 2:23, 3:21, 4:2, 5:2, and 5:11. In 2:17 it was not that they boasted in God, because Paul does this in 5:11 – it was because in doing so they 'relied on the Torah', whereas he is boasting though the Lord Jesus the Messiah through whom he received reconciliation.

The phrase 'not before God' uses a Greek term (*pros theon*), which means *towards God* rather than *in the presence of God* (see the same word *pros* in Romans 5:1, 10:1, 15:17 and 15:30). Abraham might be renowned for his works, but could not direct his boast towards God because Genesis 15:6 implied that justification was not a due but a gift. Abraham had faith in God and it was *'credited to him'* as rightstanding.

Chrysostom (*Homily VIII*) had a lovely thought:

> For a person who had no works, to be justified by faith was nothing unlikely. But for a person richly adorned with good deeds, not to be made just from hence, but from faith, this is the thing to cause wonder, and to set the power of faith in a strong light.

Paul makes the point that Abraham's faith is 'credited to him'. This is a kind of accounting term, meaning to account as equivalent to, and the NASB brings this out better than for example the NKJV. So, just as stock in a company may be 'credited' as though equivalent to a cash asset, in this case it was God's decision to credit faith as righteousness.

Some theologians have suggested that God credited to Abraham the righteous ethical perfection of Jesus. There are two real problems with this. The first is that first century Old Testament-believing Jews did not imagine that 'righteousness' meant ethical perfection. The second is that the text simply does not say this. Yes Paul has just said that the basis on which God forgave past sins was the faithfulness in death of Jesus the Messiah. However it is Abraham's own *faith* that is credited as righteousness, not anyone else's. Paul's point is that it was Abraham's faith that God credited, not some kind of works. Actually in Psalm 106:30 almost exactly the same phrase is used of the act of Phinehas which was 'accounted to him for righteousness' to all generations forevermore. It was not someone else's act that was somehow credited. The idea of some kind of imputed ethical perfection of Jesus (ie that His sinless ethical perfection is counted as though ours) may be popular in some circles but it just does not fit the text.

Abraham's faith was not a 'work' and it earned nothing. It was God's decision to credit it as righteousness, and as Paul has already explained Abraham's sins (like all those who had a faith-life before Jesus) were forgiven on the basis of the later act of sacrificial faithfulness of Jesus the Messiah.

Paul then quotes Psalm 32 which uses the same Hebrew word for 'accounted' or 'credited' as Genesis 15:6, but speaks of the blessing of the man whose sin has *not* been credited to him. The Psalmist goes on to speak not of any works of the Law, but simply says *'I said, "I will confess my transgressions to the LORD," and you forgave the iniquity of my sin.'* David is praising God that God has chosen not to credit his sin to him; God has forgiven him freely, and this is not because of any particular works. David is, of course, in the Mosaic covenant times, but is not relying on the works of the Law to bring forgiveness, just the mercy of God.

Questions for Thought and Discussion

- How common is the view that 'justification' means the initial act of God in forgiving and accepting people at conversion?

- How does Paul's key use of Abraham at this point show this is mistaken?

- How would we say today that people are shown to be in a right relationship with God through Jesus – by what they believe or by their lifestyle? How did Jesus say people would know we are His disciples?

Text 4:9–12

[9] Is this blessedness, then, pronounced only on the circumcised, or also on the uncircumcised? We say, 'Faith was reckoned to Abraham as righteousness.' [10] How then was it reckoned to him? Was it before or after he had been circumcised? It was not after, but before he was circumcised. [11] He received the sign of circumcision as a seal of the righteousness that he had by faith while he was still uncircumcised. The purpose was to make him the ancestor of all who believe without being circumcised and who thus have righteousness reckoned to them, [12] and likewise the ancestor of the circumcised who are not

only circumcised but who also follow the example of the faith that our ancestor Abraham had before he was circumcised. (NRSVA)

Commentary

Actually the justification in Genesis 15:6 was not only before Abraham was circumcised (chapter 17), but even before any covenant was made with him (15:18). So faith is primary. The reckoning or accounting as righteous is therefore dependent neither on Abraham keeping even the most basic part of the Law (circumcision), nor on any specific covenant. Abraham is the spiritual father of *anyone* who is not Jewish (either in the sense of keeping the Law or in the sense of being part of a divine covenant) but has a faith like his (presumably in a sense including Job his contemporary). He is also the father of Jewish people *if* they walk in his way of faith (like David, Jepthah, Habakkuk, Isaiah and all those listed in Hebrews 11).

Text 4:13–22

[13] For the promise to Abraham or to his descendants [Lit: seed] that he would be heir of the world was not through the Law, but through the righteousness of faith. [14] For if those who are of the Law are heirs, faith is made void and the promise is nullified; [15] for the Law brings about wrath, but where there is no law, there also is no violation. [16] For this reason it is by [Lit: out of] faith, in order that it may be in accordance with grace, so that the promise will be guaranteed to all the descendants [Lit: seed], not only to those who are of the Law, but also to those who are of the faith of Abraham, who is the father of us all, [17] (as it is written, 'A father of many nations have I made you') in the presence of Him whom he believed, even God, who gives life to the dead and calls into being that which does not exist. [18] In hope against hope he believed, so that he might become a father of many nations according to that which had been spoken, 'So shall your descendants [Lit: seed] be.' [19] Without becoming weak in faith he contemplated his own body, now as good as dead since he was about a hundred years old, and the deadness of Sarah's womb; [20] yet, with respect to the promise of God, he did not waver in unbelief but grew strong in faith, giving glory to God, [21] and being fully assured that what God had promised, He was able also to perform. [22] Therefore it was also credited to him as righteousness. (NASB)

Commentary

The promises made in Genesis 15 and 17 to Abraham and his seed to be heirs of the world both came before his circumcision. Abraham's faith did not earn any right to be central in God's plans to redeem the world – that was God's free gift. Moreover it was not any ritual works because even if (as some Jews believed) Abraham did go on to keep the Torah (though this seems highly unlikely), God's promise was definitely made before he was circumcised. What is credited as righteousness is a faith in a miracle-working God, who can produce life where naturally there would be none.

Many Jews gave 18 benedictions daily, the second of which was *'Blessed be you, Lord, who gives life to the dead.'* Paul's teacher Gamaliel was reputed to have used these benedictions. 2 Baruch 21:4 refers to one 'whom at the beginning of the world called that which did not yet exist and they obeyed You' (see also 2 Baruch 48:8). All this, then, is very much in the Jewish tradition and thinking.

Questions for Thought and Discussion

- If non-Christians have strong ideas of right and wrong, how can we challenge them about what this shows in regard to God?

- Is there much consciousness today of the fact that sin not only wrongs others but also wrongs a God who loves them and in whose image they were made?

- When people think of being held accountable to God, what kinds of things might they think to plead? What does Paul imply about them?

Romans 4:23–6:23 | Christians and the Freedom from Sin's Power

Text 4:23–25

²³ Now not for his sake only was it written that it was credited to him, ²⁴ but for our sake also, to whom it will be credited, as those who believe in Him who raised Jesus our Lord from the dead, ²⁵ He who was delivered over because of our transgressions, and was raised because of our justification. (NASB)

Commentary

In Romans 1:16 Paul launched into his themes about the two streams of humanity – righteous and unrighteous (amongst both Jew and Gentile) and the faith-basis of justification. He has spoken of the atoning death of Jesus the Messiah as the basis throughout history by which a righteous God could forgive sin and declare people who had sinned to be right before Him. All this has been about *faith in God*. Here Paul starts to turn specifically to *Christian faith*. We (like Abraham) have faith in God – but we know He is the God who raised Jesus from the dead. We know that human sin is forgiven because of Jesus' death, and His resurrection vindicates or 'justifies' those who base their lives on a faith-relationship with God.

Text 5:1–11

¹ Therefore, having been justified by faith, we have [two early mss read *let us have*] peace with God through our Lord Jesus Christ, ² through whom also we have obtained our introduction by faith into this grace in which we stand; and we exult [or *let us exult*] in hope of the glory of God. ³ And not only this, but we also exult [or *let us also exult*] in our tribulations, knowing that tribulation brings about perseverance; ⁴ and perseverance, proven character; and proven character, hope; ⁵ and hope does not disappoint, because the love of God has been poured out within our hearts through the Holy Spirit who was given to us.

⁶ For while we were still helpless, at the right time Christ died for the ungodly. ⁷ For one will hardly die for a righteous man;

146

though perhaps for the good man someone would dare even to die. [8] But God demonstrates His own love toward us, in that while we were yet sinners, Christ died for us. [9] Much more then, having now been justified by His blood, we shall be saved from the wrath of God through Him. [10] For if while we were enemies we were reconciled to God through the death of His Son, much more, having been reconciled, we shall be saved by [or *in*] His life. [11] And not only this, but we also exult [or *also exulting*] in God through our Lord Jesus Christ, through whom we have now received the reconciliation. (NASB)

Commentary

For us Christians, we know that we are declared to be in rightstanding with God through faith. What then?

On Romans 5:1 the ancient Greek New Testament manuscripts differ: some have 'let us have', while others 'we have' (the difference in Greek is just one letter: an 'o' or an 'ω'). Longenecker (*Romans*, p.548) makes a good textual case for 'let us have' and also points out that the early Christian teachers were virtually unanimous in having it as 'let us have'. This is probably not just a statement about a passive state of being, but an urge to live out the consequences of our faith-justification in the knowledge of Jesus. A similar idea is in Colossians 3:15 – *Let the peace of Christ rule in your hearts.*

The word 'peace' here does not mean mere lack of hostility, but the Hebrew word *shalom* שָׁלוֹם which as Longenecker remarks:

> included such ideas as 'an absence of conflict', 'tranquillity', and 'contentment', but primarily carried nuances of 'completeness', 'fullness of health (including not just physical but also spiritual and mental health)', and 'one's overall welfare'. (*Romans*, p.556)

The ultimate Jewish passion was for the *shalom* of God, but how could this be experienced in the face of adversity? In a sense, Habakkuk asked this question and the answer was Paul's whole starting point for his exposition: the righteous lives by faith. The NASB brings out the paradox that as Christians we are urged not only to 'exult' in the well-founded hope of the glory of God but also exult about our present difficulties. We do so because difficulties can lead to character, character to hope, so it is all part of the same experience. Moreover, for Christians we also have the love of God poured into us through the Holy Spirit.

We note here that we have righteousness (justification, v1), peace (v1) and joy or exultation (v2, 3), and these are central to the Kingdom of God (Romans 14:17). A new Kingdom is challenging the reign of sin, as we shall see.

Paul, of course, accepts the usual Jewish belief that there are righteous men and women, and the contrast between the righteous and the wicked has formed his argument thus far. But when Jesus died for us we were *not* righteous but were ungodly sinners. This is, in a sense, a logical rather than chronological priority. Jesus the Messiah died for the sins of Job and Abraham, and in chronological time order this was after they lived. However, He did not die *as a result of* their godly lives, His death was *the basis on which* God was able to pass over their sins and to be in relationship with them. Likewise with, for example, the woman to whom Jesus says: 'Your sins are forgiven you' (Luke 7:48) though of course He has not yet died for her. His faithful death had an effect both backwards and forwards in actual time. He died for the ungodly so that the ungodly could be declared righteous and live in a faith-life with God.

We will be saved from the 'wrath' of God through Messiah, not only from the wrath at the judgement day but the wrath that (Romans 1:18) is now being revealed against the wicked. We will be 'saved' not only at the last day, but as a salvaging process going on now. The gospel is the power of God unto salvation for those who have faith.

The ultimate exulting, though is neither in our hope nor our tribulations but in God Himself. We can contrast this with the Jew in 2:17 who 'rests in the Torah and exults in God' or even just 'exults in the Torah' (2:23). Our exulting in God is not resting on the Torah Law but on the Lord Jesus Messiah through whom we have this standing.

Text 5:12–19

> [12] Therefore, just as sin came into the world through one man, and death came through sin, and so death spread to all because all have sinned— [13] sin was indeed in the world before the law, but sin is not reckoned when there is no law. [14] Yet death exercised dominion from Adam to Moses, even over those whose sins were not like the transgression of Adam, who is a type of the One who was to come.
>
> [15] But the free gift is not like the trespass. For if the many died through the one man's trespass, much more surely have the grace of God and the free gift in the grace of the one Man, Jesus Christ,

abounded for the many. [16] And the free gift is not like the effect of the one man's sin. For the judgement following one trespass brought condemnation, but the free gift following many trespasses brings justification. [17] If, because of the one man's trespass, death exercised dominion through that one, much more surely will those who receive the abundance of grace and the free gift of righteousness exercise dominion in life through the one Man, Jesus Christ.

[18] Therefore just as one man's trespass led to condemnation for all, so one Man's act of righteousness leads to justification and life for all. [19] For just as by the one man's disobedience the many were made sinners, so by the one Man's obedience the many will be made righteous. (NRSVA)

As we shall see in the following Discussion Topics, some of the historical controversies over these verses are more easily decided than others. Cultural and textual backgrounds can guide us on some issues.

Discussion Topic: Physical and Spiritual Death

God warned in Genesis 2:17 that in the day 'the man' ate the fruit he would surely die. Paul's contemporary the renowned Jewish commentator and philosopher Philo suggested that since after sinning Adam lived and had children, the phrase 'you shall die the death' refers to the 'death of the soul' which is 'the decay of virtue and the bringing in of wickedness'. Another work, the book of 2 Baruch which dates from around 100 AD, was probably translated (into Syriac) from Hebrew. It contains the following interesting passage:

> For although Adam sinned first and has brought death upon all who were not in his own time, yet each of them who has been born from him has prepared for himself the coming torment. And further, each of them has chosen for himself the coming glory. For

truly the one who believes will receive reward. But now, turn yourselves to destruction, you unrighteous ones who are living now, for you will be visited suddenly, since you have rejected the understanding of the Most High. For his works have not taught you, nor has the artful work of his creation which has always existed persuaded you. Adam is, therefore, not the cause, except only for himself, but each of us has become his own Adam. (2 Baruch 54:15–19 tr Kiljn (1983))

Philo and Baruch were Jewish contemporaries of Paul, but are these ideas reflected in Paul? Justin Marston in a 2000 article in the journal *Science and Christian Belief* rightly notes:

The parallels with the Pauline Romans here are startling. In Romans God may be known by what He has made (1:20), destruction is in store for those who have rejected God from their understanding (1:28), whilst reward is for those who believe (3:22). To Paul, we note, Adam has 'brought death on' those who followed (5:12). Surely the Pauline 'because all sinned' (5:12 and cf 7:9) is also reflected in the phrase 'each of us has become his own Adam'? What is, of course, missing, is the Pauline insistence that to believe is efficacious only because of the faithfulness of Jesus the Messiah (3:22 correctly translated). Much else, though, shows the parallels with Paul who was reinterpreting not abrogating Jewish approaches.

In Romans 7:9 Paul says that at one time he was 'alive' because he had no sense of law, but then he recognised a moral law, 'sin revived and I died'. This, plainly, speaks of spiritual death, and is his personal experience of (spiritual) death spreading to all men because all men sin.

Discussion Topic: Adam – Individual and Corporate

Was Paul insistent that 'Adam' was a literal individual? Well, in Genesis 1–3, *ādām* is not a name but means 'the man' or 'humanity' as most modern versions show. Paul, in rabbinical style, is more interested in what it teaches us than in literality. Here in Romans it is 'one man' who sins first and whose act is countered by the one Man Jesus who brought us life, but in 1 Timothy 2:13–15 he says:

> [13] For Adam was formed first, then Eve; [14] and Adam was not deceived, but the woman was deceived and became a transgressor. [15] Yet she will be saved through childbearing [Greek: through *the* childbearing], provided they continue in faith and love and holiness, with self-restraint.

Here it is the *woman* who first 'falls into transgression' and whose one act is to be countered by the one act of '*the* childbearing' which must refer to the promise in Genesis 3:15 that through Eve's 'seed' the serpent's head will be crushed. Ultimately this came through a later woman, Mary, without any male aid. This understanding explains the complex switch from singular to plural and the use of the definite article.

But in any event, who really sinned first, the man or the woman? Paul's concern is simply not with such issues of literality.

Moreover, his use of the term 'Adam' is itself ambivalent. Paul plays on the plural/singular nature of the words. Compare:

– Our old man has been crucified with Him (Christ) that the body of sin might be done away with. (Romans 6:6)

– You have put off the old man with his practices and have put on the new. (Colossians 3:9–10)

– For He (the Messiah) is our peace, the one having

made us both one . . . that he might create in Himself one new man in the place of the two . . . that you put off, concerning your former conduct, the old man which grows corrupt according to the deceitful lusts, and be renewed in the spirit of your mind, and that you put on the new man which was created according to God in true righteousness and holiness. (Ephesians 2:15, 4:22–24)

1 Corinthians raises the same theme:

- For as through man (or 'a man') came death also by man (or 'a man') has come resurrection from the dead. For as in Adam all die, so in the Messiah shall all be made alive. (15:21–22)

- And so it is written, the first man Adam became a living being, the last Adam became a life giving spirit . . . The first man was of the earth, made of dust, so also are those who are made of dust: and as is the heavenly man so also are those who are heavenly. And as we have borne the image of the man of dust, so also shall we (or *'let us'*) bear the image of the man of heaven. (15:45–49)

In *Reason, Science and Faith* we argued in more detail that Paul's language leaves it open as to whether *ādām* was a literal or a 'federal' head of humanity.

Dunn also asserts of Romans 5:12 etc:

It would not be true to say that Paul's theological point here depends on Adam being a 'historical' individual or on his disobedience being a historical event as such. Such an implication does not necessarily follow from the fact that a parallel is drawn with Christ's single act: an act in mythic history can be paralleled to an act in living history without the point of comparison being lost. So long as the story of Adam as the initiator of the sad tale of human failure was well known, which we may assume (the brevity of Paul's presentation presupposes such a knowledge) such a comparison is meaningful. Nor should modern interpretation encourage patronising generalisations about the primitive mind naturally understanding the Adam stories as literally historical . . . such tales told about the dawn of human history could be and were treated with a considerable degree of sophistication, with the literal meaning often discounted. Indeed, if anything, we should say that the effect of the comparison between the two epochal figures, Adam and Christ, is not so much to historicise the individual Adam as to bring out the more than individual significance of the historic Christ. (*Romans*, pp.289–290)

This was recognised as early as Origen (c248 AD) who wrote:

In the Hebrew language Adam signifies man, and that in those parts of the narrative which appear to refer to Adam as an individual, Moses is discoursing upon the nature of man in general. For 'in Adam' (as the Scripture says) 'all die;' and were condemned in the likeness of Adam's transgression, the word of God asserting this not so much of one particular individual as of the whole human race. (Origen *Against Celsus* iv 40 (*Ant Nic Fath* iv, 516))

If the main point of Paul's teaching about the earthly *ādām* was that he was a 'type' of the one man the Messiah, then his argument certainly depends upon accepting the divine inspiration of the Genesis account of 'the man', but it is less clear that his argument requires this to be a literal individual – even if on other grounds we may conclude that it was.

Discussion Topic: 'Original Sin'

The phrase in 5:12 'because all sinned' (*eph ho pantes hemarton*) has been controversial and Cranfield lists all the seven options! In *Reconsidering Key Biblical Ideas* chapter 7 we show how Augustine wanted to translate the Greek phrase *eph ho* as 'in whom' (ie, in Adam), and how he (not Ambrosiaster as sometimes claimed) was the first to teach a doctrine of inherited guilt, that all humans sinned 'in Adam', and so inherit the guilt of the first man's sin. Cranfield (as all modern commentators) rightly discounts this rendering of *eph ho* as linguistically invalid. As Lonegnecker (*Romans*, p.589) states, the vast majority of modern scholars see *eph ho* as simply meaning 'because'. Some, however, want to cling to the Augustinian idea that we all sinned 'in Adam' anyway. The problem with this is that it reads into the text a doctrine that is contained nowhere else in Scripture and in no contemporary rabbinical writing. The only other verse Augustine could produce for his novel doctrine was his new interpretation of Psalm 51:5, which was no more meant as literal theology than 51:4 (*'against you and you only have I sinned'*) and in any case says nothing about inherited guilt. The Bible clearly says that each person is responsible only for his own sin (Deuteronomy 24:16, Ezekiel 18:20 etc). Reading any novel idea of inherited guilt into a 'because' which makes no such implication is bad exegesis.

Cranfield, Longenecker and many others have favoured some idea that everyone has sinned because they inherited a sinful nature. However, it seems strained to find 'inherited depravity' here in Romans 5:12, and there are some other issues with this because if half of Jesus' genetics were from Mary then surely he would not only have been 'in the likeness of sinful flesh' but would he have not inherited its sinful nature? (For Augustine this problem would be even worse because he believed that Mary was also born sinless, and she had two lots of guilty genetics!) Some say that we are not sinners because we sin, but we sin because we are born sinners. But Paul in Romans 7:9 says that he was alive once before he recognised a moral law, but when he did recognise one then sin revived and he died. Had he already been born a sinner surely wouldn't he have been born spiritually dead?

Longenecker does, though, usefully clarify that by 'all have sinned' in 5:12 Paul 'evidently meant "all people have sinned throughout the course of history"' (*Romans*, p. 592).

Was Paul's first sin from nurture, nature or free choice? We don't really have enough biblical data to decide. All we do know is that empirically speaking every single human to whom we can tell and explain the gospel has sinned.

Commentary

Paul steps back from the Jewish question and looks here at a sweep of human history. Through the first man who sinned, sin entered the world and became a part of human environment. It would be dangerous to try from the theological words of Paul to deduce definitely whether this is due to genetics or 'nurture'. But spiritual death entered our world and environment, and has spread to everyone because all have sinned. This phrase 'all have sinned' reflects his earlier comment in 3:23: the sins are their own sins not some inherited from anyone else. Sin counts as sin only if someone recognises that they are breaking a moral law. Adam had been given an explicit law, and committed a 'transgression' or 'trespass' *parabasis* which is a violation of such a law (it could also be rendered as 'deviation' or 'fault', the same word 'debt' as used in the 'Lord's prayer'). Similarly, after the Jews received the specific laws of Moses, sin for them was breaking those laws. Those people between Adam and Moses had no such directly given divine laws, yet (Paul points out) spiritual death reigned throughout, so we can only conclude that 'sin was in the world' during this era. Sin is the explanation for the spread of spiritual death, and Paul does not further explain this, but we presume that it is (as he earlier explored in Romans 2) that these people had an instinctive conscience recognition of right and wrong. Even if this knowledge of a moral law was imperfect they could be conscious of breaking it – and could have known (as some like Job and Epimenides did) that God's goodness was meant to lead to repentance and faith. They committed sin and so experienced spiritual death – death was using sin to reign.

Adam was a 'type' or 'pattern' of the coming Messiah. But before explaining in what way this was so, Paul strongly states two ways in which they are contrasted rather than similar. Through one deviation or transgression many came to be dead, but much more through the Messiah grace has super-abounded. The one first 'transgression' also contrasts with the gift, because the transgression brought judgement and condemnation and the gift brought exoneration and declaration of rightstanding.

Here is a more exact rendering of verses 17–19:

> [17] For if by the offence of the one the death did reign through the one, much more those, who the abundance of the grace and of the free gift of the righteousness are receiving, in life shall reign through the One – Jesus Messiah.

> [18] So, then, as through one offence to all men [it is] to condemnation, so also through one righteous act [it is] to all men to justification of life;

> [19] for as through the disobedience of the one man, the many were constituted sinners: so also through the obedience of the One, shall the many be constituted righteous. (Adapted from Young's Literal Translation)

The word *man's* is not there in verse 17 in the Greek, and the word 'one' *enos* could be masculine or neuter. So, is it the one act (of Adam and of Messiah respectively) rather than the one man which is the primary emphasis? This whole idea of the 'righteous act' of Messiah has already been laid down, because it is the *faithfulness of Jesus the Messiah* in dying an atoning death which is the whole basis for God being able to forgive sin and declare righteous those with faith. Isaiah 53:11 prophesied 'My righteous servant shall justify many. For He shall bear their iniquities.' Philippians 2:8 notes that the Messiah humbled Himself and became obedient in undergoing death on the cross. In Galatians 2:20, as we noted, Paul lives through the faithfulness of the Messiah who loved him and gave Himself for him. Verse 19 is explicit: the contrast is between the effects of the one unrighteous transgression and the one act of obedience and service.

It seems here as though both the sin and the grace were things that came to 'all people' (the word *anthropous* means people rather than just men), and this is explicit here – the translators have not added any words! Obviously we know that not all people have *accepted* this grace that came to them, so we presume the 'opting in' is voluntary.

Verse 19 gives the actual effects: many were constituted sinners and many were constituted righteous according to their opting in. Not 'all' were made righteous because Jesus died for the sins of the world but this is effective only to those who react in repentance and faith.

Some of Paul's language here reflects other first century Jewish ideas, but they are transformed. For example, in his contemporary the Jewish philosopher Philo, the 'earthly man' is the 'earthly and perishable mind' while the 'heavenly man' is the pure mind 'after the image' and set in God. In Paul the 'earthly man' is the one in Genesis 2, the 'heavenly Man' is the Messiah. In Philo immortality is a property of the human soul; in Paul it is a resurrection gift to those who have identified with the Messiah (Romans 6:5–6, 1 Corinthians 15:54 etc). Some rabbis held that the 'second man' and suffering servant were the nation of Israel, but Paul is clear that it is the Messiah (see also N.T. Wright *What St Paul Really Said*, p.262 etc).

Text 5:20–21

> [20] But law came in, with the result that the trespass multiplied; but where sin increased, grace abounded all the more, [21] so that, just as sin exercised dominion in death, so grace might also exercise dominion through justification [or righteousness] leading to eternal life through Jesus Christ our Lord. (NRSVA)

Commentary

The Law in itself just brought more condemnation; it simply increased knowledge of God's standards and so increased the reign of sin and death. But through the work of Jesus the Messiah (our Lord) God's grace was even greater and it is on this basis that God declares any person throughout history to be in rightstanding with Him. The 'eternal life' promised in Romans 2:2 would be given at the last judgement to those in pre-Christian times with faith, but for us with Christian faith we know we have it now. In both cases this eternal life comes only through the faithfulness in sacrificial death of Jesus the Messiah. However guilty a person knows himself to be, God's grace through the work of Messiah can exceed it, and declare that person to be in rightstanding with God.

Questions for Thought and Discussion

- *Have you ever met anyone who claimed that he or she had never sinned?*

- *What dimensions of the idea of being 'saved' are real to you in your life?*

Text 6:1–14

[1] What then shall we say? Shall we continue in sin that grace may abound? [2] Certainly not! Since we died to sin how can we live any longer in it? [3] Or are you unaware that as many of us as were baptized into Jesus the Messiah were baptized into His death? [4] Therefore we were buried with Him through baptism into death, that just as Messiah was raised from the dead by the glory of the Father, so we also should walk in newness of life. [5] For if we have been united together in the very likeness of His death, we shall certainly also be in the likeness of His resurrection, [6] knowing this, that our old man was crucified with Him, that the body of sin might be done away with, that we should no longer be slaves to sin. [7] For He who has died has been declared free from sin. [8] Now if we died with Messiah, we believe that we shall also live with Him, [9] knowing that Messiah, having been raised from the dead, dies no more. Death no longer has dominion over Him. [10] For the death that He died, He died to sin once and for all; but the life that He lives, He lives to God. [11] Likewise you also, reckon yourselves to be dead indeed to sin, but alive to God in Messiah Jesus. [12] Therefore do not let sin exercise dominion in your mortal body, to obey it in its passions, [13] and do not present your members to sin as instruments of unrighteousness,

but present yourselves to God as being alive from the dead, and your members as instruments of righteousness to God. [14] For sin will have no dominion over you, for you are not under law but under grace. (Our own translation).

Discussion Topic: What is Our 'Old Man'?

The phrase 'our old man' or 'our old humanity' (Greek: *anthropos*) is in verse 6. Several versions and commentators render it as 'our old self' (including both NASB and NRSV which is why we give our own more literal rendering here), and some commentators are specific in identifying the old man as our old pre-conversion self, and the new man as the post-conversion self. In some ways this sounds like a nice simple exegesis, but there are three problems with it and overall it just doesn't seem to fit the text.

The first issue is that the 'death' of the old man seems to be *with Christ* – it is a single death. But if it were our pre–conversion self then surely it would be at the time of each of our conversions that our old man died? So we would all have different times.

The second is that Paul says our (plural) old man (singular). He never refers to our old *men*. If it referred to our old self then we each have a pre-conversion self, so it should be 'our old selves' or 'our old men'.

The third relates to the second in that Paul also uses the phrase in Ephesians 4:22–24 telling us to 'put off' the old man and 'put on' the new man. But earlier in Ephesians 2:15 he said that from the Jews and Gentiles Messiah has created in Himself 'one new man'. If the new man is singular, then surely so is the old man?

What Paul really has in mind is more complex than pre- and post-conversion selves. There is one old man/humanity, and it was crucified with Messiah.

So suggestions like that of Cranfield that 'in baptism our sinful selves were crucified and died' seem really to miss the whole point of the collectivity and singularity in the 'old man'. Dunn's analysis in his commentary really helps here:

> The singular (lit. 'old man', instead of 'old men') is normal style, but does help emphasize the idea of a common humanness worn out by its bondage to sin and death (cf 8:10). The societal and salvation history dimension here should not be reduced to the pietistic experience of the individual; but the reference is to Christians ('our old man') for whom the domination of sin has been broken by their identification with Christ's death . . . (*Romans*, p.318)

Dunn notes that in verse 5 the term *we have become* (united with him) is in the perfect tense, but the aorist tense is used for *crucified with* him. Dunn adds:

> The aorist denoting (as in vv 3–4) the decisive salvation-history event of Christ's death whose effect in ending the rule of sin and death enters the experience of those who are identified and identify themselves with that event in the commitment of baptism and thereafter (the aorist passive does not exclude the active imperative; cf. Col 3:9-10; Eph 4:22; and Rom 13:14 with Gal 3:27) The centrality of the cross in Paul's gospel, as the (only) means by which the rule of sin and death could be broken, is clear here and coherent with the theology of Christ's death as sin offering outlined in 3:25. (p.319)

The imperative Dunn speaks of is the instruction to 'put off' the old man in Colossians 3:9–10 and Ephesians 4:22. The old humanity is dead, but we have to reckon it so by putting it off!

We are identified with the old man/humanity which was earthy, but God regards this as crucified once for all in His Messiah. In baptism we accept this judgement, and so come to share in the new resurrected life of Messiah, the new man/humanity from heaven.

Discussion Topic: What is the 'Body of Sin'?

The word body (*sōma*) is different from the word for flesh (*sarx*). It is used a lot in the Greek Old Testament (LXX) and standardly means the physical body (or a corpse). This is in spite of a claim (in *The Dictionary of New Testament Theology* i p.232) that '*sōma* in the Old Testament has virtually the meaning of the whole person'. It just doesn't (and the verses cited there have no such meaning). This means that when it is claimed that: 'In Paul *sōma* has "a specialised meaning in the sense of person"' we may find this doubtful. The starting point at least is that *sōma* means a physical body.

In Genesis 2:7 we read that

> . . . the Lord God formed man from the dust of the
> ground, and breathed into his nostrils the breath of life;
> and the man became a living being [or living soul].

So we find contrasts between body and soul (Matthew 10:28), and soul and spirit (Hebrews 4:12). Our self-conscious person seems to 'reside' or to have its consciousness in the living soul but appears to come into being only by having a body, which is given life by the spirit. Animals, like humans, are also body, soul and spirit (Genesis 2:19). One difficulty is that in Hebrew or Greek the same word means 'spirit' or 'breath', so in some contexts having the breath of life can simply mean that the animal is breathing, ie alive. God is said to 'breathe' into the man, whereas this is not stated to be so for animals, but it is hard to know how far this is significant.

Paul's single reference to 'body soul and spirit' (1 Thessalonians 5:23) has sometimes been taken as a kind of technical schema, but we doubt that the terms can be taken as precise ones in this way. The 'soul' or *psyche* is not some kind of real ethereal 'us' that somehow *resides* in the body like a Dalek in a machine (as Descartes has sometimes been misunderstood to be naively stating!) The first human *became* a living soul as he was embodied and given the breath (spirit) of life which is in all animals (Genesis 2:7, cited in 1 Corinthians 15:45). I don't 'have' a soul, I *am* a soul, and an embodied soul like Adam. The idea of an 'immortal soul' is a Greek one not a Hebrew one, and for humans immortality is a gift not an inherent part of our makeup (Romans 2:7, 6:23, 1 Corinthians 1:53–54, 1 Timothy 6:16 etc).

This all means that although the primary meaning of *sōma* is a physical body, because our *psyche* is embodied it can extend beyond this. So for example when Paul speaks of giving one's body to be burned (1 Corinthians 13:3) the focus is indeed on the physical body but of course at the same time if my body is burned then my psyche is no longer embodied and it is 'me' that suffers the pain of burning.

1 Corinthians says that 'your body (*sōma*) is the Temple of the Holy Spirit' (6:19). For a first century Jew the Temple was extraordinarily holy, and sometimes today we miss the revolutionary extremity of Paul's statement. Christianity was such a revolution – not only did it have no human high priest or specialised priesthood, but no 'sacred places' save in the hearts and bodies of Christians! (It was too revolutionary, of course, for the Christians who went on to invent a priesthood, sacred buildings, etc!) But if the only sacred place is our bodies, of course we should glorify God in our bodies rather than, for example sexually bond with a promiscuous person (1 Corinthians 6:13ff). But collectively we are the body (*sōma*) of the Messiah (1 Corinthians 12:27 etc), we became a part of the physical presence of Jesus on earth when we (Jews or Gentiles) were 'baptized into one body (*sōma*)' (1 Corinthians 12:13). In the resurrection what is 'sown' as a 'natural' body will be raised as a spiritual one. The natural body, he says, is earthy, as the first Adam was from the earth – but the second Man (the Messiah) is heavenly.

In Romans, we are not to let sin reign in our 'mortal' body (6:12) and in a sense the body is dead because of sin (8:10), but we are to present our bodies as living sacrifices (12:1) which are acceptable (and so not to be regarded as inherently evil). Our bodies will one day be redeemed (8:23) as we fulfil our destinies in regard to the creation. Each of these references uses the word *sōma*.

Paul's intense personal struggle with the sin of covetousness is shown in Romans 7. Cranfield takes these verses to 'depict vividly the inner conflict characteristic of the true Christian' (p.341). Surely, however, Paul's 'certainly not' in Romans 6:2, and his triumphant words in 7:25a and 8:1 mean that he did not expect this life of failure and struggle to be 'normal' for a Christian. Of course Christians do sometimes fall back into experiences as in Romans 7, but surely Paul is speaking in Romans 7 mainly of his fleshly struggles as a pre-Christian Pharisee? The Torah/Law was a good law in his mind (v23), but the Torah sowed covetousness and bad thoughts in his body (or 'members') and as a Torah of Sin and Death warred against his mental love for it. Only when it becomes a Torah of Spirit and Life, in the realisation that there is no condemnation, is the Torah good for him (8:2). This complex way of regarding the Torah is paralleled in the complexity of the way he regards his *sōma*. It is a 'body of death' (7:24) or 'body of Sin' (6:6) – in each case this is his only use of the phrase. In his 'flesh' that is in his natural strength, he can do nothing (7:18; 8:9). Only by the transforming power of the Spirit will his mortal body be given life, now (8:11) and at the previously mentioned final day (8:23). As for Paul's personal struggle with covetousness, he can say as a mature Christian in Philippians 4:11–13:

> [11] I have learned to be content in whatever circumstances I am. [12] I know how to get along with humble means, and I also know how to live in prosperity; in any and every circumstance I have learned the secret of being filled and going hungry, both of having abundance and suffering need. [13] I can do all things through Him who strengthens me. (NASB)

Paul's use of the term *sōma* (flesh) is loose rather than precise. But the 'body of Sin' – the body dominated by Sin, becomes the Temple of the Holy Spirit and can be enlivened through that Spirit if our minds are set on it.

Discussion Topic: Sinless Perfection?

All Christians understand that everyone has sinned, that no one can earn forgiveness for sin, but that this is God's free grace and gift. In general, also, most Christians accept that (if their faith is real) Christians should be showing some kind of fruit of the Spirit in their lives. But just how Christ-like a life can a Christian expect to live? If God is all-powerful and wants Christians to live holy lives, then how can we put any limit on what could be achieved? Christians have differed radically on this. At the one extreme some have said that all Christians will live permanently in the tensions of a Romans 7 experience, unable to control their passions. On the other hand John Wesley claimed that, through a crisis or a process, some could reach a state where they had temptation and still sometimes made 'mistakes' but did not sin. Wesley did not claim this for himself and though in practice we may all meet with Christians who are Christ-like in character, few of us have met any we think of as *never* sinning. But surely God's call to 'be holy as I am holy' (1 Peter 1:15–17) should make us at least *aim* to be holy in *all* our conduct.

So, whatever nuance of understanding we arrive at on Paul's complex and metaphorical analysis of Christian life in Romans 6–8, it seems clear that he believes that God through His Spirit empowers Christians to walk worthy of the Lord, fully pleasing Him, being fruitful in every good work and increasing in the knowledge of God (Colossians 1:10).

Commentary

This question in 6:1 is not the same question as in 6:15, though some commentators take it as the same. In 5:21 Sin was seen as reigning, so at this point in 6:1 Paul is not asking whether Christians should *choose* a life of Sin (as 6:15) but asking whether they have any choice. Do they have to remain enslaved by the reign or dominion of Sin?

The question in 6:1 is: 'Should Christians remain in the power and dominion of sin and just keep getting forgiven?' One cannot help believe that many Christians would actually answer 'Yes'. Even Cranfield later says that the sad story of failure in the verses 7:13–23 'depict vividly the inner conflict characteristic of the true Christian' (p.341). But Paul here exclaims 'Certainly not!'

However we understand the details of his rather complex arguments, surely he thinks that Christians who have received the Kingship of the Messiah are freed from Sin's reign over them, and they have a choice. They can choose to sin or live in self-effort and live lives of spiritual death and failure, or they can choose to live in the Spirit and have a victorious Christian life.

We were formerly 'dead in Sin' (Ephesians 2:1) as a state, but the phrase 'died to sin' in 6:1 is aorist tense and means the single death when Messiah was crucified. Ephesians 2:15 shows that to Paul there is only one 'new Man' and this is the Messiah in whom we have a part. So later in the same letter we read that we should: . . . *put off, concerning your former conduct, the old man which grows corrupt according to the deceitful lusts, and be renewed in the spirit of your mind, and that you put on the new man which was created according to God, in true righteousness and holiness* (Ephesians 4:23–24). This is not about old and new selves, it is about renouncing the old humanity and identifying with the one new Man Jesus the Messiah.

For Christians we have some relevant symbolism right before us. When we were baptised it was not just John's baptism showing repentance and asking for cleansing. It was identification with the implication that the old humanity could not just be 'fixed up' a bit – it needed replacing. Baptism is a kind of burial. Baptism is a participation in His death, and in it we have also 'grown together' in the *likeness* of His death. This was a new meaning for the baptismal rite, and 'Do you not know that . . .' may indicate that Paul was not inventing this but the Early Church had already had this thought. Dunn says that most commentators think this, though Paul is introducing a new idea in regard to its implications. In accepting Christian baptism we accept the verdict of God on the old humanity. The old humanity, then, was enslaved to Sin, but, because the old humanity has been crucified with the Messiah, in accepting this in baptism we are 'baptised into His death'. In Ephesians

1:3–14 Paul lists a whole lot of things that we have 'in Christ', but in our act of baptism we are also (in a sense) opting in to His death, the death of the old humanity. That death frees us from Sin.

At the same time, after God had placed the sin of the old humanity on the Messiah and judged Him for it, He raised Him up. This was not only to vindicate those who have faith (4:25) but also that we might share in His resurrection Life. As we share now in His resurrection Life, we are part of the new Man, but of course this will culminate when we rise again with a body like His glorious body (Philippians 3:21).

Jesus died once and for all. The Roman Catholic idea that the 'mass' is some kind of sacrifice is a really odd one, because the breaking of bread/communion is to remember Jesus' death not to re-enact it.

So we died 'with Messiah', seems to indicate that the once and for all death was on the cross not at the time of our conversion. As we have seen, Galatians 2:20 says:

> I have been crucified with Messiah; it is no longer I who live, but Messiah lives in me; and the life which I now live in the flesh I live by faithfulness of the Son of God, who loved me and gave Himself for me.

The old humanity, of which we were a part, has been crucified once and for all with the Messiah, and we share in His resurrection Life.

Paul says 'the body of sin' has been 'made ineffective' (*katargeō*). Sometimes this term may mean destroy (as in 2 Thessalonians 2:8) but more commonly it means to render ineffective or paralyse, to make idle. It is not our physical body that is paralysed of course, but the 'body of Sin' means the body insofar as it is sin-dominated. The same Torah can be the 'Torah of Sin and death' or the 'Torah of the Spirit of life in Messiah', and the same body can be a 'body of Sin' or a body which is the Temple of the Holy Spirit presented daily as an acceptable living sacrifice to God (Romans 12:2).

The old humanity is judicially dead, and yet Christians are also told to 'put off' the old humanity and put on the new. But Paul's picture is that, because the old humanity has been crucified, we are freed from any guilt which could keep us in bondage to Sin. Paul himself evidently experienced that guilt was above all what kept him from living as he wanted to – so in Romans 8:1 the freedom from condemnation is a key to spirit-filled living.

In verse 11 we get the equivalent of 'put off' the old humanity. The old humanity *is* dead, but we need to *reckon* it as dead!

Sin had a reign but now we have a choice – so verse 12 says do not let Sin reign in your mortal bodies. We now share in the resurrection life of Messiah, and can choose to present the parts of our bodies to God as instruments of righteousness. This prefigures Romans 12:2, presenting our bodies as living sacrifices. So the body itself is not evil, it can be both a Temple of the Holy Spirit and an acceptable offering to God. Once we understand that we are not bound to try in self-effort to keep the Law, but are under grace, we understand that we are free to reject the dominion of Sin

So the power of Sin has been destroyed, and we have a choice. We can *choose* to let Sin reign in our mortal bodies, and follow our lusts, ie we can present our bodies to be used by Sin. Or we can *choose* to present our bodies for God to use. Sin, as a power and principality, no longer has power over us – we have a choice.

All this is a complex set of metaphors and models, but it seems the only way to make consistent sense of the text.

Text 6:15–23

¹⁵ What then? Should we sin because we are not under law but under grace? By no means! ¹⁶ Do you not know that if you present yourselves to anyone as obedient slaves, you are slaves of the one whom you obey, either of sin, which leads to death, or of obedience, which leads to righteousness? ¹⁷ But thanks be to God that you, having once been slaves of sin, have become obedient from the heart to the form of teaching to which you were entrusted, ¹⁸ and that you, having been set free from sin, have become slaves of righteousness. ¹⁹ I am speaking in human terms because of your natural limitations. For just as you once presented your members as slaves to impurity and to greater and greater iniquity, so now present your members as slaves to righteousness for sanctification.

²⁰ When you were slaves of sin, you were free in regard to righteousness. ²¹ So what advantage did you then get from the things of which you now are ashamed? The end of those things is death. ²² But now that you have been freed from sin and enslaved to God, the advantage you get is sanctification. The end is eternal life. ²³ For the wages of sin is death, but the free gift of God is eternal life in Christ Jesus our Lord. (NRSVA)

Commentary

Verse 6:1 was asking whether we have no choice but to stay in Sin's power and keep getting forgiven. Verse 6:15 asks a different question: 'OK, so if we are free and have a choice then why not sin anyway and 'enjoy ourselves' because grace means it will all get forgiven?'

Paul is crystal clear that holy living is not mere self-effort, and that our forgiveness comes from a free gift of God. But he is also clear that Christians can choose to walk in the way of sin, and if they do this then it will lead to spiritual death. Romans 6:23 is not said to people wondering whether or not to become Christians, it is said to Christians! They can choose to become servants of Sin or servants of God and righteousness. Paul, of course, thanks God that they 'obeyed from the heart' to give themselves to God. But his repeated call to his converts to 'walk worthy' of their calling (Ephesians 4:1; Colossians 1:10; 1 Thessalonians 2:12) implies that they have a choice not to.

The choice, as always, is between death and life. These are ultimate, but are also outworked in our present beings. When we sin it sows death in our psyches, and when we give ourselves to God it sows life. If we enslave ourselves to Sin, we receive our due, our wages – death. If we choose to make ourselves slaves to God we do not receive a wage or what is due, but a gift of eternal life. In *God's Strategy in Human History* (volume 1 pp.141ff), we look at the idea of 'eternal life'. It is not just life that goes on interminably (though in some senses it is this) but a different quality of life. It is life in the new Man/ Humanity, in Jesus the Messiah. To Paul it seems incredible that someone should choose to return to the slavery of Sin and the spiritual death of the illicit, rather than the joy and life in getting closer to God. Being 'sanctified' doesn't mean becoming miserable (even if some give that impression!) but having the release and joy of the new quality of eternal life.

Chapters 7–8 | Working Out Our Spirit Freedom and Working With God

Text 7:1–6

¹ Do you not know, brothers and sisters [Greek: brothers] – for I am speaking to those who know the law – that the law is binding on a person only during that person's lifetime? ² Thus a married woman is bound by the law to her husband as long as he lives; but if her husband dies, she is discharged from the law concerning the husband. ³ Accordingly, she will be called an adulteress if she lives with another man while her husband is alive. But if her husband dies, she is free from that law, and if she marries another man, she is not an adulteress.

⁴ In the same way, my friends [Lit: brothers], you have died to the law through the body of Christ, so that you may belong to another, to Him who has been raised from the dead in order that we may bear fruit for God. ⁵ While we were living in the flesh, our sinful passions, aroused by the law, were at work in our members to bear fruit for death. ⁶ But now we are discharged from the law, dead to that which held us captive, so that we are slaves not under the old written code but in the new life of the Spirit. (NRSVA)

Discussion Topic: What is the 'Flesh'?

The NIV translation 'sinful nature' is really not helpful. For one thing Paul adds the adjective 'sinful' when he wants to say that Messiah was only *in the likeness of* sinful flesh (Romans 8:3). But elsewhere he says Messiah also reconciled us through the body of His flesh (Colossians 1:22) so the flesh is not inherently sinful. What Paul seems to emphasize by it is the purely human, the lack of spiritual dimension, though again it is not a strictly technical term. Messiah was a 'descendant of Abraham, according to the flesh' (Romans 1:3 also 9:5), ie in terms of is purely human descent. In Galatians 2:20 and Philippians 1:22 for Paul to live 'in the flesh' just means to live in his physical body. In Galatians, though, Paul notes that he lives in the flesh in a particular way:

> I have been crucified with Messiah and it is no longer I that live, but it is Messiah who lives in me. And the life I now live in the flesh I live by the faithfulness of the Son of God who loved me and gave Himself for me.

In Galatians 2:20 living in a human body is what we all do, but it should be done in the power of Messiah. In Romans 7:5 and 8:9 Paul gives the phrase 'in the flesh' a quite different meaning, saying that they are *not* in the flesh, and seeing such a state as being a bad thing in their past. In the Romans verses it means living in the purely natural human dimension, *without* linking in to the power of God.

Actually this could be done in two contrasting ways. It could be living in simple self-indulgence and enjoyment of sin, but for Paul the Pharisee it meant unaided human effort to try to keep the Torah. Either of these is focussing on the purely human. Ironically, the licentious person and the law-bound religious fanatic are both 'living in the flesh' even if they may loathe each other!

Commentary

The 'law' in verse 1 must surely mean the Jewish Torah-law, because other laws differed anyway (for example, in Roman Law a woman was not freed by her husband's death but had to remain unmarried for a year or lose anything she had from him). But the analogy he uses here is hard to apply in its details. The general principle is clear enough: the marriage law applies only 'until death us do part'. But who is the 'husband' here and who dies? Is the 'husband' the Law, or is it the 'old humanity'? Some Commentators plausibly see verses 2–3 simply as an illustration of the fact that the Law binds only during life. If so, then verses 2–3 do not give an exact analogy so that we have to identify a 'husband'; rather the 'you also' (*kai humeis*) in verse 4 refers back to verse 1. If we want to identify the 'husband' specifically it/he must be Sin as already personified as 'reigning' or having dominion in 6:12. Sin is using the Law to bind people to it. But of course even then it is not an exact analogy because it is not the 'husband', ie Sin, that dies but the 'wife', ie Christians (the 'you also' which includes us). So, however we interpret it, the analogy cannot be pressed too far.

'Sin' attacks us in various ways. Sin attacks us as a king seeking to reign with authority over us (5:14), as a slave-master seeking to control us (6:16) and as a 'husband' using the Law to bind people to it/him (7:1).

We Christians were 'put to death through the body of Messiah'. In Him the fullness of the Father dwelt, and He reconciled us 'in the body of His flesh through death' (Colossians 1:22). So we are free from being bound by the law.

The analogy switches rather confusingly in verse 4. Dying in Christ means we are no longer bound by the Law to Sin, but we are not just left in limbo. The widow is free to marry another, and the one we are now bound to is the resurrected Christ. This does not lead to licentiousness but to fruit. So the Christian life is not one of legalism, but of a dynamic relationship with God through Jesus that leads us to spontaneous good.

Paul had found that the Torah did not aid him in living a righteous life because (we presume) he had not sought it in faith. As he goes on into chapter 7 we see more how the Torah actually had the opposite effect. His realisation that covetousness was wrong (as one of the Ten Commandments) only made him covet the more, and increased his guilt. But once someone realises that the old humanity has been crucified in the body of Messiah, then they are free to serve God in newness of Spirit.

Text 7:7–12

> [7] What then should we say? That the law is sin? By no means! Yet, if it had not been for the law, I would not have known sin. I would not have known what it is to covet if the law had not said, 'You shall not covet.' [8] But sin, seizing an opportunity in the commandment, produced in me all kinds of covetousness. Apart from the law sin lies dead. [9] I was once alive apart from the law, but when the commandment came, sin revived [10] and I died, and the very commandment that promised life proved to be death to me. [11] For sin, seizing an opportunity in the commandment,

deceived me and through it killed me. [12] So the law is holy, and the commandment is holy and just and good. (NRSVA)

Discussion Topic: Who is the 'I'?

Paul switches here dramatically to talk about 'I'. Who is he talking about? Is it himself as a pre-Christian Pharisee, himself in a Christian experience, or some kind of symbolic reference to Adam, to the nation of Israel or to 'everyman'? Is there a distinction in that in verses 7–12 it is in the past tense but in verses 13–25 in the present tense?

Fanciful interpretations such as that of Käsemann that 'the story of Adam is projected into the present as the story of the "I"' (p.196), are unlikely because they expect a complicated jump to be made by those listening (as Paul's letter is read out) that the text does not indicate. His hearers would know the story of Adam, and might well see some reflection of it in what Paul says, but there is nothing in first century literature which would indicate any preparedness for them to conclude that when Paul repeatedly says 'I' he really means Adam. Paul may have used the devices of rhetoric (as Witherington argues) but is unlikely to have expected this level of sophistication in a general audience. Moreover in verse 9 he says that sin 'revived' or came back to life, which cannot describe the experience of Adam. Paul must surely be speaking about himself, even if his experience parallels that of Adam in the way 2 Baruch 54:15–19 (as on p.149–150) indicated.

W.G. Kümmel in 1929 (followed by others), argued that this could not be Paul as a Pharisee, because Paul claimed in Philippians 3:6 that he was 'according to righteousness under the law blameless'. Can this argument be answered?

The key is to remember that in Philippians 3 Paul is speaking about those who 'have confidence in the flesh'. He was, he claims, an exemplary Pharisee – whose zeal ironically was shown in persecuting the Church. So in this sense as far as concerned 'righteousness in the Law' he was 'blameless'. This did not mean sinless, but (as two commentators put it) 'appears to describe an exemplary way of life that is in conformity with the Old Testament as interpreted along Pharisaic lines' (O'Brien *Commmentary on Philippians*, p.380), or 'Torah observance understood as observable conduct' (Fee *Paul's Letter to the Philippians*, p.308). There is no contradiction at all between living an 'exemplary' (or 'blameless') religious life and having an inner struggle with covetousness. Acts 26:14 seems to indicate that even as he was zealously persecuting the Church Paul had inner turmoil and doubts 'kicking against the goads'. Pharisee Paul was irreproachable in his Jewish human standing, but the 'righteousness within the Law' in this context is not real rightstanding before God. Soon after in Philippians 3 he speaks of the contrast between trying to set up his own righteousness from the Law and having one that comes through the faithfulness of Messiah the Son of God, righteousness based on faith (3:9). So we have the paradox: outwardly blameless but inwardly guilt-ridden. Plainly at that time he was not living out the Law in the faith-related manner that it was meant to be lived, but this is certainly not to say that no other Jews were doing so. Zechariah and Elizabeth were not only 'walking in all the commandments and regulations of the Lord blameless' (ie, living lives above reproach in Torah terms) – they were also 'righteous before God' (Luke 1:6). Their piety was not merely external but an internal one of faith. They were not, however, 'Christians' but were pre-Christian Jews living a faith-life with God.

So could a man born in a Pharisee family really say 'I was alive once without the Law'? Some commentators have cited second century rabbis to the effect that the Torah became legally binding for a boy only at bar mitzvah. However it would be very odd to suggest that at the age of (say) ten, a Jewish boy would have no understanding that covetousness was wrong. If, as we believe, babies are born innocent, then at the very beginning of anyone's life (Jew or otherwise) there would be a time when there was no consciousness of right and wrong. At the time when first a moral law was recognised and broken, spiritual death begins in that person's experience. What exact age was it for Paul? Only God can know. For Paul's particular experience his first recognition of right and wrong would have been inextricably linked with the Jewish Torah. He is recounting a Jewish experience, but of course in a more general sense at some stage all people become aware of right and wrong and choose the wrong. This is why, as we saw earlier, death reigned from Adam to Moses. An awareness of right and wrong does not depend on having a particular set of explicit divine commandments.

Discussion Topic: The Normal Christian Life?

Jewett asserts: 'That Paul was sceptical about the human capacity to live the transformed life even after conversion remains typical of Lutheran and Calvinist exegesis' (*Romans: a Commentary*, p.466). Witherington in his commentary traces it back to Augustine (p.188). Nygren and Cranfield both take this view. Dunn, though not generally Augustinian/Reformed in his approach, also does. However, it seems plain from Paul's cry of triumph in 7:25a and description of the Spirit-led life in chapter 8 that Paul did not expect this to be the normal Christian experience. Of course genuine Christians may sometimes slip back into a futile effort to please God in the flesh and live lives of failure and guilt. Some may never even realise that a Spirit-led life is possible. But it is not where Paul expects Christians to stay. His switch from past to present in verse 13 seems to us just to be for dramatic effect – both refer primarily to the same pre-conversion Paul, though by using the present tense it may emphasize that such experience is more general.

Commentary

For Paul, circumcised on the eighth day and brought up as a Pharisee, his first experience of any moral law was of the Jewish Torah. Sin was in the world and human environment, but was dead or dormant. As a baby Paul was innocent and so in a sense spiritually alive, but at the point where he first became aware of the Law and sinned he died spiritually. Hultgren is right in saying that when Paul says 'when the commandment came' it means 'when the commandment came *to me*' (*Paul's Letter to the Romans*, p.279). The Jewish law forbidding covetousness made him aware that even to covet was sinful, and this just bound him up in a cycle of guilt, fixation and sin. This was sowing spiritual death in his psyche and being.

It seems plain from his cry of triumph in 7:25a and description of the Spirit-led life in chapter 8 that he did not expect this to be the normal Christian experience. Of course genuine Christians may sometimes slip back into a futile effort to please God in the flesh and live lives of failure and guilt. But it is not how Paul expects Christians to stay. There is no need (as some have done) to imagine that the Torah is somehow summed up in covetousness, Paul just uses it as an example, and maybe the one he found hardest in his own life.

When Paul first realised (and at what stage in his early life we don't know) that there was a binding moral code of human conduct, the effect on him was twofold. First, he could 'recognise' (*egnōn*) and 'perceive' (*ēdein*) that there was now Sin in his life. These two Greek words translated as 'known' are slightly different, though this is their overall meaning. But there was also a second effect: knowing that the 'fruit' was forbidden made him all the more fascinated with it – so Sin (personified as a kind of Principality) actually used his knowledge and recognition of the commandment to *produce* more sin in him. For someone just to know that thought-sin like lust or covetousness is wrong, often not only fails to help them avoid it but actually increases their fascination with it. Forbidden fruit can seem the more sweet.

Text 7:13–25

13 Did what is good, then, bring death to me? By no means! It was sin, working death in me through what is good, in order that sin might be shown to be sin, and through the commandment might become sinful beyond measure.

14 For we know that the law is spiritual; but I am of the flesh, sold

into slavery under sin. [15] I do not understand my own actions. For I do not do what I want, but I do the very thing I hate. [16] Now if I do what I do not want, I agree that the law is good. [17] But in fact it is no longer I that do it, but sin that dwells within me. [18] For I know that nothing good dwells within me, that is, in my flesh. I can will what is right, but I cannot do it. [19] For I do not do the good I want, but the evil I do not want is what I do. [20] Now if I do what I do not want, it is no longer I that do it, but sin that dwells within me.

[21] So I find it to be a law that when I want to do what is good, evil lies close at hand. [22] For I delight in the law of God in my inmost self, [23] but I see in my members another law at war with the law of my mind, making me captive to the law of sin that dwells in my members. [24] Wretched man that I am! Who will rescue me from this body of death? [25] Thanks be to God through Jesus Christ our Lord!

So then, with my mind I am a slave to the law of God, but with my flesh I am a slave to the law of sin. (NRSVA)

Commentary

So poor lost Pharisee. Desperate to keep what he knew to be the good Torah of God ('You shall not covet'), but just unable in his own strength to do it. The passage is a cry of anguish, and we should be careful not to expect too much of a precise language as Paul expresses it. When in anguish David cries out 'Against you and you only have I sinned' (Psalm 51:4) of course it is not literally true – he certainly *did* sin against Uriah. But he expresses his overwhelming awareness that he has offended a holy and loving God. So here 'It is no longer I that do it' is clearly not literally true, it really is Paul. But the point he makes is that it is in a sense involuntary, against his better instincts, that he covets.

In 7:7–13 the tense is past but in 7:14 Paul switches to the present tense. It may be that this reflects a movement from his intensely personal memories of struggle as a pre-Christian Pharisee to 'a general sense of people who try to live out their lives in their own strength' (Longenecker *Romans*, p.642). It does not indicate any pre- and post-conversion self of Paul.

Some have tried to take 'in my flesh nothing good dwells' to deduce some kind of doctrine of 'total depravity', but this is a poor translation as for example Cranfield, Käsemann and Jewett insist. Actually the text reads: 'I know that dwells not in me, that is in my flesh, the good (*agathon*), I can will is present with me but to work good (*kalon*) is not'. Someone who was really 'totally depraved' in any meaningful sense, would not be able to will to do what is good.

Jewett also suggests that in a sense when Paul was striving to do 'the good' and through persecuting the Church to advance the coming of the Messianic age, he found on the Damascus road that actually it was the Messiah he was persecuting.

The 'law' (*nomos*) throughout this passage is the Torah, as we shall expand below. The Greek word *nomos* was not used in the English sense of 'law' to mean an observed principle. For verse 21 the NASB has 'I find then a principle that . . .' and the NRSVA 'I find a law that . . .' But the word *nomos* was a very common word, meaning some kind of written or unwritten legal code that people should try to keep. Attempts to find it used to mean some kind of regularity of nature are unconvincing – this is a much later idea. Nothing important hangs on this issue, but we therefore find the NASB/NRSVA renderings unlikely. It can read something like the Meyer translation: *'It results to me therefore, that, while my will is directed to the Law in order to do the good, the evil lies before me'* (see Jewett, *Romans a Commentary,* p. 469). Dunn renders 7:21 – *'I find then the law, in my case wishing to do the good, to be that for me evil lies ready to hand.'* The Torah in his mind is good, but the Torah as it operates in his flesh is the Torah of Sin and Death.

Verse 24 summarises his anguish. His human flesh is weak, unable to resist as Sin uses the Torah to enslave him. Who will rescue him? Before his final summing up he cannot resist the burst of praise: 'thanks be to God through Jesus the Messiah our Lord.' God did not intend to leave His people in a Romans 7 experience!

Questions for Thought and Discussion

- How often do we find ourselves as Christians in an experience like that of Romans 7?
- How do we escape from it?

Text 8:1–4

> [1] There is therefore now no condemnation for those who are in Christ Jesus. [2] For the law of the Spirit of life in Christ Jesus has set you free from the law of sin and of death. [3] For God has done what the law, weakened by the flesh, could not do: by sending His own Son in the likeness of sinful flesh, and to deal with sin [or *and as a sin-offering*], He condemned sin in the flesh, [4] so that the just requirement of the law might be fulfilled in us, who walk not according to the flesh but according to the Spirit. (NRSVA)

Commentary

Romans 8:1 is a core verse. 'In Christ' we have redemption (3:24), and we can 'consider ourselves dead to sin but alive to God in Christ Jesus' (6:11) in whom we have eternal life (6:23). Romans 6 stated the objective position (we died in Christ so are dead to Sin), while Romans 7–8 goes through how it all works in personal experience. Paul's bond with Jesus is personal, relational, and in a sense mystical. What is the 'Law of the Spirit of life'? 'Spirit of life' may just be a Jewish expression for 'life-giving Spirit' (as in 2 Corinthians 3:6), but what about the 'Law'? Well, as already mentioned, 'Law' (*nomos*) means a code of human conduct, and the epitome of this to Paul is the Jewish Torah (not just its ritual but its real meaning of what God wants from us). To be 'in Christ' does not mean simply lawlessness and licentiousness. We still follow a divinely given code of conduct, but this is fulfilled in dynamic relationship with the indwelling Christ, not in self-effort.

But can Paul really now be speaking positively about some kind of Torah when he has said so strongly that it cannot bring life? Käsemann, for example, thinks not, calling it the 'irreparably perverted law of Moses'. But this misses the point. Paul has already said that the Law itself is 'holy' (7:12) 'spiritual' (7:14) and 'good' (7:16). It is because he once approached it in fleshly effort that what was good did him harm and enslaved him to Sin. A sharp knife can be a good kitchen tool, but in the hands of a robber or a three year old is not good. It depends how it is used. Dunn makes this point about the Torah:

> Paul is able to think of the law in two different ways: the law caught in the nexus of sin and death . . . but the law rightly understood and responded to in (spirit not letter) is pleasing to God. (*Romans*, 2:29)

As a Christian, Paul's relationship to the Torah has radically changed. It is no longer a bearer of Sin and death, but because he knows that the old humanity has been judged and there is no condemnation he can now follow its underlying meaning in the power of the Spirit and in Life. If we are in Jesus we do not walk by human fleshly effort but according to the Spirit. Paul often talks about life as a 'walk' and the implication is usually that we have a choice (Galatians 5:16, Ephesians 4:1 etc). We know, of course, that in a sense we remain 'in the flesh' but in 2 Corinthians 10:3 he says that although we walk *in* the flesh our spiritual life and warfare is not *according* to the flesh but the Spirit.

How is the 'righteous requirement' of the Law fulfilled in us? The word *dikaiōma* is little used in the New Testament. Paul's friend Luke uses it in Luke 1:6 when he asserts that Elizabeth and Zechariah 'were righteous before God walking in all the commandments and *dikaiōma* of the Law blameless.' We might pause to note that according to many commentators, since they lived before the New Covenant (and being old probably died before the crucifixion) this was impossible because all that the Law did for the Jews was to increase their guilt. But, clearly, living such a life was possible before the New Covenant period or epoch that started around 33 AD. Paul was unable to do it as a Pharisee because he approached it in the purely human effort of the flesh, but not all Jews were such Pharisees.

Paul himself says that Gentiles who suppress the truth in unrighteousness instinctively know the *dikaiōma* (God's just moral requirements) are against what they do, but do them anyway (1:32). On the other hand, he says that there are other Gentiles who keep the *dikaiōmata* of the Torah and so show up the unfaithful amongst the Jews (2:26). The 'just requirements' seems not to mean the letter, but the underlying spirit of the Torah, what it was really signifying. The other two Pauline uses are in Romans 5:16 (*dikaiōma*) and 5:18 (*dikaiōmatos* = righteous act). So does it mean, as some claim, that it is 'fulfilled in us' in the sense that 'Jesus is our righteousness' and so God 'looks on us and sees *His* ethical perfection'? We don't believe that this is its meaning.

Of course the just demands of the Law *were* fulfilled through Jesus' death and our participation in it. However, Romans 5:18 does not refer to some kind of transferred ethical perfection but to His righteous *act* – His sacrificial death. And here in chapter 8 there are two reasons why it seems to mean something about our lifestyle. The first is that when Luke applies *dikaiōma* to Elizabeth and Zechariah he is speaking neither about ethical perfection nor some kind of imputed righteousness from someone else – it is their lifestyle he speaks of. The second is that Paul goes on to speak of us as being 'those who walk not according to the flesh but according to the spirit'. If all that mattered was some kind of artificially imputed righteousness of someone else then it really would not make much difference how we walked.

Paul is not speaking of people who fulfil all the written ordinances of Torah, but of those who live in fulfilment of its righteous requirements through faith and the Spirit.

There is absolutely no need to think that Paul diverges in any way from the plain statements of the apostle John in 1 John 3:5–8.

> [5] You know that He was revealed to take away sins, and in Him there is no sin. [6] No one who abides in Him sins; no one who sins has either seen Him or known Him. [7] Little children, let no one deceive you. Everyone who does what is right is righteous, just as He is righteous. [8] Everyone who commits sin is a child of the devil; for the devil has been sinning from the beginning. The Son of God was revealed for this purpose, to destroy the works of the devil. (NRSVA)

John has also said that if we say we have no sin we are liars – we have sinned and need forgiveness. He is aware that we need to confess sins and claim the blood of the Messiah for forgiveness. But if we are righteous it is not just that we somehow claim a transfer of the ethical perfection of Jesus, we *live* righteously. In Paul's terms, we walk according to the spirit.

Text 8:5–11

> [5] For those who live according to the flesh set their minds on the things of the flesh, but those who live according to the Spirit set their minds on the things of the Spirit. [6] To set the mind on the flesh is death, but to set the mind on the Spirit is life and peace. [7] For this reason the mind that is set on the flesh is hostile to God; it does not submit to God's law—indeed it cannot, [8] and those who are in the flesh cannot please God.
> [9] But you are not in the flesh; you are in the Spirit, since the Spirit of God dwells in you. Anyone who does not have the Spirit of Christ does not belong to Him. [10] But if Christ is in you, though the body is dead because of sin, the Spirit is life because of righteousness. [11] If the Spirit of Him who raised Jesus from the dead dwells in you, He who raised Christ from the dead will give life to your mortal bodies also through His Spirit that dwells in you. (NRSVA)

Commentary

In Romans 8:1–4 Paul covered the objective way in which God has freed us to live in the Spirit. Now he turns to urge them to make the choice to do it. *How* are they to walk in the Spirit? It is all about mindset. If we focus purely on the physical realm – whether that be in the 'flesh' in the sense of just enjoying sinning or in the sense of purely human self-effort to be good – then it leads to spiritual death. To 'set their minds upon' in verse 5 is a Greek phrase that Cranfield points out generally implies to 'take the side of'. Verses 6–7 literally say: 'For the mind of flesh is death but the mind of Spirit is life and peace because the mind of flesh is against God.' The genitives in this verse indicate that these are minds belonging to flesh and spirit respectively. So in us we have two alternative 'minds' and we choose on which to focus.

Those who are 'in the flesh' in the sense of focussing on the purely human cannot please God because the flesh in this sense is naturally lawless and so cannot relate to God. As already noted 'in the flesh' is not a technical term used consistently by Paul. In 2 Corinthians 10:3 Paul contrasts Christians walking 'in the flesh' (*en sarki*) with warring 'according to the flesh' (*kata sarka*) – whereas here the two phrases are equivalent. In Galatians 2:20 Paul says he himself lives 'in the flesh' but is living by faith. His language is not, then, precise and technical, but whatever the details, we get the gist!

However, Paul assures the Roman Christians that they are not 'in the flesh' but 'in the Spirit'. Christians are in the Spirit, and the Spirit (whether called the 'Spirit of God' or 'Holy Spirit' or 'Spirit of Messiah') is in Christians. This applies whether we think of 'in the spirit' as meaning living on a spiritual level, or more specifically in the Holy Spirit, because for Christians this is the same thing. For some there can be a second experience (or second blessing) which brings consciousness of the Spirit's power within, brings specific spiritual gifts. The Spirit can be experienced at different levels, in a sense from a kind of paddling to a total immersion, and people's experience as they progress in their Christian life can be different. The filling of the Holy Spirit (usually *pleitho* in the aorist tense) can be at a specific time for a specific manifestation, for example a prophecy (Luke 1:15, 1:41, 1:57, Acts 2:4, 4:8, 4:31, 9:17, 13:9). There is also a continuous filling (usually *pleroo*) in the sense that we are told to be *being* filled with the Spirit (Ephesians 5:18 – also Luke 4:1, Acts 2:2, 6:3 & 5, 7:55, 11:24, 13:52).

But Paul seems to say here that someone who does not have the Spirit at all is not a Christian. Dunn puts this more actively: 'only those whose lives demonstrate by character and conduct that the Spirit is directing them can claim to be under Christ's lordship' (*Romans*, p.429). Dunn suggests that the point is not that some verbal confession or ritual act defines who is a Christian and we deduce from this that the person must have the Spirit even if their behaviour is bad. Rather, he says, it is that if there is no fruit of the Spirit or indication of the Spirit's presence we may doubt that they really belong to Christ. John very similarly says that is not words but the love in us that tells us we belong to Christ. But John adds a word for sensitive souls who may start on an introspective obsession about looking within themselves for signs of Spirit presence:

> [18] Little children, let us love, not in word or speech, but in truth and action. [19] And by this we will know that we are from the truth and will reassure our hearts before Him [20] whenever our hearts condemn us; for God is greater than our hearts, and He knows everything. [21] Beloved, if our hearts do not condemn us, we have boldness before God. (1 John 3:18–21, NRSVA)

Faith is not mere belief but reflects in lifestyle. However, we all have failings and if we focus over much on them then this is just another way of setting the mind on the flesh.

Jesus was raised as the firstfruits of the dead (1 Corinthians 15:20) and through Him our mortal bodies will be transformed in the receipt of immortality.

Text 8:12–17

> [12] So then, brothers and sisters, we are debtors, not to the flesh, to live according to the flesh— [13] for if you live according to the flesh, you will die; but if by the Spirit you put to death the deeds of the body, you will live. [14] For all who are led by the Spirit of God are children of God. [15] For you did not receive a spirit of slavery to fall back into fear, but you have received a spirit of adoption. When we cry, 'Abba! Father!' [16] it is that very Spirit bearing witness with our spirit that we are children of God, [17] and if children, then heirs, heirs of God and joint heirs with Christ—if, in fact, we suffer with Him so that we may also be glorified with Him. (NRSVA)

Commentary

Always Paul moves from what God has done and is doing to our response. Again we find here that Christians have a choice and if they choose to live according to the flesh they will die. Does this mean they 'lose their salvation and go to hell'? Maybe, but this does not seem to us to be what Paul is really thinking of. All the time he sees flesh-sin as leading to spiritual death and spirit-life as leading to spiritual life. He implies that by the Spirit they *can* put to death the deeds of the body. Not by self-effort and teeth gritting, but by latching on to the power of the Spirit within.

The reference to being led by the Spirit probably relates back to the Israelites being led through the desert by the Spirit – as maybe chapter 6 could be thought to relate to their 'baptism' through the Red Sea (see also 1 Corinthians 10:2). This is an ongoing daily experience, not a once-for-all one. And all those (men or women) who allow themselves to be Spirit-led are 'sons'! In their first century cultural terms, all have the position and privileges of 'sons' whether they are men or women, slaves or free, Jews or Gentiles.

The Holy Spirit Christians have received is not a spirit of slavery but of 'son-placing' – perhaps rather misleadingly translated here as 'adoption'. This is a future event of the redemption of the body for which we wait (Romans 8:23) and it is our future destiny (Ephesians 1:5). It does not mean 'adoption' in the sense of the English word, but an entry into the inheritance we have when Christ comes again. So the Holy Spirit is the 'Spirit of son-placing' or the 'guarantee of our inheritance' (2 Corinthians 5:5, Ephesians 1:14).

It is the Holy Spirit within which makes us cry out 'Abba!' or 'Daddy' to God. This shows that we are genuinely children of God, and so are heirs, awaiting our son-placing or coming into our inheritance to rule with Christ. Christian faith is an amazing thing that enables us to recognise that God is the Lord and creator of all the universe, and yet allows us to call Him Daddy in a family bond.

To share, however, in the rule that is part of being co-heir with Christ, means that we must also be prepared to suffer with Christ. There is a cost in sharing the glory. When is the time when we will be 'glorified together'? John 12 speaks much about this, but it is not entirely clear whether Jesus is to be 'glorified' going to the cross, or being resurrected, or maybe both. 'The hour is come' He says 'when the Son of Man will be glorified' – but that hour seems to be His crucifixion. In 2 Thessalonians 1:10–12 Paul seems to imply both that in the Day of Judgement Christ will be glorified in His saints, but also that the name of Jesus may be glorified in them presumably in the present age too.

Questions for Thought and Discussion

- *How often do we fall back into a human fleshly struggle with sin?*

- *How in practice can we set our minds on the spirit rather than the purely human?*

- *How far do you feel the inner conviction of the Spirit that you are a child of God and led by Him?*

Text 8:18–25

[18] I consider that the sufferings of this present time are not worth comparing with the glory about to be revealed to [Greek: *eis*] us. [19] For the creation waits with eager longing for the revealing of the children of God; [20] for the creation was subjected to futility, not of its own will but by the will of the One who subjected it, in hope [21] that the creation itself will be set free from its bondage to decay and will obtain the freedom of the glory of the children of God. [22] We know that the whole creation has been groaning in labour pains until now; [23] and not only the creation, but we ourselves, who have the first fruits of the Spirit, groan inwardly while we wait for adoption, the redemption of our bodies. [24] For in hope we were saved. Now hope that is seen is not hope. For who hopes for what is seen? [25] But if we hope for what we do not see, we wait for it with patience. (NRSVA)

Commentary

This is clearly speaking of future glory which is to be revealed *in* us or *to* us (*eis* could mean either). The revealing or son-placing of the sons of God is to be for the redemption of creation.

When was creation subject to futility? Paul does not say. Many take it to be at the fall, but this is not specified. In Genesis, humanity (*ādām*) is commanded to 'have dominion' and also to 'subdue' the earth. Maybe it was already groaning awaiting the revealing of the sons of God but *ādām* instead chose sin. In verse 22 Paul pictures it as a kind of birth-pangs. After someone has gone through birth-pangs the pain may be forgotten in the joy of the new arrival. But in the meantime the creation is groaning.

We Christians also groan. The 'firstfruits' of a harvest were the first of the new crop. The Spirit within has given us this, but, as Paul has already explained, we are still tied to our body-flesh. This is not because flesh is inherently evil, but until it is redeemed it is contaminated. When we rise again we will have a spiritual body, a body like His glorious body (1 Corinthians 15:37–44, Philippians 3:21). Our bodies will be redeemed, we do not become disembodied spirits but re-embodied beings/souls. This is our 'hope' but of course it does not mean hope in the sense of 'just hope for the best', rather it is a sure and certain expectation.

Text 8:26–30

> [26] Likewise the Spirit helps us in our weakness; for we do not know how to pray as we ought, but the Spirit Himself intercedes for us with sighs too deep for words. [27] And He who searches the hearts of men knows what is the mind of the Spirit, because the Spirit intercedes for the saints according to the will of God. [28] We know that in everything God works for good with those who love Him, who are called according to His purpose. [29] For those whom He foreknew He also predestined to be conformed to the image of His Son, in order that He might be the first-born among many brethren. [30] And those whom He predestined He also called; and those whom He called He also justified; and those whom He justified He also glorified. (RSV)

Discussion Topic: Working Together

Here are various English translations of verse 28:

NKJV: All things work together for good to those who love God, to those who are the called according to His purpose. (KJV is similar)

ESV: And we know that for those who love God all things work together for good.

RSV: In everything God works for good with those who love Him, who are called according to His purpose.

NRSVA: All things work together for good, for those who love God

NASB: God causes all things to work together for good to those who love God, to those who are called according to His purpose.

NIV: In all things God works for the good of those who love Him, who have been called according to His purpose.

NIV Margin: In all things God works together with those who love Him to bring about what is good.

NEB: In everything, as we know, [the Spirit] cooperates for good with those who love God.

So first, is it 'things' (KJV, NKJV and ESV) or God who 'works'? Well there is nothing anywhere else in Scripture to indicate that 'things' could somehow 'work', but the idea of God working or working together with Christians is clearly found. That it is God rather than 'things' working was also the apparent understanding of the Early Church, and some important early manuscripts contain an extra nominative 'God' (*ho theos*) to put this beyond doubt. The KJV/NKJV/ESV rendering is therefore unacceptable.

This *ho theos* also makes the NEB rendering attractive, because their strong trinitarian understanding would make working with the Spirit the same as working with God – and working together with the Spirit in prayer was the topic in Romans 8:26.

One key term in the verse is *sunergei* = work (*ergei*) together (*sun*) making 'work-*together*'. The NIV main rendering must surely be wrong because it leaves out the 'together' altogether.

So, is it God *causing* all things to work together as the NASB? The word *energia* does not mean 'cause', it is the word from which we get 'energy'. The picture is of God 'energising'. Indeed, we find in Ephesians that God is energising in things (1:11). God energises in us (3:20) but also Satan energises in the children of disobedience (2:2). We also find that the prayer of a person in rightstanding with God is an effective energising power (James 5:16). The idea of Christians working together with God to energize for good is therefore an obvious one.

Moreover would the God who loved the world and sent the Jesus who told us to love our enemies and do good to those who treat us badly, want to do good *only* to those who presently love him? We know that:

> . . . the eyes of the Lord are on the righteous, and His
> ears are open to their prayer. But the face of the Lord
> is against those who do evil. (1 Peter 3:12, NRSVA)

But He still wants to bring good to those who do evil because He would rather they turn and repent. So God certainly does not only 'work for the good of *those who love him*'. He works for the good of *everyone*. While we were still sinners and did not love God, Christ died for us (Romans 5:8), and whether someone loves God, does not yet love God, or will never love God, He works for their good and sent His Son to die for them because God 'so loved the world'.

The NASB not only gives a misleading picture of God, but it encourages Christians simply to sit back and feel smug: *'Don't worry, God is working all things for your good, you don't need to do anything!'* Actually the verse is a call to action, for those 'called according to His purpose' are called to be the body of Christ seeking to work with God to bring good into the world.

The idea of Christians as God's fellow energisers or workers appears elsewhere. In Mark 16:20 we find that as the disciples preached the Lord 'worked together' with them. In 1 Corinthians 3:9 Paul says that 'we are God's fellow workers'. In 2 Corinthians 6:1 he again describes himself as 'working together' with God *using the same term as in Romans 8:28*. It is also possible that the NEB translation is correct. The word 'God' in the earliest manuscripts is not in the Greek and the NEB very naturally takes the Holy Spirit to be the continuing subject of the sentence:

> In the same way the Spirit comes to the aid of our weakness. We do not even know how we ought to pray, but through our inarticulate groans the Spirit Himself is pleading for us, and God who searches our innermost being knows what the Spirit means because He pleads for God's own people in God's own way; and in everything, as we know, He co-operates for good with those who love God . . . (NEB)

In any event, the basic idea is Christians working together with God to bring good into any situation. They are to: i) pray in the Spirit as they fight against spiritual hosts of wickedness in the armour of God, letting that Spirit intercede with and for them, and ii) cooperate with God to bring good into any situation.

Discussion Topic: Foreknowledge

The word 'foreknow' (*proginōskō*) simply means to know beforehand. In our work *Reconsidering Key Biblical Ideas* chapter 5 we show that there is absolutely nowhere that the word 'know' (in Greek or Hebrew equivalent *yādā*) can ever mean simply to 'choose'. The many commentaries that claim that it does, all repeat the same verses (particularly Genesis 18:19, Deuteronomy 9:24, Jeremiah 1:5, Amos 3:2, Hosea 13:5) to 'prove' it, and in no case in these verses does it mean to choose. It means to know personally, to recognise, or to know about. Of course there *is* an element of choice in getting to know someone in a relationship, but this does not mean that 'know' is equivalent to 'choose'. To use an analogy: to train a dog you have to choose one, but it would be odd to say that 'I trained a dog' could mean 'I chose one without yet having met it'.

So 'fore-know' must mean to 'know about' in advance, to 'recognise' in advance, or to 'have a relationship' in advance – not merely to choose in advance.

So could it mean to know personally, to have a relationship with them, in advance of their birth? To say that God could have a personal relationship with a group of people before they existed would surely be nonsense. God can do what is impossible to us, but to put 'God can' in front of nonsense does not make it mean anything.

Why not take foreknowledge in its simple sense of knowing about beforehand? Often such a sense is taken (by advocates and critics) to mean that God knew something specific about the *individuals* who would make up the Church, ie that they would repent – but of course this is not stated in the text. We believe that this idea is, in any case, misleading. It seems to us to reflect the post-Augustine self-absorbed obsession with getting individual tickets to heaven. Likewise the same individualistic obsession has made people change the Ephesians 1 concept of being 'chosen *in* Christ' to being 'chosen (as individuals) *to be put into* Christ'

– this is another issue we look at in *Reconsidering Key Biblical Ideas*. But Paul sees them *collectively* as the body of Christ, and surely this whole thing is about God's plan and vision for the Church as a body. God knew in advance that he would call people to repent and the Church would be formed. He decided on the destiny for this Church. He planned (as Daniel shows) that those to be called/named saints would rule with Messiah. He planned that the Church is justified in Messiah, and the Church will be glorified (and indeed in one sense is already being glorified). It is not about singling out individuals, though of course it affects the individuals who enter the Church.

Discussion Topic: Predestination and Election

'Predestination' is widely misconceived to be about 'election' which in turn is misunderstood to be about a supposedly arbitrary choice of God as to who to make repent (which many think of as 'Calvinism'). It is interesting, though, that on the first of these misconceptions even Calvin himself said that 'predestination does not refer to election, but to that purpose or decree of God by which he has ordained that the cross is to be borne by His people;' (Calvin *Commentary on the Epistle to the Romans,* p.343). The term translated as predestination (*proorizō*) means 'setting out a horizon' and concerns our destiny as Christians, not how we became Christians.

The terms 'election' and 'predestination' are both analysed in depth in our *Reconsidering Key Biblical Ideas*. Election is something we receive *in Christ* (Ephesians 1:4), it is not that we were chosen *to be put into* Christ based on some kind of arbitrary selection process. The Messiah was the chosen servant of God (Matthew 12:18, Luke 9:35). If we enter into Christ we then share in His election. We also receive a destiny 'in Christ' to receive the 'son-placing' or 'adoption' (Ephesians 1:3) which is our destined inheritance (Ephesians 1:11). Their destiny, then, is for Christians to be conformed to the image of His Son (Romans 8:29) when we receive the 'son-placing' (8:19, 23) and so share with Christ in the redemption and ruling of creation.

As *proorizō* means 'setting out a horizon', it is not about choosing who should or should not become Christians, it is about the future destined task of those who are chosen in Christ. As usual, though, to Paul our present lifestyle should also reflect our future destiny.

Commentary

Verse 26 does *not* say that we don't need to be praying because the Spirit does it all for us. Rather, the picture is of us striving in prayer but cooperating in it with the indwelling Holy Spirit. We don't always know what to pray for, but our hearts cooperate with the Spirit to pray 'Your Kingdom come, Your will be done on Earth as it is in Heaven.' Christians are not called to passively enjoy God's favour while He does everything. In Ephesians Paul says:

> [10] Finally, be strong in the Lord and in the strength of His power. [11] Put on the whole armour of God, so that you may be able to stand against the wiles of the devil. [12] For our struggle is not against enemies of blood and flesh, but against the rulers, against the authorities, against the cosmic powers of this present darkness, against the spiritual forces of evil in the heavenly places . . . [18] Pray in the Spirit at all times in every prayer and supplication. To that end keep alert and always persevere in supplication for all the saints. [19] Pray also for me, so that when I speak, a message may be given to me to make known with boldness the mystery of the gospel. (NRSVA)

It is not in our own strength that we fight, but in God's – but nevertheless we are called as saints of the Most High to spiritual warfare. Prayer is to be 'in the Spirit', but at times as we strive in prayer we do not know the right thing to be asking for. We can reach that point before God where only our hearts can speak, and we experience a deep oneness with the Spirit. For some, speaking in tongues may be a way to express not only praise but intercession, though this is not Paul's specific reference here. The Spirit intercedes in our behalf, but for this to happen we ourselves need to be deeply in prayer communion. It is a cooperation.

Verse 28, properly translated, continues this idea of cooperation. We not only cooperate in prayer to bring in good, we energise together with God to see it happen. So, *in everything God energises for good together with those who love Him, who are called according to His purpose.* Christians don't passively sit there and forget intercessory prayer on the supposed grounds that God is controlling everything anyway. Christians don't wait smugly and let God 'work all things' for our benefit (and forget about anyone else). We seek to work together with God to bring good into and out of any situation, however bad it is. The mistranslations of verse 28 have sometimes led Christians facing some very awful tragedy to try to convince themselves that God has somehow caused it for their good. This is mistaken. What they should rather be saying is 'How can I work *with* God (in both prayer and action) to bring good into this dreadful situation?'

God foreknew that He would have a body of people called/named according to His purpose to work for good and to have the destiny of son-placing when they would be conformed to the image of Jesus and help Him to redeem creation. Jesus died to take away the sins *of the world*, and God is not willing that any should perish but desires all to come to repentance. Some people, we know, have rejected both God's will (Matthew 7:21 etc) and His plan for them (Luke 7:30), but those who *have* accepted His offer of undeserved forgiveness and salvation He has named saints, justified and glorified in the Messiah.

Text 8:31–39

> [31] What then are we to say about these things? If God is for us, who is against us? [32] He who did not withhold His own Son, but gave Him up for all of us, will He not with Him also give us everything else? [33] Who will bring any charge against God's elect? It is God who justifies. [34] Who is to condemn? It is Christ Jesus, who died, yes, who was raised, who is at the right hand of God, who indeed intercedes for us. [35] Who will separate us from the love of Christ?

Will hardship, or distress, or persecution, or famine, or nakedness, or peril, or sword? [36] As it is written,

'For your sake we are being killed all day long;
we are accounted as sheep to be slaughtered.'

[37] No, in all these things we are more than conquerors through Him who loved us. [38] For I am convinced that neither death, nor life, nor angels, nor rulers, nor things present, nor things to come, nor powers, [39] nor height, nor depth, nor anything else in all creation, will be able to separate us from the love of God in Christ Jesus our Lord. (NRSVA)

Commentary

Little can be added to this wonderful doxology! Satan is the accuser who seeks to twist us with guilt, but 'there is no condemnation' and God has declared He is for us. It is Messiah who is our High Priest and intercessor at the right hand of God Himself. Whatever our apparent circumstances, we are bound up in the Love of God.

However this is no 'prosperity gospel'. Paul does not say that faithful praying Christians will never experience tribulation and persecution – he just says that *in* all these we are more than conquerors. It is not (in the words of one hymn) that 'in his presence our problems disappear,' it is that even if they are still there we are more than conquerors as we pass through them.

There are spiritual powers and principalities (Ephesians 6:8) against which we are in conflict, but even these can never separate us from God's love.

Questions for Thought and Discussion

- How exciting do you find this future destiny of being son-placed, conformed to the image of Jesus, and sharing in the redemption of creation?

- What does it imply about living now?

Part 2: God's Faithfulness and His dealings with the Jews 9:1–11:36

Romans 9–11 | Israel and God's Historical Strategy

Discussion Topic: The Place of Judaism and the Mosaic Covenant

In his earlier section Paul has dealt much with faith as the only basis of being right with God, and ways of approaching the Jewish Law or Torah. But there remain some very basic issues: i) has God now completely rejected Israel? ii) If he has then does this mean He is unfaithful to His covenants with Abraham and through Moses? Central to these is the issue of the meaning of the Old Covenant with the Jews.

Two particular, usually competing, schema have been suggested on this: Covenant Theology and Dispensationalism.

Covenant Theology is a generally 'Reformed' approach that posits three covenants:

1. A 'covenant of redemption' between the persons of the Trinity before creation to sovereignly select out various humans to become the bride of Christ.

2. A 'covenant of works' made with Adam.

3. A 'covenant of grace' which is a one-sided decision
    of God to unconditionally forgive and redeem
    sovereignly-selected individuals.

The various actual covenants mentioned in Scripture are then seen
as part of one or the other of these last two, sometimes a mixture.
So, for example the Abrahamic covenant is grace, but the Mosaic
one is mostly works, but also has elements of a typology of Christ
and so grace.

The problem with all this is that it seems to impose a structure
which is not actually indicated in Scripture. The covenant of
redemption is pure invention. There is no Scriptural mention of
any 'covenant' with Adam, and on offer in the garden was the
'tree of life' – meaning that he was offered a choice between sin
or entering a union with the Son who is represented by that tree.
Thus, while we agree that the only basis of being right with God is
faith-grace, the overall schema is confusing and imposes a language
that is just not there in Scripture.

Dispensationalism dates from the early nineteenth century and
has held that there are seven 'dispensations' in which God deals
differently with humankind:

1. Innocence (or freedom) (Genesis 2:8–17, 25), prior
    to Adam's fall

2. Conscience (Genesis 3:10–18; Romans 2:11–15),
    Adam to Noah

3. Government (Genesis 9:6; Romans 13:1), Noah to
    Abraham

4. Patriarchal rule (or promise) (Genesis 12:1–3; 22:17–
    18; Galatians 3:15–19), Abraham to Moses

5. Mosaic Law, (Exodus 20:1–26; Galatians 3:19), Moses
    to Christ

6. Grace (Romans 5:20–21; Ephesians 3:1–9), the current Church Age

7. Millennial, a literal future earthly 1000 year Kingdom (Isaiah 9:6–7; 11:1–9; Revelation 20:1–6).

Dispensationalists say God deals differently with people in different dispensations. So Jewish people can be saved through keeping the Mosaic Law. The nation of Israel remains the chosen nation, and has not been 'replaced by' the Church (Dispensationalists accuse Covenant theologians of 'replacement theology'). Israel the nation continues as a central part of God's purpose, and will have a role in the millennium after (as they believe) the Christians are 'raptured' out of this world to avoid any tribulation or serious difficulties.

Dispensationalists inevitably vary amongst themselves, and some 'progressive dispensationalists' have amended the strict categorisation. But we have some basic issues with the schema. Chief is that Paul seems to teach that the only basis to receive justification is faith in God. Not only Abraham, but David and Habakkuk and (according to Hebrews) all the Old Testament saints were living by faith. The faith might be expressed differently or based on different amounts of revelation, but faith-grace is the only basis of justification – whether this is inside or outside any specific 'covenant'. The Pharisees were all meticulously keeping the Law, but Jesus says some harsh things about them in Matthew 23; many or most of them were evidently not living a faith-life in relationship with the Father. Rather, they were a 'brood of vipers' dramatically fulfilling the prophecy in Genesis 3:15! Jesus also says that if they are really wanting to follow God then they will know whether His teaching is true (John 7:17). Paul is desperate for his countrymen to be saved (Romans 9:1) but elsewhere says this will be by turning to Christ, not by continuing in a covenant of Law (2 Corinthians 3:16).

Has the Church 'replaced' Israel as the people of God? This is a misleading question. Paul is very clear that *as a nation* Israel failed to live up to acting as a light to the Gentiles. But he is also clear that even in dark times there was a *remnant* (like the 7000 in the days of Elijah – Romans 11:4) who were the 'true Israel' (Romans 9:6) and had the 'true circumcision' which is of the heart (Deuteronomy 10:16, 30:6; Jeremiah 4:4). Paul uses the term 'Israel' (like the word 'circumcision') usually in a literal but occasionally in a spiritual sense. Throughout much of Romans 'Israel' plainly means the nation; but he also says 'not all are Israel who are of Israel' (9:6). The *true* Israel in Old Testament times were the faithful remnant of Jews, and his later use of the term in 11:26 must be read in this light. In New Testament times the 'Israel of God' (Galatians 6:16) began entirely as Jewish, but then seems to include the Gentiles who were in Messiah. The true badge of being part of the people of God is not works of the Law but a faith-relationship with God, and this applies to Jews and Gentiles in the Church Age.

Peter actually goes further and says to the Church (Jews and Gentiles):

> [9] But you are a chosen race, a royal priesthood, a holy nation, a people for God's own possession, so that you may proclaim the excellencies of Him who has called you out of darkness into His marvellous light; [10] for you once were not a people, but now you are the people of God; you had not received mercy, but now you have received mercy. (1 Peter 2:9–10, NASB)

This is applying to the Church the words of Exodus 19:5–6:

> [5] 'Now then, if you will indeed obey My voice and keep My covenant, then you shall be My own possession among all the peoples, for all the earth is Mine; [6] and you shall be to Me a kingdom of priests and a holy nation.' These are the words that you shall speak to the sons of Israel. (NASB)

The nation of Israel was chosen to prepare the way for the Messiah to come (this was the promise to Abraham that through his seed all nations would be blessed), so of course the Church has not 'replaced' it in that calling. God also continues to call those who are part of physical Israel to live up to their calling, ie by accepting Messiah and living as His people. God also has an especial affection for Israel as the physical descendants of the patriarchs (11:28). But though Jews would be the natural branches of the olive tree of God's visible presence on Earth, yet when Messiah came to His own His own received Him not (John 1:11). So the unbelieving branches are not part of that olive tree, though naturally they can be grafted back in. There is no indication in Paul or anywhere in the New Testament that Jews who reject Jesus as Messiah can be justified through the Torah.

We have empathy with the more thoughtful of modern 'Messianic Jews'. Our lord is *Yeshua the Messiah*, and we are appalled at the antisemitism stemming from figures like Augustine and Luther and the shocking record of Christendom. If Jewish Christians want to celebrate Passover, Purim and Hanukkah as part of a national/ethnic heritage of thanks to God, this is all good. What Paul would have insisted was that: i) there should not be a separate church meeting (Galatians 2:12 etc), and ii) any Jewish symbols should not be seen as any sign of greater holiness than that possessed by Gentiles in the church.

Always faith-relationship

So we are neither 'Covenant theologians' nor 'Dispensationalists'. Post the fall, the only way to be justified before God is through a faith-relationship which involves sins forgiven based (whether that person knows it or not) on the righteous act of self-sacrifice on the cross, the faithfulness, of Jesus the Messiah. This is true whether that relationship exists inside or outside any specific covenant such as those with Abraham, David or Moses.

Text 9:1–5

[1] I am telling the truth in Christ, I am not lying, my conscience testifies with me in the Holy Spirit, [2] that I have great sorrow and unceasing grief in my heart. [3] For I could wish that I myself were accursed, *separated* from Christ for the sake of my brethren, my kinsmen according to the flesh, [4] who are Israelites, to whom belongs the adoption as sons, and the glory and the covenants and the giving of the Law and the *temple* service [Greek: *latrea*] and the promises, [5] whose are the fathers, and from whom is the Christ according to the flesh, who is over all, God blessed forever. Amen. (NASB)

Commentary

Following the great paean of praise at the end of chapter 8, we get a cry of anguish from Paul the Israelite. We have seen how the Jewish-Gentile issues are not peripheral in his context, but a central concern. He has said that the Jews have an 'advantage' in having the 'words of God' (3:1) and yet as a nation they have done no better than the Gentiles (3:9). We have seen how the Law can operate with the Spirit producing life, but alternatively with the flesh producing death. So what was God's strategy in choosing Abraham and through him Israel? In Romans 9–11 Paul analyses this.

Brian Abasciano in *Paul's Use of the Old Testament in Romans 9:1–9* chapter 3, convincingly argues that, although there is no similarity in wording, Paul's offer in Romans 9:3 to be cut off for the sake of his people reflects Moses' intercessory prayer in Exodus 32:32, where he pleads with God to spare the wayward Israelites:

[32] 'But now, if you will only forgive their sin—but if not, blot me out of the book that you have written.' [33] But the LORD said to Moses, 'Whoever has sinned against Me I will blot out of my book.' (NRSVA)

God's reply is 'sovereign' but far from some arbitrary exercise of power. God has declared that faith is to be accounted as rightstanding, and that choosing a way of sin will lead to judgement.

The word for 'wish' in 9:3 is rendered prayer in the only other two uses Paul makes of it (2 Corinthians 13:7, 9) which would make it even more like the prayer of Moses. Paul, however, realises that the prayer/wish is unattainable, and Cranfield (*A Critical and Exegetical Commentary on The Epistle to the Romans*, p.456) well argues that the language implies this.

Consistently in Exodus and throughout the prophets it is clear that the choice is theirs, there is no kind of hidden puppetmaster strings determining who will repent and who not. To suggest to Moses that 'really' God (the God who 'changed His mind' in response to Moses' prayer in Exodus 32:14) does not want the Israelites to repent and turn to Him would surely have produced a reaction of total incredulity. It would likewise never have occurred to Paul to imagine that the reason most of Israel had not accepted their Messiah was that God wanted it that way, and cared less about them than Paul himself who was willing to be cut off for them. Whenever God 'hardens' or 'turns away' it is in response to peoples' own unrepentance, not the initial cause of the unrepentance.

Three aspects make Israel the nation (called 'Israelites' by the special name God gave to Jacob) especially precious, though for the first one the functions intended are now seen in the Church:

1. They have been given and should be the natural heirs of:

    a. **the 'son-placing'** (*huiothesia*)
        Israel was 'God's Son' called out of Egpyt (Hosea 11:1), though later this Sonship was fulfilled by the Messiah, and the 'son-placing' is given in 8:23 as the destiny of those who are in Christ.

    b. **the glory** (*doxa*)
        Present in the desert (Exodus 16:7–10) the tabernacle (Exodus 40:34–35; Leviticus 9:6 etc) the giving of the Torah (Exodus 24:16–17) and in the Temple (1 Kings 8:11). This glory is given in 8:17 to those who are joint-heirs in Christ and suffer with Him.

    c. **the Abrahamic and Mosaic covenants**
        Though in a sense all those of faith, especially Christians, are heirs of Abraham (Romans 4:11).

    d. **the Torah**
        Although others may fulfil by faith the real meaning of Torah (Romans 2:14).

    e. **the priestly temple service** (*latrea*)
        Though in Romans 12:1 he will say Christians fulfil this by presenting their bodies as living sacrifices instead of sacrificial animals.

    f. **the promises**
        The best textual tradition has this (like the 'covenants') as plural. In Romans 4 Paul spoke of the promise to Abraham in Genesis

15:5, and in Romans 15:8 says that Messiah has become a servant to confirm the promises made to the patriarchs. These are to Abraham (Genesis 12:2–3 etc) to Isaac (Genesis 26:3–5) to Jacob (Genesis 28:13–15) to Moses (Deuteronomy 18:1–19) and David (2 Samuel 7:8–16). The 'children of promise' (Romans 9:8) are those who are in the chosen line of descent to the Messiah who would fulfil those promises.

2.   **The patriarchs**
      Abraham, Isaac, Jacob etc, who were the ancestors of the Israelites.

3.   **The ancestry of the Messiah**
      who came in physical descent from the nation of Israel.

The words at the end of verse 5 could have either of two readings:

   i) 'came the Messiah who is God over all blessed forever amen'

   ii) 'came the Messiah. God who is overall be blessed forever amen'.

The first reading would assert the Trinity, the second has the last part as a separate doxology. Virtually all Early Church figures went for reading i), including Irenaeus, Origen, Chrysostom, Theodore of Mopsuestia, Theodoret, Ambrosiaster, Augustine and Pelagius! More recent commentators are split. Favouring i) are for example, Sanday & Headlam, Bruce, Brunner, Metzger, Nygren, Cranfield, Abasciano and Longenecker, while favouring ii) for example, are Beet, Barth, Käsemann, Dodd, Dunn and Hultgren. We are Trinitarians, but don't depend heavily on a Trinitarian implication here, so it does not seem that a great deal hangs on which you decide is the right interpretation. On balance we believe that i) is more likely correct, and for example Longenecker and Cranfield both argue that the linguistic considerations favour this.

Text 9:6–9

[6] But it is not as though the word of God has failed. For they are not all Israel who are *descended* from Israel; [7] nor are they all children because they are Abraham's descendants [Lit. seed], but: 'through Isaac your descendants [Lit. seed] will be named.' [8] That is, it is not the children of the flesh who are children of God, but the children of the promise are regarded as descendants [Lit. seed]. [9] For this is the word of promise: 'At this time I will come, and Sarah shall have a son.' (NASB)

Discussion Topic: Israel

Usually by 'Israel' Paul means the nation of Israel, and by 'Jews' those of that nation in his own day. However, the word 'Jew' comes from 'Judah', which means 'praise', and he also says:

> [26] So if the uncircumcised man keeps the requirements of the Law, will not his uncircumcision be regarded as circumcision? [27] And he who is physically uncircumcised, if he keeps the Law, will he not judge you who though having the letter of the Law and circumcision are a transgressor of the Law? [28] For he is not a Jew who is one outwardly, nor is circumcision that which is outward in the flesh. [29] But he is a Jew who is one inwardly; and circumcision is that which is of the heart, by the Spirit, not by the letter; and his praise is not from men, but from God. (NASB, (2:26–29))

Likewise with the word 'Israel' he says in Galatians 6:15–16 as noted:

> [15] For neither is circumcision anything, nor uncircumcision, but a new creation. [16] And those who will walk by this rule, peace and mercy be upon them, and [Greek: *kai*] upon the Israel of God. (NASB)

In this verse in Galatians the 'Israel of God' refers to Christians, as we have shown above, not to the physical nation of Israel.

The name 'Israel' is a combination of the words 'wrestle' and 'God'. It comes from Genesis 32 where Jacob wrestled all night with someone and refused to let go until that one blessed him. The wrestler, whom Jacob identified as God, said: *'Your name shall no longer be called Jacob, but Israel; for you have struggled with God and with men, and have prevailed'* (32:28). Later, in Genesis 35, God repeated this name change, and repeated the covenant: *'The land which I gave Abraham and Isaac I give to you; and to your descendants after you I give this land'* (35:12). During the Exodus the people are called 'the children of Israel' but also simply 'Israel' (eg Exodus 19:1–2). Later sometimes 'Israel' is distinct from 'Judah' when the ten and two tribes split, but it consistently means the physical descendants. In the eighth century BC the ten tribes were taken into Exile by the Assyrians, and 'Israel' came to mean the remaining groups mostly from Judah and Benjamin, and eventually 'Jew' also came to apply to all of these. From the sixth century BC, the terms 'Jews' and 'Israel' are used fairly interchangeably (for example in Ezra and Nehemiah).

The synoptic gospels all state Jesus' acceptance of the title 'King of the Jews' (which some bystanders rephrased 'King of Israel') though each gospel uses the term (meaning the nation) in just one other place (Matthew 28:15; Mark 7:3, Luke 7:3). John was probably written much later, and 'the Jews' usually implies the part of the nation who rejected Jesus (remembering that Jesus and all the disciples were Jews). The word 'Israel' is common throughout all the gospels and in Acts, and it means the nation. Luke tells us that He will turn many of the children of Israel to their God (1:32), He is Israel's consolation (2:25), glory (2:32), redeemer (24:21) though will cause many to rise or fall in Israel (2:34).

Usually, then, 'Israel' means the physical nation of Israel and 'Jews' means those of that nation, but can also refer to the 'real Jew' and the 'Israel of God' in a spiritual sense. Paul does this in Galatians 6:15–16 and also in Romans 11:26. In the latter verse it was so taken by early figures like Irenaeus, Clement of Alexandria, and Theodore, while Origen takes it differently in different contexts (see Fitzmyer *Romans*, p.624). It seems to mean either all believers or possibly all the faithful of physical Israel.

Commentary

So have God's words or promises to Abraham and to Jacob (Israel) failed? This is what this whole section addresses. Some commentators seem to think Paul is asking '*Why* have most of the Jews disbelieved?' – and that he answers 'it is

God's Sovereign will for them to disbelieve'. But this is neither his question nor the answer, and 'might is right' would certainly be no answer at all to a question about God's faithful righteousness.

Abasciano (*Paul's Use of the Old Testament in Romans 9:1–9*) puts it:

> Practically, if it is the unbelief of Israel that Paul addresses, then Romans 9–11 can tend to be read as seeking to explain Israel's unbelief and God's responsibility for it. On the other hand, if it is rather God's rejection of Israel that is the issue, then, with most interpreters, Paul is defending God's response to Israel's unbelief. (p.330)

Has God's promise of a glorious future for His people failed? Paul says not.

He begins with the cryptic 'they are not all Israel who are of Israel'. This can only mean that the physical descendants of Jacob are not all 'Israel' in the true sense. Maybe this reflects the statements of John the Baptist and Jesus:

> [37] 'I know that you are descendants of Abraham; yet you look for an opportunity to kill Me, because there is no place in you for My word. [38] I declare what I have seen in the Father's presence; as for you, you should do what you have heard from the Father.'
>
> [39] They answered Him, 'Abraham is our father.' Jesus said to them, 'If you were Abraham's children, you would be doing what Abraham did, [40] but now you are trying to kill Me, a man who has told you the truth that I heard from God. This is not what Abraham did. [41] You are indeed doing what your father does.' They said to Him, 'We are not illegitimate children; we have one father, God Himself.' [42] Jesus said to them, 'If God were your Father, you would love Me, for I came from God and now I am here. I did not come on My own, but he sent Me. [43] Why do you not understand what I say? It is because you cannot accept My word. [44] You are from your father the devil, and you choose to do your father's desires. He was a murderer from the beginning and does not stand in the truth, because there is no truth in him. When he lies, he speaks according to his own nature, for he is a liar and the father of lies. (John 8:37–44, NRSVA)

Paul has already argued that it is those of faith who are Abraham's true seed (Romans 4:16–17) and heirs of the covenant – it is faith that is reckoned as rightstanding, not works of the Law. Of course this was *open* to any physical descendant of Abraham, but Paul also already quoted many Old Testament indications that often the bulk of Israel and well as other nations were unrighteous (Romans 3:9–18). His core answer to the question about the faithfulness of God is that all God's promises are conditional, and throughout history there were only a remnant who sought rightstanding through faith and received the grace of God.

Romans 9:7 could be confusing. The 'true Israel' distinct from the physical Israel would be a ready concept, as the words of John and Jesus show. But in this verse 7 Paul seems to be alluding to an allegory he had already used at length in Galatians several years earlier. To have several different levels of interpretation, including one of allegory, was common in Jewish thinking. Aquila and Priscilla, now in Rome, would very likely be familiar with this particular allegory of Paul, which it seems likely he would have repeated in his ongoing debates with Jews as it is so explicit in Galatians. As we have noted, he wrote to the church there, Jew and Gentile:

> [22] For it is written that Abraham had two sons, one by a slave woman and the other by a free woman. [23] One, the child of the slave, was born according to the flesh; the other, the child of the free woman, was born through the promise. [24] Now this is an allegory: these women are two covenants. One woman, in fact, is Hagar, from Mount Sinai, bearing children for slavery. [25] Now Hagar is Mount Sinai in Arabia and corresponds to the present Jerusalem, for she is in slavery with her children. [26] But the other woman corresponds to the Jerusalem above; she is free, and she is our mother. (Galatians 4:22–27, NRSVA)

Ishmael and Isaac were both sons of Abraham. This passage in Romans is not about their individual eternal destinies. Hagar was actually given a promise not a lot different from Abraham's (compare Genesis 12:2, 17:20, 21:18). It also says that 'God was with the lad', ie with Ishmael (Genesis 21:20). The choice was about which of Abraham's physical sons would be the designated one from whom all nations would be blessed in the Messiah, the covenant people. But, in the allegory in Paul's mind, Ishmael represents Abraham's fleshly effort to fulfil the prophecy and Isaac a miracle child of the promise. So even in the election of Isaac it points to the miraculous grace of God and not human self-effort.

Surely Paul cannot mean that the Sinai covenant was *intended by God* to bring bondage? If so it would be very odd to say as a plus point of the Jews 'theirs are the covenants' (9:4). Nor is he saying that the Sinai covenant itself was a result of human self-effort, as though they formed a committee and came up with ten commandments.

Jesus asked '. . . what man is there among you who if his son asks for bread, will give him a stone? Or if he asks for a fish, will he give him a serpent?' The context is of God's gift of the Holy Spirit, but surely the principle would apply more generally? God said: *When Israel was a child, I loved him, and out of Egypt I called my son'* (Hosea 11:1). If the Mosaic covenant and gift of Torah put *all* Old Testament Israelites (including presumably Zechariah, Elizabeth, Simeon and Anna, not to mention David and the list in Hebrews 11) into bondage, then it was a poor gift from a father. The Torah did 'give birth to bondage' wherever it was pursued by the flesh, but this was not its only effect. Interesting, too, that here in Galatians we find that Paul not only has two 'Israels', and two 'Jews', but two 'Jerusalems'. The true spiritual Jerusalem, the bride of Messiah, is free.

Commentators differ as to whether the 'spiritual Israel' is just made up of believing Jews or also includes Gentile Christians. In the context of Galatians 6:16 it seems most likely to have the inclusive meaning, and, though at this point in Romans Paul may leave it open, his later comments would surely mean that those in the Messiah are all part of a spiritual Israel, spiritually circumcised.

'Reformed' commentators like Piper and Moo see Romans 9:6b as important to their belief that God has elected particular individuals to become faithful and get salvation. Most commentators now rightly think that 'Paul implies nothing about the salvation of individuals in Romans 9' (Abasciano *Paul's Use of the Old Testament in Romans 9:1–9*, p.185). Abasciano goes on to show how the election concept is corporate (see also the Discussion Topic on Election, pages 233–238).

Text 9:10–13

[10] And not only so, but when Rebecca also had conceived by one man, even by our father Isaac [11] (for not yet being born, nor having done any good or evil, that the election purpose of God though election might stand, not of works but of Him who calls), [12] it was said to her, 'The older shall serve the younger.' [13] Even it has been written, 'Jacob I have loved, but Esau I have hated.' (Our own translation)

Commentary

In Romans 9:11b, the phrase has sometimes been taken to imply that the purpose was about election. Abasciano (*Paul's Use of the Old Testament in Romans 9:10–19*) shows that both grammatical and contextual indications are that it means 'election as the means to fulfilling God's purpose'. He adds:

> . . . what is the purpose of election that Paul speaks about? It is none other than God's purpose to bless the world in Abraham. (p.49)

God's election of the nation to be the named seed (through whom Messiah would come to bless the world) did not result from works. It was God's strategy.

This passage is not about the individual destinies of Jacob and Esau. We have used our own translation here because most versions insert 'the children' or 'the twins' when actually the Greek does not contain this phrase. Paul knew perfectly well that this was not about individual eternal destinies. He quotes from Genesis 25:23

> [23] And the LORD said to her, 'Two nations are in your womb, and two peoples born of you shall be divided; one shall be stronger than the other, the elder shall serve the younger.' (NRSVA)

This is about nations not individuals. In fact the individual Esau certainly did not ever serve Jacob, but Jacob came and grovelled before Esau and said Esau's face was like the face of God to him (Genesis 33:10). The election is of the nation of Israel as the path to prepare for and bear God's Messiah. The actual quotation 'Jacob have I loved but Esau have I hated' is from Malachi 1:2–3 and came a millennium after the individuals had lived and died – again it is about nations not individuals. The love and hate pairing here are a Jewish hyperbole – the 'hate' means 'love less than'. Genesis 29:30–31 says that 'Jacob loved Rachel more than Leah', and then 'God saw that Leah was hated'. Jesus tells us to 'hate' all our relatives (Luke 14:26) but as Matthew 10:37 makes clear He means that we should love Him *more than* our relatives. Isaac blessed both Jacob and Esau in faith (Hebrews 11:20), but recognised primogeniture would not apply and the Israelites would have the greater role in God's salvation plans for humanity. Hebrews 12:16 also recognises that Esau was an immoral and godless person who sold his birthright and then could not get it back, but this was about his heritage as he himself was prosperous enough. It is all about God's strategy to ultimately fulfil the promise that through the chosen seed of Abraham all nations will be blessed by the coming of Messiah. The election is about nations, not individuals, and the love and hate are relative, not absolute.

The election is 'sovereign' and not a reward for any works. But this does not mean it is *arbitrary* (as some seem to take 'sovereign' to mean). The idea of primogeniture is laid down in the Torah (eg Deuteronomy 21:17), but God prophesies to Rebecca that it will not apply here. Abasciano also explores how many commentators (Jewish and Christian) have seen in the characters of Jacob and Esau some good reasons why God may have made this choice – and indeed Esau's own contemptuous view of the firstborn blessing was an immediate cause of its loss. Jacob was certainly not ethically perfect, and indeed perhaps not likeable, but he did value spiritual things. To suggest that God's choice was arbitrary or capricious, just to show off His power, would be demeaning to the God of Israel.

Abasciano argues that Piper's assumption that divine election is the 'an effectual summons that produces faith' is mistaken (Abasciano *Paul's Use of the Old Testament in Romans 9:10–19*, p.54). He notes that in Romans 4:16–17 Paul had already insisted that God 'grounds grace in faith' as far as concerns being the real seed of Abraham. Abasciano also shows that in both Genesis 15 and Malachi 1 the interest is in corporate not individual election.

Text 9:14–18

[14] What shall we say then? There is no injustice with God, is there? May it never be! [15] For He says to Moses, 'I will have mercy on whom I have mercy, and I will have compassion on whom I have compassion.' [16] So then it does not depend on the man who wills or the man who runs, but on God who has mercy. [17] For the Scripture says to Pharaoh, 'For this very purpose I raised you up, to demonstrate My power in you, and that My name might be proclaimed throughout the whole earth.' [18] So then He has mercy on whom He desires, and He hardens whom He desires. (NASB)

Commentary

The faithfulness and righteousness of God were already asserted in Romans 3:3–5 and here Paul revisits it.

The form of speech in 9:15 is taken by Reformed commentators like Piper to mean that God is totally unconstrained in His decisions, effectively making them arbitrary. Abasciano (2011) shows that actually:

> . . . when the idiom signals freedom of action elsewhere, it never appears to speak of unconditional action. Rather, in every such instance the context or circumstances suggest that the subject would take factors external to himself in deciding how to perform the action. (p.177)

All the following passages are analysed in some depth in our book *God's Strategy in Human History* (volumes 1 & 2), but here we will mention two key points about Moses and Pharaoh.

The context of God's words to Moses are that Moses had been pleading with God to 'go down' amongst the Israelites and finally God agreed. Moses also asked to see the glory of God, and it was then that God said:

> I Myself will make all My goodness pass before you, and will proclaim the name of the Lord before you; and I will be gracious to whom I will be gracious, and will show compassion on whom I will show compassion. (Exodus 33:19, NASB)

Had God gone down openly amongst the Israelites most of them would have been consumed (Exodus 33:5) – they had trouble even bearing to look on the radiance of Moses' face when he came down (Exodus 34:30). God knows how best to distribute His favour, and He does it according to a strategy.

The hardening of Pharaoh's heart is looked at in detail in *Reconsidering Key Biblical Ideas* chapter 6. Abasciano in *Paul's Use of the Old Testament in Romans 9:10–19*, gives an even more detailed scholarly analysis of the whole issue, rightly concluding:

> The specific use of the vocabulary of hardening in Exodus portrays Pharaoh with a will already fixed upon keeping Israel under Egyptian bondage and oppression before any hardening activity on the part of YHWH. God's hardening activity emboldened Pharaoh's will to persist in an already chosen course, despite the immense pressure applied by the signs and wonders of God, resulting in a stubbornness indicated by all three words used for hardening. (p.108)

Basically, Pharaoh had already decided on a moral path of evil long before God did anything to him, and the primary action of God was to strengthen him in his resolve when most people would have given way not in repentance but in fear. To oppose a God whose strength Moses has so well demonstrated even to Pharaoh's magicians (Exodus 8:19) was foolhardy in the extreme. Pharaoh has been 'raised up' as ruler so that God's power will be shown and this will help His people as they enter the Promised Land. In the Torah it is always the enemies of Israel who are 'hardened', for example in Joshua 11:20, to aid the progress of the Israelites as God prepares for His Messiah. But it is not that Moses was a bad man and God made him good and Pharaoh was a good man and God made him bad! We agree with the words in the *Dictionary of New Testament Theology*:

> Hardening, according to the Old Testament understanding, results from the fact that men persist in shutting themselves to God's call and command. A state then arises in which a man is no longer able to hear and in which he is irretrievably enslaved. Alternatively, God makes the hardening final, so that people cannot escape from it. (vol 2 p.154)

In Pharaoh's case the most common word used in Exodus is to 'make stubborn'.

The exact meaning of 'raised you up' (v17) has been hotly debated. Abasciano gives good reasons to take it simply to mean 'spare/allow to remain alive' (p.164). Actually, then, Paul does not here even mention the fact that Pharaoh was 'hardened' or 'made stubborn'. The issue is why God has let him live in his defiance of God. It is so that God can use him to show His creation and redemption power to all the earth. It is part of God's strategy.

Text 9:19–24

[19] You will say to me then, 'Why does He still find fault? For who resists His will?' [20] On the contrary, who are you, O man, who answers back to God? The thing moulded will not say to the moulder, 'Why did you make me like this,' will it? [21] Or does not the potter have a right over the clay, to make from the same lump one vessel for honourable use and another for common use? [22] What if God, although willing to demonstrate His wrath and to make His power known, endured with much patience vessels of wrath prepared for destruction? [23] And He did so to make known the riches of His glory upon vessels of mercy, which He prepared beforehand for glory, [24] even us, whom He also called, not from among Jews only, but also from among Gentiles. (NASB)

Discussion Topic: The Potter

To us the picture of God as a potter might indicate that we (the clay) had no freewill. But the Old Testament potter picture is far from this. The immediate reference may be to Isaiah 29:16:

> Shall the potter be considered as equal with the clay, That what is made would say to its maker, 'He did not make me'; Or what is formed say to him who formed it, 'He has no understanding'? (NASB)

The context is speaking of those who try to hide their plans from God. Later the people themselves say:

> Why, O Lord, do You cause us to stray from your ways? (Isaiah 63:17, NASB)

> But now, O Lord, You are our Father, We are the clay, and You our potter; And all of us are the work of Your hand. (Isaiah 64:8, NASB)

But this attempt to blame God is rejected by God who replies in Isaiah 65:

> [2] I have spread out My hands all day long to a rebellious people,
> Who walk in the way which is not good, following their own thoughts,

> [3] A people who continually provoke Me to My face,
> Offering sacrifices in gardens and burning incense on bricks . . .

> [12] I will destine you for the sword,
> And all of you will bow down to the slaughter.
> Because I called, but you did not answer; I spoke, but you did not hear.
> And you did evil in My sight
> And chose that in which I did not delight. (NASB)

Their inference is rejected, it is their own refusal to respond to His continual pleas and invitations that is to blame for their woes, not some sovereign act of God in hardening and making them stray. The potter parable which is surely in Paul's mind is even more clearly shown in Jeremiah 18:

> [1] The word that came to Jeremiah from the Lord: [2] 'Come, go down to the potter's house, and there I will let you hear My words.' [3] So I went down to the potter's house, and there he was working at his wheel. [4] The vessel he was making of clay was spoiled in the potter's hand, and he reworked it into another vessel, as seemed good to him.
>
> [5] Then the word of the Lord came to me: [6] 'Can I not do with you, O house of Israel, just as this potter has done?' says the Lord. 'Just like the clay in the potter's hand, so are you in My hand, O house of Israel. [7] At one moment I may declare concerning a nation or a kingdom, that I will pluck up and break down and destroy it, [8] but if that nation, concerning which I have spoken, turns from its evil, I will change My mind about the disaster that I intended to bring on it. [9] And at another moment I may declare concerning a nation or a kingdom that I will build and plant it, [10] but if it does evil in My sight, not listening to My voice, then I will change My mind about the good that I had intended to do to it. [11] Now, therefore, say to the people of Judah and the inhabitants of Jerusalem: "Thus says the Lord: Look, I am a potter shaping evil against you and devising a plan against you. Turn now, all of you from your evil way, and amend your ways and your doings."' (NRSVA)

The word 'relent' used in some versions here means to change one's mind as the NRSVA correctly renders it, and God does it repeatedly (for example Genesis 6:6, Exodus 32:14, Judges 2:18, 1 Chronicles 21:15, Psalm 106:45, Jonah 3:10). Now, Numbers 23:19 and 1 Samuel 15:29 say that God 'is not a man that He should change His mind' but the context there is of a capricious or fickle mind change. In 1 Samuel 15:11 and 35, ie in the same chapter, (using the same Hebrew word for 'to change one's mind') it says that God was sorry and *regretted* He had made Saul the king. God changes His mind, to judge or to bless, according to human reactions, but He is emphatically not fickle. The interactivity of the potter allegory is plain. To 'change His mind' cannot mean 'to do what He always intended to do to them anyway because He decides who will turn from evil and who will not'. This is as though God originally lied about His intentions because He really knew all along what He would do, and He is the one determining it all. But the allegory makes it clear that God varies His action according to how the clay reacts. So, for example Jonah told Nineveh that it would be destroyed – no escape clauses. But the Ninevites (Jonah 3:9) and Jonah (4:2) both knew that God could change His mind if they repented.

God uses the clay to work out His purposes, but whether the 'clay' is blessed or judged depends on their reactions – and God can change His mind about what to do with it. Ultimately God is not some kind of puppet master, He is fundamentally relational.

In another analogy, God is like a master chess player – except that the 'game' is with millions simultaneously. A master chess player knows just what move they will make whatever their opponent does – though he does not know what that opponent *will* do. God varies His actions according to human moral choices – but is never taken by surprise. Actually such a God is infinitely greater than a mere puppet master would be following out a blueprint preordained in every detail.

Commentary

The Greek does *not* say 'Who *is able* to resist His will?' (NIV), but 'Who resisted His will?' In other words, if God got what He really wanted why is He cross? The use of the perfect tense probably means that the question is specific to the unbelieving questioners – ie effectively 'If God wanted us to be unbelieving then we haven't resisted His will, so why is He angry with us?' Throughout Romans Paul imagines a critic questioning him (see also Romans 3:1, 3:8, 6:1,) but sometimes (as in 3:8) the questioner is clearly misunderstanding Paul's position in a ludicrous way and Paul contemptuously dismisses him. So a key issue here is whether the 'critic' has actually correctly interpreted what Paul is saying. Is Paul really saying that God deliberately decided that the bulk of Israel would stay unrepentant? Or is this another woeful misrepresentation of Paul's thought, as inaccurate as the idea that we should do evil that good may come (3:8)?

Actually, in spite of what some theologians have claimed, Scripture makes it very clear that neither God's plan (Greek: *boulomai, boulē, boulēma*) nor His will (Greek: *thelō, thelēma, ethelēsa*) are always done. He does not always get what He wants. We look at this in depth in our book *Reconsidering Key Biblical Ideas*, but very briefly comment here. Paul's friend Luke says that *'the Pharisees and lawyers rejected the **plan** (boulēn) of God for themselves'* (Luke 7:30). Jesus also said that God's *will* (*ethelēsa*) (was to gather Israel, but it did not happen because their will (*ethelēsate*) was against this (Matthew 23:37; Luke 13:34), and that *'whoever does the **will** (thelēma) of My Father in heaven is My brother and sister and mother'* (Matthew 12:50; Mark 3:35). But it is not just a matter of a couple of 'proof texts'. The whole of the Old Testament is full of instances where God's will and plan for His people is rejected by them, and any reading without particular theological blinkers would get this picture – even though the Hebrew prophets also had a vision of God as powerful and ultimately acting in justice. Reformed theologians have to do all kinds of exegetical oddities to avoid this obvious conclusion, making up different kinds of 'wills' not mentioned in Scripture and sometimes may finish with nonsensical assertions like 'God effectively wills their resistance to His will'. But it is plain that when God says He wants something (for example, that Israel will turn to Him), He is not lying but really does, and is sorry when what He wants doesn't happen.

Theologians like John Piper claim that Paul does not actually say that the questioner at this point has misunderstood him, but this is misleading. The idea that no one has resisted God's will is not what Paul means, and his response in 9:20 'on the contrary' (*menounge*) is a denial. Jesus used it in Luke 11:28 where it is translated 'No rather . . .', and in Romans 10:18 it again implies denial. The only other New Testament place the term is used is Philippians 3:8 where is it used with *alla* and *kai* in a slightly different construction. Paul is not agreeing with the premise, but saying that it is an avoidance of the real issue.

The NASB renders it here as 'on the contrary . . .' to capture this. The critics are using this slur to avoid facing the real question.

Paul saying, 'Who are you, O man, who answers back to God?' was never a put down to someone asking a real question about love and justice. When Job or Habakkuk ask such a real question God answers them, He does not just say 'Shut up you!' This would be no answer at all to the charge. On a human level, if someone questioned the injustice of some act of an autocrat who forced people to do something and then punished them for it, to simply say 'Shut up you!' would be no answer at all. It would be akin to an autocratic state imprisoning and silencing lawyers who exposed injustices. Paul discerns that the real base of the misrepresentation of what he is saying is a Jewish objection to the way in which God is treating Israel, as God differentiates between the faithful remnant and the bulk of unrighteous.

Paul refers to the Potter allegory. To us the allegory of the potter might sound as though God is determining everything and the clay is purely passive, but to those familiar with Jeremiah 18 this is far from the case. The whole allegory speaks of God adapting and *changing* His response according to the freewill responses of the 'clay'. However, Paul introduces something new. In Jeremiah the lump represented a whole 'nation or kingdom'. But now God is using *one* lump to make *two* pots. The nation of Israel will no longer be treated as a single unit. From the single lump of Israel God is making one pot which will bring Him honour, and one which is to be judged and brings Him no honour. And how can the lump question the potter's right to make two pots instead of one?

Those Jews who were theoretically 'His own' but (in John's words) 'received Him not', were to become vessels of wrath. But to those who received Him (Jews and Gentiles) and became children of God, He would show the riches of His glory as vessels of mercy. Interestingly, Paul says that God 'endured with much patience' these 'vessels of wrath'. These are not words Paul would use if actually God wanted them to be such vessels. But He endured them in order to be able to show His mercy on those who were receptive.

The new dimension is that Christian Jews (or Messianic Jews if this is a preferred title) may be still part of the Jewish nation, but are part of another transnational 'vessel', the Church, the body of Messiah, in which *'There is neither Jew nor Greek, there is neither slave nor free, there is neither male nor female; for you are all one in Christ Jesus'* (Galatians 3:28). This is the vessel unto honour. And it was this divine incorporation of those who were formerly 'not My people' (ie

Gentiles) that really infuriated Paul's opponents (see also Acts 22:21–22).

The word *kaleō* can mean called (in the sense of invited) or named. In *Paul's Use of the Old Testament in Romans 9:10–19,* Abasciano well argues that most usually in the New Testament it means 'naming' rather than calling in the sense of a summons (p.201ff). In verse 24 it seems to mean 'even those whom He has *named*' as the following verses show, because it is about being named as His people. So the vessels of mercy, Jews and Gentiles, now make up the pot which shows God's honour.

Text 9:25–29

> [25] As indeed He says in Hosea, 'Those who were not My people I will call "My people", and her who was not beloved I will call "beloved".'
> [26] 'And in the very place where it was said to them, "You are not My people", there they shall be called children of the living God.'
> [27] And Isaiah cries out concerning Israel, 'Though the number of the children of Israel were like the sand of the sea, only a remnant of them will be saved; [28] for the Lord will execute His sentence on the earth quickly and decisively.' [29] And as Isaiah predicted, 'If the Lord of hosts had not left survivors [Greek: seed] to us, we would have fared like Sodom and been made like Gomorrah.' (NRSVA)

Discussion Topic: Remnant Theology

In the Old Testament, four different words are used for 'remnant':

1) *š'r* (about 220 times) – used for example in 1 Kings 19:18 of the 'remnant' who have not worshipped Baal. The term is common in the Old Testament. In Isaiah we find a remnant related to judgment (Isaiah 10:19–22), and a remnant is left by the LORD (37:32) in His mercy (46:3). The LORD will purify so that the remnant are holy (Isaiah 4:2–3) and He will redeem them (11:11) and will be a glorious crown for them (28:5) and from them form the nucleus of a new faith community (37:31–32).

2) *ytr* (about 220 times) for example Ezekiel 6:8 where God promises to leave a remnant – its meaning seems similar to 1), with an idea of something left over.

3) *šə·'ê·rît* (about 70 times) for example Isaiah 37:32 a remnant shall go out of Zion. It means a remainder or residue. In Zephaniah 3:13 and Haggai 1:12 the remnant of Israel turn to the Lord.

4) *pᵉlêtâ* (about 30 times) for example Ezekiel 14:22 with overtones of escape and deliverance.

The terms themselves are very general, and word studies on them will not be all that helpful. Longenecker in his commentary points out that the eighth century prophet Amos develops the idea:

1. To refute the claim that all the people of Israel constitute 'the remnant' . . .

2. To show that there will be a surviving remnant that exists within Israel by the fact that destruction will come to those other people of Israel who do not return to God – which pronouncement of judgement also entails the idea of salvation for those who choose to return to God.

3. To enlarge by his inclusion of the 'remnant of Edom', along with his allusion to neighbouring nations, the remnant concept to include all those who will be recipients of God's promise to David (p.806).

Longenecker also says 'the promise of divine salvation is conditioned by Israel's response', and for example in 5:4–6 the prophet urges them to turn back to God – 'Perhaps the Lord God Almighty will have mercy on the remnant.'

Longenecker points out that Joel also prophesied judgement but that the Lord has reserved a remnant within Israel on whom God will pour out His Spirit (2:28–32), then adds, 'For the prophet

Joel, therefore, the one who truly trusts in God is to "call on the name of the Lord" in believing faith' (p.807).

Isaiah, Micah, Zephaniah and Jeremiah all developed remnant theologies.

Remnant ideas continued in Sirach 47:22 and 1 Maccabbees 3:35, and later into 2 Esdras 12:34. The Qumran community and the Pharisees both regarded themselves as holy remnants who through strict Torah observance prepared the nation for the coming Messiah. The whole idea was prominent in Jewish thinking.

In all of this Old Testament material, the prophets squarely put the blame for judgement and reduction to a faithful remnant on the people themselves. The Jeremiah potter parable, as just considered, made judgement contingent on their own reaction. At the end of Isaiah the unrighteous people try to blame God, saying:

> 64 ¹O that You would tear open the heavens and come down, so that the mountains would quake at Your presence—
>
> . . . But You were angry, and we sinned; because You hid Yourself we transgressed.
>
> ⁶ We have all become like one who is unclean, and all our righteous deeds are like a filthy cloth . . .
>
> ⁷ There is no one who calls on Your name, or attempts to take hold of You;
>
> for You have hidden Your face from us, and have delivered us into the hand of our iniquity.
>
> ⁸ Yet, O LORD, You are our Father; we are the clay, and You are our potter; we are all the work of Your hand.
> (NRSVA)

This sounds like a lot of modern theologians – the reason (they say) that the people are unrighteous is because God chooses to leave them as such! What they need (they say) is a sovereignly sent revival. Verses 6 and 8 may even be quoted by modern preachers. But God will have none of it and responds:

> 65 ¹ I was ready to be sought out by those who did not ask, to be found by those who did not seek Me.
>
> I said, 'Here I am, here I am' to a nation that did not call on My name.
>
> ² I held out My hands all day long to a rebellious people, who walk in a way that is not good, following their own devices . . .
>
> 66 ⁴ when I called, no one answered, when I spoke, they did not listen, but they did what was evil in My sight, and chose what did not please Me. (NRSVA)

The blame is all theirs – God was all the time calling them and ready to bless them if they came. It was their own choice to do what did not please Him and was no part of His plan for them.

Throughout his whole development of thought Paul has been quoting Scripture – *in context* – to show:

- There have always been two streams of people – the righteous and unrighteous – as Habakkuk saw.

- God has always judged impartially – the righteous and unrighteous amongst both Jews and Gentiles will be judged accordingly.

- Taken as a whole the Jewish nation has been criticised as much by prophets as Gentile ones.

- But there have always been those accounted righteous because of faith, and this (and forgiveness of Sin) is done through the faithfulness and sacrificial death of the Messiah.

- God's strategy in planning the path from Abraham to the Messiah is based on His own considerations, not on any kind of ritual works.

> — The fact that only a remnant of national Israel are faithful in Paul's day is nothing new, only that God chooses to treat differently the believing and unbelieving parts of the nation – as two 'lumps' for different pots.
>
> — Also new is the combination of Gentiles 'in Messiah' as the visible presence of God's people on Earth, the originally Jewish olive tree into which they have been grafted.

Commentary

Paul then makes two basic points. The first is that God can decide who He will name as His people. The Old Testament context (Hosea 2) was God renaming a repentant Israel as 'His people' again – indeed much of the early part of Hosea is about naming. Paul here applies it to the Gentiles: surely God can also now name them as 'His people' if He so wishes, even though formerly they were not?

The second point is that what is now happening is consistent with remnant theology throughout Old Testament history. As the above Discussion Topic explains, a variety of terms are used throughout the Old Testament (and especially in later prophets) to develop the theme that only a remnant of Israel will be faithful and blessed by God. The LXX has two usual terms used for remnant: *kataleimma* and *hupoleimma*. Neither term is used elsewhere in the New Testament, but in Romans 9:27 Paul uses *hupoleimma* and in 11:5 *leimma*.

The wording in the first part of the quotation in 9:27 is actually not from Isaiah but from Hosea again. The Isaiah 10 quote says:

> [20] On that day the remnant of Israel and the survivors of the house of Jacob will no more lean on the one who struck them, but will lean on the Lord, the Holy One of Israel, in truth. [21] A remnant will return, the remnant of Jacob, to the mighty God. [22] For though your people Israel were like the sand of the sea, only a remnant of them

will return. Destruction is decreed, overflowing with righteousness. [23] For the Lord God of hosts will make a full end, as decreed, in all the earth. (NRSVA)

This prophecy seems to have had an immediate Old Testament context fulfilment, for the next verse says: *'Therefore do not be afraid of the Assyrian . . .'* But chapter 11 in Isaiah is clearly Messianic, referring both to the present age and the New Heaven and Earth, and it is not unreasonable for Paul to take it to also refer to the Church Age. But his point is also that the remnant idea is not new, and God never intends utter destruction as for Sodom and Gomorrah.

Text 9:30–33

[30] What shall we say then? That Gentiles, who did not pursue righteousness, attained righteousness, even the righteousness which is by faith; [31] but Israel, pursuing a law of righteousness, did not arrive at that law. [32] Why? Because they did not pursue it by faith, but as though it were by works. They stumbled over the stumbling stone, [33] just as it is written,

'Behold, I lay in Zion a stone of stumbling and a rock of offense, And he who believes in Him will not be disappointed.' (NASB)

Commentary

To Paul the Law is holy and good, and pursuing the 'law of righteousness' is not a bad thing. The problem is with how they went about it. Verse 30 is a typically Jewish overstatement. Compared with the Jewish obsession with righteousness/rightstanding-with-God, the Gentiles had little interest! Yet, paradoxically, Gentiles obtained it while 'Israel' did not. Paul does not of course mean *all* Gentiles attained it, nor that *all* Jews didn't. The Jews who did not achieve it failed because they were not approaching the Torah out of (*ek*) faith but out of (*ek*) *works of the Law*. Now of course some of them even before Jesus' mission and death (Zechariah, Elizabeth, Anna, Simeon . . .) *did* approach it through faith and attained righteousness. But how we know that others were approaching it through works of the Law rather than faith is precisely because they rejected their Messiah. The quotation is a mixture of Isaiah 8:14 and 28:16. The Messiah is both a foundation stone and a 'stone of stumbling'. But those in Israel who were in faith-relationship with God were drawn to accept the Messiah – as Jesus Himself said (John 6:44).

Questions for Thought and Discussion

- Does this stuff about God's moving through the patriarchs and the birth of Israel seem distant to us today?

- How can we get more excited about God's plan and movement in history?

Text 10:1–4

¹ Brethren, my heart's desire and my prayer to God for them is for their salvation. ² For I testify about them that they have a zeal for God, but not in accordance with knowledge. ³ For not knowing about God's righteousness and seeking to establish their own, they did not subject themselves to the righteousness of God. ⁴ For Christ is the end of the law for righteousness to everyone who believes. (NASB)

Commentary

Again, of course, 'Israel' later in 10:31 means the great part of Jews who have not accepted their Messiah. Paul knows nothing of some kind of 'Dispensation of Law' under which they can be saved just through keeping it assiduously. Verse 3 seems more likely to refer to God's righteousness than 'the righteousness that comes from God' as the NRSVA has it, though the meaning is in the end similar. As Paul has said (3:26) God is righteous and justifies people out of His Messiah's faithfulness in dying a sacrificial death. Their own righteousness is in seeking to be justified purely by works of the Law. Messiah is the end (*telos*) of the Law. The word *telos* can either mean 'termination' or 'the goal or end being led towards'. If Paul really meant termination then it would be a puzzle why he himself still kept the Law and had Timothy circumcised. We believe that here *telos* means the goal or end led towards. For everyone who has faith, Messiah is ultimately what the Torah leads to. This was reflected (as we saw) in reference to the *paidagogus* Paul mentioned in Galatians (pages 43–44), in the instance of those Jews who have now become Christians. But maybe throughout Israel's history it was meant to lead them into a faith which would ultimately lead to the expectation of a Messiah. The verse does not mean that formerly the Law was a way to righteousness but is now no longer, because righteousness has always been through faith. As Romans 9:32 says, the problem was not that they sought a Law of righteousness but that they did not seek it *through faith*, which has always been God's way.

Text 10:5–13

⁵ Moses writes concerning the righteousness that comes from the law, that 'the person who does these things will live by them.' ⁶ But the righteousness that comes from faith says, 'Do not say in your heart, "Who will ascend into heaven?"' (that is, to bring Christ down) ⁷ 'or "Who will descend into the abyss?"' (that is, to bring Christ up from the dead). ⁸ But what does it say? 'The word is near you, on your lips and in your heart' (that is, the word of faith that we proclaim); ⁹ because if you confess with your lips that Jesus is Lord and believe in your heart that God raised Him from the dead, you will be saved. ¹⁰ For one believes with the heart and so is justified, and one confesses with the mouth and so is saved. ¹¹ The scripture says, 'No one who believes in Him will be put to shame.' ¹² For there is no distinction between Jew and Greek; the same Lord is Lord of all and is generous to all who call on Him. ¹³ For, 'Everyone who calls on the name of the Lord shall be saved.' (NRSVA)

Discussion Topic: What's in a Name?

A Jewish website states:

> In Judaism, a name is not merely a conglomeration of letters put together as a convenient way to refer to someone. Ideally, it is a definition of the individual – a description of his personality and an interpretation of his traits. It may even be a portent of the person's future, or perhaps a prayer that the person bearing this

particular name shall live up to the potential expressed in the name.

Joseph was told that Mary would have a son and *'you shall call His name JESUS, for He will save His people from their sins'* (Matthew 1:21). His name 'Jesus' or 'Yeshua' ישוע came from the word 'to save'. John tells us: *'Yet to all who did receive Him, to those who believed in His name, He gave the right to become children of God'* (John 1:12). God (as John will go on to say) has sent Jesus to die for us so that *'whoever believes in Him shall not perish but have eternal life'* (John 3:16). But to 'believe' is more than to 'believe about' Him. The Greek word implies having faith in Him. To have faith in His name means to accept Him as Saviour. God sent Him to die for the sin of everyone – but to get the benefit of this someone has to accept or receive it.

The name of 'Jesus' is not a magic word. In Acts 19:13–16 some non-Christians tried to use the name of Jesus in exorcism and it ended badly. The name has power only if used in a relationship with the person of Jesus.

The idea of 'calling on the name of the Lord' is found in:

Prehistory: Genesis 4:26

Patriarchs: Genesis 12:8, 13:4, 26:25

Israel: 1 Kings 18:24, 2 Kings 5:11, Psalm 116:4,13,17, Zephaniah 3:9

Prophecy of Messianic age: Joel 2:32

New Testament: Acts 2:21, Acts 22:16, Romans 10:13, 1 Corinthians 1:2

In the Old Testament the name is YHWH (הָוָה) but the LXX translates it *kurios,* or LORD. Peter quotes the Messianic prophecy of Joel 2:32 in Acts 2:21 *(whoever calls on the name of the Lord will be saved)* using the Greek *kurios,* and then later says that God has made Jesus both Messiah and Lord. He urges them to be baptised in the name of Jesus. Jesus himself told us to baptise in the name (singular) of the Father, the Son and the Holy Spirit (Matthew 28:19). Paul says Christians 'call on the name of our Lord Jesus Messiah' (1 Corinthians 1:2). There is absolutely no New Testament or early church evidence for claims of so-called 'Jehovah's Witnesses' that Christians should call on the name of הוהי. In Romans 10:9 we are to confess the LORD Jesus, in 10:12 it is the same LORD who is rich over all, and in 10:13 we are to call on the name of the LORD. The anti-Trinitarian Jehovah Witness New World translation renders the first two as 'Lord' and the third as 'Jehovah'.

To whom should we pray? God is a relational triune God. We can pray to the Father (Matthew 6:9) and to Jesus (John 14:14), and as the Spirit intercedes for and with us and witnesses to our spirits there seems no reason not to address the Spirit sometimes (it could be argued that there are two Old Testament types where the Spirit seems to be addressed: Numbers 21:17–18, Ezekiel 37:9).

Does it matter if we call the Father 'God' or YHWH (הוהי) or theos (θεος), or maybe if we are Chinese Shan-di (上帝)? Does it matter if we call the Son 'Jesus' or Yeshua (ישוע) or Iesus ('Ιησοῦς)? Well there is some evidence that in early copies of the Old Testament LXX, written in Greek by Jews and for Jews, the tetragrammaton הוהי was used rather than the later *kurios*. There are, however, no early copies of the New Testament writings themselves in which this tetragrammaton is used rather than the Greek words *theos* (God) or *kurios* (Lord). No New Testament manuscript uses ישוע rather than Jesus. So if the apostles were happy to use terms in Greek rather than in Hebrew or the Aramaic Jesus spoke, then it seems that God does not much mind what particular term we use as long as our use of the name occurs within a relationship recognising His person. Maybe if anything God prefers *Abba*, this seems to be the Holy Spirit choice (Romans 8:15, Galatians 4:6).

Discussion Topic: Law and Faith

The main divine covenants described in Scripture are:

1. That after Noah (Genesis 6:18; 9:9 etc) not to send another flood

2. That with Abraham (Genesis 15:18; 17:2–21; Exodus 2:22) which had two parts:

   a) The descendants of his son (Isaac) would inherit the land

   b) Through his descendant(s) all nations would be blessed

3. The covenant through Moses (Exodus 19:5, 24:7; Deuteronomy 5:2; etc) also called the 'Old Covenant' or the 'First Covenant' (Hebrews 8:7 etc)

4. The 'New Covenant' (Jeremiah 31:31; Matthew 26:28; Hebrews 8:6-13, 9:15 etc).

The book of Hebrews deals a lot with the Old and New Covenants. The Jewish sacrifices, it says, cannot really take away sin, they are just pictures or shadows of the real sacrifice made by Jesus. The writer introduces the key verses Habakkuk 2:3–4 in Hebrews 10:38: *'The righteous shall live by faith'*. But Habakkuk 2:3–4 is not merely prophetically referring to faith in the New Covenant age because the writer goes on in Hebrews 11 to point out that faith was the basis by which all righteous people lived, in prehistory, the patriarchal period, and throughout Jewish history. The Jew-Gentile issue is not mentioned, but Hebrews 8:13 says that the New Covenant has made the first 'obsolete – growing old and ready to vanish away'. It does not deal with meticulous law keeping, but the assumption is presumably that the ordinances and sacrifices were applied and given in faith, and pointed forward to the real sacrifice of Messiah.

To Jesus, the central commandments were to love God and

love others, and without these any meticulous law keeping was pointless. But He sees this as following the prophets 'I desire mercy and not sacrifice' (Matthew 9:13 quoting Hosea 6:6). He did not come to destroy the Law but to fulfil it (Matthew 5:17) and went on to say that His standards were even higher because they concerned the heart and love even for enemies.

In our commentary on Galatians we explored the distinction between the real meaning of the Law (which is about love fulfilled by faith) and the 'works of the Law' which are specific ordinances elaborated in traditions which mark off the nation of Israel. Attempts to make these latter a general badge of holiness are misguided, and miss the fact that the curse of not fulfilling all such details has been taken by Christ. The Law itself was a constraining guideline given to Israel until the coming of Christian faith.

Commentary

Romans 10:5 is a quotation from Leviticus 18:5 where Moses is contrasting what God expects from His people with Canaanite behaviour. It is really about idolatry rather than salvation. The introductory word of 10:6, *'gar de'*, is rendered 'but' by the NRSVA, though Davies (*Faith and Obedience in Romans*, p.190) points out that in the bulk of uses of this phrase by Paul, no contrast is intended. More often it indicates a supplementary or parallel statement. Most of the rest from verse 6 onwards is a loose quotation (with a couple of bits from Psalm 107 and possibly Job) from Deuteronomy 30:9–20. We will quote this main passage here in full:

> [9] And the Lord your God will make you abundantly prosperous in all your undertakings, in the fruit of your body, in the fruit of your livestock, and in the fruit of your soil. For the Lord will again take delight in prospering you, just as He delighted in prospering your ancestors, [10] when you obey the Lord your God by observing His commandments and decrees that are written in this book of the law, because you turn to the Lord your God with all your heart and with all your soul.

¹¹ Surely, this commandment that I am commanding you today is not too hard for you, nor is it too far away. ¹² It is not in heaven, that you should say, 'Who will go up to heaven for us, and get it for us so that we may hear it and observe it?' ¹³ Neither is it beyond the sea, that you should say, 'Who will cross to the other side of the sea for us, and get it for us so that we may hear it and observe it?' ¹⁴ No, the word is very near to you; it is in your mouth and in your heart for you to observe.

¹⁵ See, I have set before you today life and prosperity, death and adversity. ¹⁶ If you obey the commandments of the Lord your God that I am commanding you today, by loving the Lord your God, walking in His ways, and observing His commandments, decrees, and ordinances, then you shall live and become numerous, and the Lord your God will bless you in the land that you are entering to possess. ¹⁷ But if your heart turns away and you do not hear, but are led astray to bow down to other gods and serve them, ¹⁸ I declare to you today that you shall perish; you shall not live long in the land that you are crossing the Jordan to enter and possess. ¹⁹ I call heaven and earth to witness against you today that I have set before you life and death, blessings and curses. Choose life so that you and your descendants may live, ²⁰ loving the Lord your God, obeying Him, and holding fast to Him; for that means life to you and length of days, so that you may live in the land that the Lord swore to give to your ancestors, to Abraham, to Isaac, and to Jacob. (NRSVA)

There are two very different possible understandings of Paul's interpretation of these verses:

1) Paul believes that only Christians can fulfil any of this, and the Torah was given just to prove that no one could do it. Moses' words seem to say that it is possible for them to do this but actually this only applies over a millennium later in the Christian era.

2) Paul believes that Moses' hearers also could fulfil this through faith, and those who fulfil it in the present Messianic age are simply superlative examples of what is true for all who have had faith throughout history.

Linguistically, 1) is possible, but in the wider context it makes no sense. A modern politician who said 'Vote for me and you will get a good standard of living' would hardly be regarded as honest if he 'really' meant 'Vote for me and in a millennium's time your remote descendants will do well.' If 1) were true, then either Moses knew that actually they had no chance for the next millennium or so (in which case it was a con) or he didn't (in which case he was duped or mistaken). Only understanding 2) can maintain the integrity both of God and His prophet.

Dunn says that this Deuteronomy 30 passage 'was a subject of considerable reflection among Jews, both in Palestine and in the diaspora' (p.604), and that fairly free interpretations were common. Moses' central and first commandment is 'Love the Lord your God . . . and walk in His ways.' His real point is then to go on to say *'Look, don't make it over complicated or mysterious. Don't feel that it involves some stupendous religious acts. It's simple! Love God and listen to Him. Hold fast to or 'cling' to Him – He is the Life.'* The word used for 'cling to' or 'hold fast to' in Deuteronomy 30:20 is the same as the one in Genesis 2:24 for husband and wife 'clinging' to each other in marriage. It means a close unifying bond, which is what they need with God to fulfil what He asks. The word (*rhema*) is very near you. Do it – love God!' In contrast the Pharisee interpretation of Torah (sometimes called 'the oral law' or 'traditions of the elders' and later embodied in the Mishnah) became a 'heavy yoke'. In Luke 11:37–54 and Matthew 23:1–36 Jesus castigates the Lawyers and Pharisees because they put heavy burdens on people but *'have neglected the weightier matters of the law: justice and mercy and faith'.* In other words, they had not done at all what Moses urged, they constructed amazingly strict detailed ritual regulations but missed out the essentials, and were not truly 'clinging' to God as shown by their rejection of His Messiah.

What we believe Paul is doing is showing that the Christian understanding of faith and justification is in line with what Moses said to the Israelites. For us as Christians, we know that the reason for all this is that our basis of justification is the faithfulness of Jesus the Messiah. There was no human effort to bring the incarnation, nor to raise Him from the dead – it was divine grace in both cases. We have just to have faith in Him to be declared righteous and to openly confess Him to begin properly to experience salvation in our lives. Paul refers back to the verse already cited in 9:33. Though the Messiah was prophesied to be a stumbling block to those who rejected Him, those who would have faith in Him would 'not be put to shame'. Jews or Gentiles, whoever calls on the name of the Lord will be saved.

Taken out of context verse 9 could simply mean that a verbal confession 'Jesus is Lord' and an intellectual acceptance of the historical truth of the resurrection is enough to be saved. But plainly from the many things he says elsewhere Paul did not believe this. To 'confess with your mouth the Lord Jesus' must mean to accept Him as Lord. To believe *on* (*ep*) Him is not to believe *about* Him, but to put trust in Him.

Calling on the name of the Lord implies a relationship with Him. If He is our 'Lord' then we are putting ourselves under Him, acknowledging our dependence. We are pledging to serve Him as Lord.

Text 10:14–21

¹⁴ But how are they to call on one in whom they have not believed? And how are they to believe in one of whom they have never heard? And how are they to hear without someone to proclaim Him? ¹⁵ And how are they to proclaim Him unless they are sent? As it is written, 'How beautiful are the feet of those who bring good news!' ¹⁶ But not all have obeyed the good news; for Isaiah says, 'Lord, who has believed our message?' ¹⁷ So faith comes from what is heard, and what is heard comes through the word of Christ.

¹⁸ But I ask, have they not heard? Indeed they have; for

'Their voice has gone out to all the earth, and their words to the ends of the world.'

¹⁹ Again I ask, did Israel not understand? First Moses says,

'I will make you jealous of those who are not a nation; with a foolish nation I will make you angry.'

²⁰ Then Isaiah is so bold as to say,

'I have been found by those who did not seek Me; I have shown Myself to those who did not ask for Me.'

²¹ But of Israel he says, 'All day long I have held out My hands to a disobedient and contrary people.' (NRSVA)

Commentary

Sometimes this passage may be used to encourage Christians to go out and preach the gospel, and there is no harm in this at all. But in the context the passage is really about the fact that the unbelief of much of Israel in the

Messianic age was prophesied by Moses and Isaiah. So first Paul is claiming that his (and other Christians') mission is fulfilling the words in Isaiah 52:7 which he paraphrases:

> How beautiful upon the mountains are the feet of him who brings good news, who proclaims peace, who brings glad tidings of good things, who proclaims salvation.

He then quotes Isaiah 53:1 exactly as in the LXX: *'Lord who has believed our report?'* This chapter of Isaiah, as most Christians well know, prophesies that Messiah will be rejected by the bulk of His own people.

So then he asks: is the problem that they didn't hear the gospel? On this he cites Psalm 19:4 (LXX 18:5) to say that the preaching of the words has gone out. So it is not that they lacked faith in the Messiah because they did not hear the message. So 'Israel' did know about Jesus.

Paul then turns to the Jewish objection about God including Gentiles in His new vessel/vase, the Church. Moses' words in Deuteronomy 32:21 are now directed towards Israel. Moses had already said in 31:27:

> For I know well how rebellious and stubborn you are. If you already have been so rebellious towards the Lord while I am still alive among you, how much more after my death! (NRSVA)

There follows this threat:

> They made Me jealous with what is no god, provoked Me with their idols. So I will make them jealous with what is no people, provoke them with a foolish nation. (Deuteronomy 32:21, NRSVA)

Then finally Paul quotes God's response to the nation's claim that they are the clay and He is the potter so it was not their fault (Isaiah 64:8 see Discussion Topic on pages 212–214). On the contrary, God has been pleading with them to turn to Him, and because they have not done so He will make Himself manifest to Gentiles for whom He had not been their God.

Text 11:1–6

> [1] I ask, then, has God rejected His people? By no means! I myself am an Israelite, a descendant of Abraham, a member of the tribe of Benjamin. [2] God has not rejected His people whom He foreknew. Do you not know what the scripture says of Elijah, how he pleads with God against Israel? [3] 'Lord, they have killed Your prophets,

they have demolished Your altars; I alone am left, and they are seeking my life.' [4] But what is the divine reply to him? 'I have kept for Myself seven thousand who have not bowed the knee to Baal.' [5] So too at the present time there is a remnant, chosen by grace. [6] But if it is by grace, it is no longer on the basis of works, otherwise grace would no longer be grace. (NRSVA)

Discussion Topic: Election

In the New Testament context 'election' (Greek: *eklektos*) means some kind of choice. In our *Reconsidering Key Biblical Ideas* chapter 4 we look in depth at the concept which we outline below. But first, just some thoughts about why it is crucial to get this biblical concept correct. It is not that we doubt the sincerity of those who do not, but that they do not seem to realise the real horror into which mistakes in this doctrine can lead them.

To illustrate this, consider how Wayne Grudem in a popular introduction *Christian Beliefs* raises an obvious question on page 90ff. If (as the Bible says) God loves everyone and is 'willing that none should perish but all come to repentance', then why does not everyone believe and be saved? In the present context the apostle Paul might be asked: 'If God loves His people Israel then whey are not all of them saved?' Grudem rightly says that Christians have given two basic alternative answers, and we can summarize them thus:

1. One is that God does not want to alter their freewill because this would dehumanise them not save them, and so it is in the end their own choice to remain unrepentant.

2. The other is that it is 'for His own glory' that He wants to torture some of them in hell forever for unbelief, so He chooses to leave them unrepentant while selecting some to be made to repent.

To Grudem, the doctrine of election (which on p.83 he wrongly equates with predestination) implies that the second is the truth. But the two alternatives are not morally equivalent. A modern tragic report was of an ISIS jihadist who prayed to Allah and read his Qu'ran before raping a twelve-year-old girl, believing it was for the glory of Allah because she was a 'sinner'. This is horrific. But according to Wayne Grudem, God could easily make this same Yazidi girl believe and have eternal life, but He would rather let her die in unbelief and suffer what Grudem calls 'eternal conscious punishment' because this brings Him 'glory'. Jonathan Edwards, whose books, alas, are also on the shelves of our local Christian bookshop, would add that unless you enjoy this thought of her suffering forever for God's glory you may not be one of the elect.

Note that Grudem's first alternative says that it is precisely *because* God loves them that He does not change unbelievers into dehumanised robots; in the end He lets them choose the absolute destruction that comes when they are finally exposed in their rebellion to the fire of the absolute Love of God. But Grudem's second alternative is that it is for God's own ego that He wants to keep some people to torture forever – presumably He enjoys it. So these two alternatives are certainly not morally equivalent.

Now those of Grudem's persuasion, like the jihadist, may say to us 'Who are you to answer back to God?' (p.89). But we have never questioned God in either case, what we are questioning is *their wrong perception of God*. And when this question was asked by Paul in Romans it was about using Israel to make two 'lumps' out of Israel to demonstrate the contrast of unbelief and faith – not about who was supposedly sovereignly selected to become believers.

Grudem presents (p.90) the contrast as being 'those who support the doctrine of election' and those who do not. But this is very misleading. The issue is about what 'election' *means* in Scripture, not whether or not it is true. We emphatically support the true biblical doctrine of election.

In *Reconsidering Key Biblical Ideas* chapter 4 we look at the various uses of the word 'chosen' or 'elect' in Scripture. Jesus is God's 'chosen' Son (Luke 9:35) though Matthew and Mark render it 'beloved' (Matthew 17:5, Mark 9:7). It does not imply 'selection'. The Church is 'chosen *in* Messiah' (Ephesians 1:4) not 'chosen to be put into Messiah'. We share His election, and also share His servanthood which so often goes along with election. With the nation of Israel there is an 'elect' within the 'elect' nation, marked out by the fact that they have received grace. They are not marked out by 'works of the Law' (ie in particular circumcision, diet and Sabbath keeping). We looked in an earlier Discussion Topic on the potter at the picture near the end of Isaiah of a disobedient people contrasted there with the elect (see page 212). Isaiah 66:2 says God really looks for a poor and contrite spirit, and goes on to imply that actually the people *are* sacrificing lambs, making grain offerings etc. But God reiterates that:

> I called, but you did not answer; I spoke, but you did
> not hear. And you did evil in My sight And chose that
> in which I did not delight. (NASB, Isaiah 66:4)

All this would be nonsense if 'really' God did *not* want most of them to repent because He had secretly decided who would be the minority selected out sovereignly to be made to believe, while the rest were deliberately left in unbelief. God does not delight in sin, He is not willing that any should perish but that all should repent. The 'hardening' and 'spirit of stupor', are judgements on their refusal to believe, not causes of their unbelief.

Kruse rejects this because, he claims that it does not explain 'why some Jewish individuals accept the gospel while others do not which is the reason Paul introduces it in chapter 9.' We do not accept his exegesis of Romans 9, and in any case this view of what it means would be strange. Paul does *not* ask 'Why do only some Jews believe?' He asks 'Is it that the word of God has failed?' (9:6)

'Has God rejected His people which He foreknew?' (11:1) Paul's central concern is to show that the Christian faith and apparent supplanting of the nation in no way implies that God has been unfaithful or unrighteous. If it were really God's ordaining that determined which Jews would believe and which not, then this would spectacularly fail to answer this question. If the reason for their unbelief were really that God decided not to elect them, then He would indeed have rejected (most of) His people whom He foreknew. But actually Paul's answer is that God's true elect have always been those who responded to God in faith and so received His grace – and those who refused to do so were confirmed by God in their choice and its results.

So our own understanding of Paul's overall answer is:

- God's purpose in choosing the descendants of Abraham through Isaac was a strategy in preparing for the Messiah.

- This was also His purpose throughout Israel's history, in raising up Pharaoh and dealings with Israel.

- However, throughout history those who have had faith amongst Israel have only been a remnant.

- God's promises to them were genuine but in personal terms always conditional – and those who refused to repent had their understanding further darkened.

- God is the potter and we cannot question what kind of vessel He makes of us, but in making His decision He also reacts to how we behave and His promises to bless or break down are always conditional.

- At present national Israel is being made into two vessels – the one for honour being the real spiritual Israel which is the foundation of the Church that now includes Christian Gentiles.

- God's 'glory' consists of wanting to show mercy to all, but working around those who are disobedient.

The answer of theologians such as Augustine, Grudem, Moo and Kruse can basically be summarised (not in their own words):

- God has not 'cast off' His people whom He foreknew because before the creation He had decided that He would sovereignly elect only a minority of them to be made to repent, and the rest He would leave unrepentant and bound for unending suffering.

- Underlying His words that He loved them and wanted them to repent was the eternal decree of election which meant that they would *not* repent, so nothing is new and He has not really changed His mind or been unfaithful.

- Since He is Almighty, no one can question His sovereign will, and He can do as He likes. His 'righteousness' and 'faithfulness' consists of sovereignly deciding which He will save and which not, and it is His decree that determines their reaction.

- God's 'glory' consists of showing His absolute power to save and bless some, and to judge and make suffer others, while He himself controls their reactions.

The rejection of the correct corporate nature of 'election' leads, in our view, to an interpretation of Romans 9 that would convince no one except those who believed 'might is right' – which was emphatically not the view of first century Jews or Christians. It is fundamentally against what Jesus says in Matthew 20:25, where He contrasts the pagan tyrant's enjoyment of arbitrary power as benefactor or destroyer with the Kingdom of heaven in which He as Lord of all is the suffering Servant.

Divine 'election' is never arbitrary selection to receive blessing or curse. Moreover, Jacques More's detailed and careful examination of the Hebrew and Greek words for 'elect' (*Deleting 'Elect' in the Bible*) concludes that the element of being special rather than selection is paramount.

Romans 11:1–2 are clearly talking about the physical nation of Israel. Paul's claim to be an Israelite is based on his physical descent from Benjamin, and the 'Israel' against whom Elijah pleads is the literal nation. He is the living proof that not all Israelites have been condemned, for some are in the faithful remnant.

Within the nation of Israel, then, there has always been a 'remnant' who are those of true faith who have received God's grace. Paul asserts that it is not by Torah keeping, but by grace that these are marked out. This implies that it is misleading to say that the covenant with Israel and the gift of Torah only brought added condemnation. It is also misleading to say that faith arrived only with the Christian Age. These seven thousand had received grace, and the only way for this to happen was through faith, which is also the case for Habakkuk and the heroes of Hebrews 11.

Commentary

God has not cast away His people as Paul himself is living proof – he is a Hebrew of the Hebrews but also a Christian. Here (as elsewhere) 'foreknew' means 'knew about beforehand'. Those theologians who want it to mean 'chose beforehand' could only apply it at this point by assuming He had chosen them for destruction! But the real point is that God knew the nature of those He called Israel. Always, throughout their history, only a remnant truly had faith and were in right relationship with Him. So at the time of Elijah there were actually 7000 (Paul says men, though the Old Testament just says people). The 'election' of grace means that they are the ones who have received grace. How did they receive it? One presumes by a faith response to the invitation of God, through a positive response to the light that enlightens everyone who comes into the world. It was not 'of works' though actually it is their lifestyle to which God refers in His conversation with Elijah. Note that God says 'I have reserved to Myself . . .' It is because they are in faith-relationship with Him that He has preserved them from the idolatry all around them. In each generation, then, there is an elect within the elect. The nation as a whole is named Israel, but there is a group within it who are fulfilling the role that Israel was meant to fulfil. The same, Paul implies, is happening in his day as in the day of Elijah – though now the remnant are those who accept Jesus as Messiah.

What determines who form that elect within the elect? This is not Paul's subject here, but the whole tenor of all the Old Testament passages is that it is to do with human choice. It is not about humans choosing to live ethically perfect lives, or choosing to clock up enough works to earn God's acceptance. It is choosing to accept God's offer of forgiveness and relationship, offered through what John Wesley called 'prevenient grace' if you like this term (though it is not a biblical one). God always initiates, and He would always like a positive response, but He has made us in His image and in this respect ultimately given us what later philosophers called 'freewill'.

Text 11: 7–10

> [7] What then? Israel failed to obtain what it was seeking. The elect obtained it, but the rest were hardened, [8] as it is written,
>
> 'God gave them a sluggish spirit, eyes that would not see and ears that would not hear, down to this very day.'
>
> [9] And David says, 'Let their table become a snare and a trap, a stumbling-block and a retribution for them; [10] let their eyes be darkened so that they cannot see, and keep their backs for ever bent.' (NRSVA)

Commentary

What is it that Israel seeks? In Paul's day it was to be 'justified', ie to be shown to be living out the signs of being the people of God. But many of them were going about it the wrong way. Because they were doing this they had become blind to the obvious fulfilment by Jesus of the Messianic prophecies, maybe looking for a different kind of messiah (as sadly the non-Christian Jews later did to their cost). So when people reject Him, God sometimes confirms them in their decision by blinding their eyes to the obvious.

Paul is citing Deuteronomy 29:3 and Isaiah 29:10. The first comes in the great passage in which Moses in his 'swan song' is setting before them a choice. We remember that Moses says things like:

> I have set before you life and death, blessings and curses. Choose life so that you and your descendants may live, loving the Lord your God, obeying Him, and holding fast to Him; for that means life to you and length of days, so that you may live in the land that the Lord swore to give to your ancestors, to Abraham, to Isaac, and to Jacob. (Deuteronomy 30:19–20, NRSVA)

'Life' is not from meticulous works of the Law, but holding fast to or *clinging to* God, *loving* God, and recognising that in God is their *life*. Moses is presenting the faith-relationship-life option as clearly as Paul in Galatians 6:7–8. If actually it were secretly God who decided who will follow Him and who will not (as some theologians since Augustine have claimed) then the whole impassioned speech of Moses would be pointless. But in reality their blindness is a judgement on refusal to repent, not the determining factor in their basic choice.

In Isaiah 29:10 why does God send a spirit of stupor?

> The Lord said: 'Because these people draw near with their mouths and honour Me with their lips, while their hearts are far from Me and their worship of Me is a human commandment learned by rote' (Isaiah 29:13, NRSVA)

Their lip service and unrepentant hearts are the cause not the result of the spirit of stupor. A repentant heart will lead a person to see how Jesus is indeed Messiah. Or as Paul puts it elsewhere:

> [15] Indeed, to this very day whenever Moses is read, a veil lies over their minds; [16] but when one turns to the Lord, the veil is removed. (2 Corinthians 3:15–16, NRSVA)

Paul's emphasis here is not on the source of the unbelief, but that it was prophesied that Israel would show it.

Verses 9–10 refer to Psalm 69:22–3 and possibly also Psalm 35:8. At first sight this is an odd choice, because David is directing this against his enemies. Psalm 69 may have been seen as having Messianic overtones, for example:

> [4] Those who hate me without a cause . . .

> [7] For It is for your sake that I have borne reproach, that shame has

covered my face. ⁸I have become a stranger to my kindred, an alien to my mother's children. ⁹It is zeal for your house that has consumed me. (NRSVA) (see also John 2:17)

Perhaps this is why Paul reapplies it to the Israelites who are Messiah's kinfolk.

Text 11:11–24

¹¹ So I ask, have they stumbled so as to fall? By no means! But through their stumbling [Lit: transgression] salvation has come to the Gentiles, so as to make Israel jealous. ¹²Now if their stumbling [Lit: transgression] means riches for the world, and if their defeat means riches for Gentiles, how much more will their full inclusion mean!

¹³ Now I am speaking to you Gentiles. Inasmuch then as I am an apostle to the Gentiles, I glorify my ministry ¹⁴ in order to make my own people jealous, and thus save some of them. ¹⁵ For if their rejection is the reconciliation of the world, what will their acceptance be but life from the dead! ¹⁶ If the part of the dough offered as first fruits is holy, then the whole batch is holy; and if the root is holy, then the branches also are holy.

¹⁷ But if some of the branches were broken off, and you, a wild olive shoot, were grafted in their place to share the rich root of the olive tree, ¹⁸ do not vaunt yourselves over the branches. If you do vaunt yourselves, remember that it is not you that support the root, but the root that supports you. ¹⁹ You will say, 'Branches were broken off so that I might be grafted in.' ²⁰ That is true. They were broken off because of their unbelief, but you stand only through faith. So do not become proud, but stand in awe. ²¹ For if God did not spare the natural branches, perhaps He will not spare you. ²² Note then the kindness and the severity of God: severity towards those who have fallen, but God's kindness towards you, provided you continue in His kindness; otherwise you also will be cut off. ²³ And even those of Israel, if they do not persist in unbelief, will be grafted in, for God has the power to graft them in again. ²⁴ For if you have been cut from what is by nature a wild olive tree and grafted, contrary to nature, into a cultivated olive tree, how much more will these natural branches be grafted. (NRSVA)

Discussion Topic: Images of God

The rest of chapter 11 can be read according to two quite different paradigms.

In the first, God is the puppetmaster who determines everything. He decides that the majority of Israelites will be hardened and not believe, that He will then save some preselected Gentiles, and then He will make Israel have a national revival. We believe that this is fundamentally mistaken. For one thing, it makes it seem as though God is just playing a game. If He determines whether or not they will be hardened or believe then why should He need to use anything to provoke them to jealousy? For another, what would be the point of Paul giving a warning in verse 21 if it were God who determined repentance or apostasy anyway?

The other way of reading this whole passage is to see Paul not as predicting what will inevitably happen, but making outcomes dependent on their reactions – as we saw the Old Testament allegory of the potter did. *If* they do not continue faithful then God will act accordingly (v21). *If* (v23) the natural Jewish branches repent then they can be grafted back in (v24). The 'all Israel' in verse 26 who will be saved is spiritual Israel, not a prophecy of national Jewish revival. The disobedience comes from their own choice, but, as always, God confirms people in their choice, shutting them up to the disobedience they chose (or in Romans 1:28 'gave them up' to the mind-paths they had chosen) in order that He might show mercy on all. This last does not mean that eventually all those who were disobedient will be saved, but mercy is always God's intention if people will only accept it.

The fall of the bulk of Israel is not irrecoverable. In what sense did this fall lead to salvation coming to the Gentiles? It may be that the stumbling (or more properly 'transgression') is rejection of the gospel, and Acts 8:1ff, 13:45–48, 18:6 and 28:24–28 indicate this led to increased emphasis on Gentile evangelism, though it is hard to see how if the Jews had not rejected the gospel the Gentiles would have been left out. Another possibility (suggested for example by Barth and Cranfield) is that it was the Jewish transgression of rejecting Jesus that led to Him being given up for death and so bringing reconciliation to both Jews and Gentiles. Actually to us this seems more likely.

Commentary

A positive result of the Gentiles receiving salvation is that this should make Israel jealous when they see the blessings on the Church. Nanos rightly points out (*The Mystery of Romans*, p.249) that it is jealousy *of his mission* that Paul speaks of. So the jealousy comes when they see how his ministry is fulfilling the Jewish expectation that through the Messiah the Gentiles also would be blessed. Surely, though, Paul's 'pride in his ministry to the Gentiles' must include the fact that they are visibly being blessed with the joy and power of the Spirit? And surely that 'jealousy' was not expected to die when Paul died, but to continue if the Church continued to show such blessing?

In any event, how utterly removed Paul's thinking is from the wicked persecution of Jewish people in Christendom, starting in the days of Ambrose and Augustine and exacerbated by the virulent anti-Semitic writings of figures like Luther! How horrific the pogroms and the misrepresentation and caricaturing of Jewish culture have been, and all the other things Christendom has done in the name of Jesus the Messiah. It only the more reflects on the failure of the Church to reflect the blessing that would attract more Jews to come and experience it.

The NKJV, NRSVA and NASB rightly have 'I am *an* apostle to the Gentiles'. Paul was one missionary to Gentiles, but there were others. So Paul personalises his previous statement. In his own ministry he has not forgotten that he is Jewish, and one hope is that when his fellow Jews see the blessings God gives to Gentile Christians they will want to be part of it. He does not mean that this is the only or even the main purpose of his work with Gentiles (any more than he meant that God gave them salvation only to make Jews jealous). But it *is* a hope that he has.

His statement in verse 14 is actually quite cautious and conditional, which the NRSVA does not really reflect. Most versions have 'if by any means' or 'in the hope that', so for example the NIV reads 'in the hope that somehow I might arouse some of them'. This is not a confident prophecy of some kind of national Jewish revival, but a conditional tentative wish.

Nanos argues (p.253 after Hays) that 'Israel undergoes rejection for the sake of the world, bearing suffering vicariously'. Hays and Nanos see this as reflecting the vicarious suffering of Jesus the Messiah. Is this plausible? Well concerning the sacrifice of Messiah we read:

> [46] And He said to them, 'Thus it is written, that the Messiah is to suffer and to rise from the dead on the third day, [47] and that repentance and forgiveness of sins is to be proclaimed in His name to all nations, beginning from Jerusalem.' (Luke 24:46–47, NRSVA)

We may not understand why this sacrifice was necessary, but the need for an atoning sacrifice was pictured throughout Scripture. Had God possessed a choice of some other way then presumably He would have positively answered Jesus' prayer in Matthew 26:27–42. But we cannot think of any conceivable reason why God should have been constrained to have to purposely harden and reject a big chunk of Israel in order to send the gospel message to Gentiles. In Jesus' commission to make disciples of 'all nations', and in God's commission to Paul, the inclusion of Gentiles is already assumed, and had the great bulk of Jews turned to their Messiah this would have made the carrying of the message to Gentiles much easier not harder. They were broken off because of unbelief, but there was no need for God to ordain such unbelief in order to reach the Gentiles.

Romans 11:16 is picturing the whole of Israel as somehow 'holy' or set apart. This leads into the picture of the olive tree. This is the visible presence of the people of God in the world. The natural branches of this would be the Jews, but those who did not believe have been broken off. Paul does not say *'well they remain in a different dispensation'*, rather the ones broken off are not part of the active people of God, but the Gentile Christians now are. The 'root' though, is Jewish – whether we think of this as the Patriarchs and prophets or as the earliest members of the Church. So Gentiles should be glad of the blessing that comes from the Old Testament, and from this spiritual heritage. It is that Gentile Christians have joined the remnant of Israel in the Church (or *ekklesia*), not that a few Jews have joined the Church.

Romans 11:20–21 emphasize human choice. Gentile Christians stand as the people of God through faith, and Paul here clearly thinks that it is their choice whether to continue to do so. They are to 'tremble' in the sense of taking their own responsibility to continue in faith seriously, not because God might unilaterally decide to make them apostate.

Romans 11:22 repeats this: God's kindness is '*if* you remain in His kindness'. Again this is not suggesting that God may just decide no longer to be kind to them, but that it is their responsibility to remain in it. The kindness is undeserved and unmerited, but they can decide whether to stay in or leave it.

Romans 11:23 is yet again conditional: '*if* they do not persist in unbelief, they will be grafted in, for God is able to graft them in again'. Again this is neither a ringing prophecy of a national revival that is certain, nor an indication that it is just if God feels like it that they will repent. Rather it *is* a certainty that God will show mercy if they turn and that the way is always open for them. *If* a person turns to the Lord the veil is removed (2 Corinthians 3:16). In a sense it would be much more natural for a Jew to recognise that Jesus is the Messiah prophesied in Isaiah and the Psalms, than for a Gentile to do so. So a Jew coming to Jesus is a natural thing.

Text 11: 25–27

[25] So that you may not claim to be wiser than you are, brothers and sisters, I want you to understand this mystery: a hardening has come upon part of Israel, until the full number of the Gentiles has come in. [26] And so all Israel will be saved; as it is written,

'Out of Zion will come the Deliverer; He will banish ungodliness from Jacob.' [27] 'And this is My covenant with them, when I take away their sins.' (NRSVA)

Commentary

In linguistic terms the word 'mystery' (Greek: *mysterion*) did not mean something impossible to understand, but a secret. Mysteries can be known (Matthew 13:11) and understood (1 Corinthians 13:2). Romans 16:25 says that this 'mystery' of the preaching of Jesus the Messiah had been a secret but was now made manifest.

What does he mean by 'all Israel will be saved? Cranfield in his commentary (vol ii p 576) lists the four possible options for the meaning of this:

i) all the elect, Jews and Gentiles.

ii) all the elect of the nation of Israel.

iii) the whole nation of Israel, including every individual member.

iv) the nation of Israel as a whole, but not necessarily including every individual member.

Kruse (p.448ff) runs through various supporters of each of these views, though himself supports ii). The term 'all Israel' is used 148 times in the Old Testament and usually has a meaning something like iv). Cranfield argues for a similar meaning here also on the grounds that 'Israel' must mean the same in 11:26 as 11:25. But neither of these points seem good to us. Paul has already spoken of the 'true Jew' and 'real circumcision', and in Romans 9:6 wrote: 'They are not all Israel who are of Israel' using the same term differently even in the same sentence. In Galatians 6:16, as we saw, he wrote:

> For in Messiah Jesus neither circumcision nor uncircumcision avails anything but a new creation. And as many as walk according to this rule, peace and mercy be upon them, even upon the Israel of God.

Whatever the 'Israel of God' means here, is it not iii) or iv) of the four just given. In the Galatians commentary we gave reasons to suppose that it meant those 'in Christ'. If Paul used this elsewhere in his preaching, then, given the relationship between Galatians and Romans, we think a similar meaning is most likely here. It most probably means all the elect (Jews and Gentiles), though it could just possibly be ii), ie the elect of the nation of Israel.

Interpretation iii) is wildly unlikely, as it would mean God suddenly treating them differently from His actions throughout history. Interpretation iv) also seems unlikely. There is no other indication in Scripture that a total national turning to Messiah is expected, and given Paul's earlier hesitancy that he 'hoped that by some means *some* might be persuaded' it would be odd here for him suddenly to predict a definite national Jewish revival. Kruse also notes that a mass conversion would 'seem to involve a special provision different from that provided for Gentiles. This flies in the face of the overall argument of Romans that Jews and Gentiles are treated alike in matters of sin, judgement and salvation' (*Paul's Letter to the Romans*, p.451).

Paul goes on in 11:26–7 to speak of a deliverer 'turning ungodliness from

Jacob', a kind of composite quote from Isaiah 59:20–21. Other New Covenant prophecies look as though they refer just to national Israel, but in fact in the New Testament they are referred to the Church:

> But this is the covenant that I will make with the house of Israel after those days, says the Lord: I will put My law within them, and I will write it on their hearts; and I will be their God, and they shall be My people. (Jeremiah 31:33, NRSVA)

Hebrews 8:10 (see the Discussion Topic below on Supersessionism) very plainly seems to apply this to the New Covenant – now, at the present time – and the assumption is that it applies both to Jews and Gentiles in the body of Christ who look to Jesus as their great High Priest.

Paul's quotation in 11:26, then, has been taken as either a prophecy that these words of Isaiah remain to be completed in the future when there will be a national Jewish turning to Jesus the Messiah, or as a statement that they are now being fulfilled in the Church Age and the 'Jacob' is the remnant-elect of Israel (joined by Gentiles in the Church). We understand it to be the latter.

Text 11:28–32

> [28] As regards the gospel they are enemies of God for your sake; but as regards election they are beloved, for the sake of their ancestors; [29] for the gifts and the calling of God are irrevocable. [30] Just as you were once disobedient to God but have now received mercy because of their disobedience, [31] so they have now been disobedient in order that, by the mercy shown to you, they too may now receive mercy. [32] For God has imprisoned all in disobedience so that He may be merciful to all. (NRSVA)

Discussion Topic: Supersessionism

Supercessionism or 'Replacement Theology' says that the Church has replaced Israel as the people of God. Is this so?

Well on the one hand, we cannot accept 'dual covenant theology' or versions of 'dispensationalism' that imply that Jews who refuse to accept Jesus as Messiah can be saved by keeping

Torah. Paul says here that they are 'enemies of the gospel' and in many places he makes it clear that they need to turn to Jesus the Messiah in repentance to be saved. Moreover, in our earlier Discussion Topic on Dispensationalism (page 195–199), we noted that in 1 Peter 2:9–10 the words of Exodus 19:4–6 including a 'holy nation' are applied to the Church. Jesus in Matthew 21:43 says that the kingdom of God will be taken from them (the Israelites) and given to a 'nation' (*ethnei*) that produces the fruit of the kingdom. It is clear that Paul regards Jesus the Messiah as fulfilling the prophecies, for example in Isaiah where Israel's Messiah achieves the task of being a light to the nations, in which Israel itself generally failed. The body of Messiah on Earth, Paul believes, is the Church, in which there is neither male nor female, Jew nor Gentile, slave nor free. He is also adamant (as in Galatians) that there are not to be two churches (Jew and Gentile) meeting separately. Finally, we presume Paul agrees with Hebrews 8 which says:

> [7] For if that first covenant had been faultless, there would have been no need to look for a second one. [8] God finds fault with them when He says: 'The days are surely coming, says the Lord, when I will establish a new covenant with the house of Israel and with the house of Judah; [9] not like the covenant that I made with their ancestors, on the day when I took them by the hand to lead them out of the land of Egypt; for they did not continue in My covenant, and so I had no concern for them, says the Lord. [10] This is the covenant that I will make with the house of Israel after those days, says the Lord. I will put My laws in their minds, and write them on their hearts, and I will be their God, and they shall be My people. [11] And they shall not teach one another or say to each other, "Know the Lord" for they shall all know Me, from the least of them to the greatest [12] For I will be merciful towards their iniquities, and I

will remember their sins no more.'

¹³ In speaking of 'a new covenant', He has made the first one obsolete. And what is obsolete and growing old will soon disappear. (NRSVA)

Verse 13 makes it clear that this is not to be projected 2000 years into the future at some time of Jewish national revival, it is *now*. And the implication is that it is being fulfilled in the Church. Hebrews goes on to say that Old Covenant sacrifices among other things were 'shadows' of the realities which are in Messiah. Jesus is our lamb, our High Priest, so neither Jewish nor Gentile Christians have need of any other.

As God's people on Earth, a royal priesthood acting between God and men, the Church which is the body of Messiah has indeed 'replaced' the nation of Israel in this sense.

So does this mean that there is no longer any real Jewish national identity? Are they no longer 'special'? Does it mean that Jewish people should cease to be Jewish? We would answer 'No' to all these questions. They remain the 'natural' olive branches to be grafted back in. They are 'beloved for the sake of the fathers', which does not mean that they are in right relationship with God, but that He has some special affection for them. Paul 'spiritualizes' many of the promises to Abraham (saying that the true children of Abraham are those of faith), but he also still recognises that Jews are his kindred in physical terms, and never says *'Well now I am a Christian and no longer Jewish.'*

Should Jewish Christians keep Torah? Well Jesus himself rejected the 'traditions of the Elders' that were later embodied in the Jewish *Mishnah*, so clearly these traditions are not binding. After the destruction of the second Temple it was also not possible to offer sacrifices – though sin offerings might have seemed anomalous anyway to Jewish Christians since Jesus is our lamb and High Priest. But if circumcision is seen as a sign of national identity rather than spiritual superiority, then in our view Paul would have had no problem with it. Celebrating national deliverance at Passover, Purim and so on makes just as much sense for Jewish Christians as for example British Christians who keep Remembrance Day on 11th November. Keeping the Sabbath is fine, as long as (and Paul addresses this in Romans 14) they do not try to impose it on Gentiles or take it as a sign of superiority.

Finally, will there be a Jewish national revival? If so will they have some special purpose outside the Church? On the first question we do not believe anyone can know. A lot of Christians emphasize the 'many prophecies' that Jews would return to Israel (in 1948). But the prophecies cited are often dubious. So for example, one website cites Zephaniah 3:8–10 selecting the KJV which says 'then will I turn to the people a pure language' and suggests this is Hebrew rather than Yiddish. The problem with this is that the word 'people' is *goyim* which usually means Gentile nations not Jews. The same website cites Isaiah 11:21–23, yet these verses come after a passage which seems to speak of the New Heaven and Earth where the lion lies down with the lamb. Other prophecies cited seem to be in passages which make any return to the land dependent on national repentance – which was the basis of the first return from exile. Yet the return in 1948 was not a part of any national turning to the Messiah. For such reasons it seems to us that confident predictions about the future place of Israel remain speculative at best.

Commentary

Biblical prophesies often have an immediate and an ultimate fulfilment. God's promises to Abraham had various layers. The promises that through his seed all nations would be blessed certainly happened literally. The promise that his descendants would inherit the land seems to have been on two levels. On the one hand the spiritual 'children of Abraham' will inherit the 'heavenly country' that Old Testament people of faith were looking out towards (Hebrews 11:16). On the other hand Abraham certainly expected that his physical descendants would inherit the physical land he was shown. This was always conditional on their faithfulness, but there is no indication that a stage would be reached where the promise was finally cancelled, apart from at the New Heaven and New Earth when the land would presumably no longer be there in the same form.

Paul's immediate application of the idea of the promises is that they are conditional upon obedience. 'God has committed them all to disobedience that He may have mercy on all' is not a statement of universalism, ie that eventually everyone will be saved. It indicates that His undeserved mercy is always there, always on offer. He would like to have mercy upon all because He says:

> Say to them, 'As I live!' declares the Lord God, 'I take no pleasure in the death of the wicked, but rather that the wicked turn from his way and live. Turn back, turn back from your evil ways! Why then will you die, O house of Israel?' (Ezekiel 33:11, NASB)

Text 11: 33–36

[33] O the depth of the riches and wisdom and knowledge of God! How unsearchable are His judgements and how inscrutable His ways! [34] 'For who has known the mind of the Lord? Or who has been His counsellor?' [35] 'Or who has given a gift to Him, to receive a gift in return?' [36] For from Him and through Him and to Him are all things. To Him be the glory for ever. Amen. (NRSVA)

Commentary

What can be added to this?

Questions for Thought and Discussion

- How far do Christians today have a vision of the way in which God always works in history, always wants to show mercy, always seeks for people to repent?

- How does this inspire you in your life?

Part 3: Theology worked out in Christian Lifestyle 12:1–16:27

Romans 12:1–15:32 | The Practical Implications for Christian Lifestyle

Text 12:1–2

[1] I appeal to you therefore, brothers and sisters, by the mercies of God, to present your bodies as a living sacrifice, holy and acceptable to God, which is your spiritual [or *reasonable*] worship. [2] Do not be conformed to this world [Lit. age], but be transformed by the renewing of your minds, so that you may discern what is the will of God—what is good and acceptable and perfect. (NRSVA)

Commentary

As he comes to practical lifestyle implications, Paul begins with our relationship with God. These wonderful verses actually follow on directly from his earlier themes. The Jewish priests presented sacrifices as part of their Temple service, and indeed this is common throughout world religions. Paul here urges them that their own bodies are to be the 'sacrifices', and that this is their 'reasonable service'. The word used is *reasonable* (*logikos*) not *spiritual* – it is only rational to react to what God has done for us in this way. The 'service' (*latria*) means service as in a Temple. In the New Covenant we no longer have to present animal sacrifices in a Temple – what God wants is ourselves, all of us, as living sacrifices. The Christian faith is such a radical new kind of religion if indeed it can be called a 'religion' at all! As N.T. Wright emphasises in his massive book *Paul and the Faithfulness of God,*

Christianity was totally radical in having no sacred places, no sacrificial offerings, and no priests. We are all, as the Church, the Temple of the Holy Spirit, a royal priesthood, and asked to give ourselves as living sacrifices. Various Christians, of course, have tried to invent 'sacred places', invented a 'priesthood', made sacred relics and icons etc, and invented not a few sets of rules or traditions of the elders! Such is the power of traditional religion!

Romans 12:2 is so central to what it is to be a Christian. Most people simply conform to whatever values and ways of living the society around them regards as norms. But the Christian is being changed from the inside out, by a divine renewing of mind. The focus is then not on what the world expects but what God expects. Change is not from increased self-effort but from God changing us from the inside out.

Text 12:3–13

> [3] For by the grace given to me I say to everyone among you not to think of yourself more highly than you ought to think, but to think with sober judgement, each according to the measure of faith that God has assigned. [4] For as in one body we have many members, and not all the members have the same function, [5] so we, who are many, are one body in Christ, and individually we are members one of another. [6] We have gifts that differ according to the grace given to us: prophecy, in proportion to faith; [7] ministry, in ministering; the teacher, in teaching; [8] the exhorter, in exhortation; the giver, in generosity; the leader, in diligence; the compassionate, in cheerfulness.
>
> [9] Let love be genuine; hate what is evil, hold fast to what is good; [10] love one another with mutual affection; outdo one another in showing honour. [11] Do not lag in zeal, be ardent in spirit, serve the Lord. [12] Rejoice in hope, be patient in suffering, persevere in prayer. [13] Contribute to the needs of the saints; extend hospitality to strangers. (NRSVA)

Commentary

Paul now turns to relationships in the Church. In several places in his epistles he refers to (spiritual) gifts (Romans 12, 1 Corinthians 12 & 14, Ephesians 4). Some of these (like healing) are supernatural, others (like administration) may be natural gifts which when used in the service of God nonetheless need

His Spiritual anointing to bring blessing. There is no definitive list of gifts, in each place he gives 'frinstances'. But his picture of the Church is always that everyone in it has gifts and should use them for edification and upbuilding of the whole body. A church where work is done by one or several 'professionals' while others look on is not a Pauline concept – even though today this is too often what is found. Another problem can be when someone thinks he or she has a gift when really they do not – whether this be, for example, leading worship or prophetic utterance.

Love (*agape*) should not be play-acting – and to really love we need the love of God poured into our hearts (5:5) and overflowing to love for others. This is not just *agape* love but also brotherly love (*philadelphia*) and warm affection. We should put each other first. Romans 12:11 is a picture of real commitment. Romans 12:12 reflects 5:3–5, where the most likely reading also gave it as an instruction: *Let us exult in tribulation knowing it produces perseverance, character and hope.* Romans 12:13 is practical. Love and brotherly love are not just warm feelings, they lead to action, and to giving if other Christians have needs. Hospitality (literally 'love of the stranger') is a general command in 1 Peter 4:9, and a necessary qualification for leadership (1 Timothy 3:2, Titus 1:8). Here, again, it is a general instruction.

Text 12:14–21

[14] Bless those who persecute you; bless and do not curse them. [15] Rejoice with those who rejoice, weep with those who weep. [16] Live in harmony with one another; do not be haughty, but associate with the lowly; do not claim to be wiser than you are. [17] Do not repay anyone evil for evil, but take thought for what is noble in the sight of all. [18] If it is possible, so far as it depends on you, live peaceably with all. [19] Beloved, never avenge yourselves, but leave room for the wrath of God; for it is written, 'Vengeance is mine, I will repay, says the Lord.' [20] No, 'if your enemies are hungry, feed them; if they are thirsty, give them something to drink; for by doing this you will heap burning coals on their heads.' [21] Do not be overcome by evil, but overcome evil with good. (NRSVA)

Commentary

Paul now turns primarily to relationships with others in general. Christians should be peaceable folk. Sometimes it becomes impossible to be at peace with some people, especially if we stand for truth, but insofar as we can we try to be at peace.

Romans 12:20 is a quotation from the LXX of Proverbs 25:21–22a. There have been commentators who took it that this meant by being kind we will increase the divine punishment on our enemies. This, however, would not fit with verse 21, and is therefore rejected with good reason. No one knows what the original meaning of the coals of fire was. One possibility (favoured for example by Cranfield, Hultgren, Jewett, Kasemann and Wright) is that it relates to an Egyptian rite of penitence where a person carried on his head a dish of burning charcoal as a self-punishment. Whatever the original context, however, the idea is that by doing good to an enemy he may be moved to remorse. Origen said that an enemy treated kindly 'will swear that as his conscience torments him for the wrong he has done, it is as if a fire were enveloping him' (quoted in Hultgren *Paul's Letter to the Romans*, p.460). We should try to overcome evil by good. This is always the hope, though of course it does not always happen.

Text 13:1–7

> ¹ Let every person be subject to the governing authorities; for there is no authority except from God, and those authorities that exist have been instituted by God. ² Therefore whoever resists authority resists what God has appointed, and those who resist will incur judgement. ³ For rulers are not a terror to good conduct, but to bad. Do you wish to have no fear of the authority? Then do what is good, and you will receive its approval; ⁴ for it is God's servant for your good. But if you do what is wrong, you should be afraid, for the authority does not bear the sword in vain! It is the servant of God to execute wrath on the wrongdoer. ⁵ Therefore one must be subject, not only because of wrath but also because of conscience. ⁶ For the same reason you also pay taxes, for the authorities are God's servants, busy with this very thing. ⁷ Pay to all what is due to them—taxes to whom taxes are due, revenue to whom revenue is due, respect to whom respect is due, honour to whom honour is due. (NRSVA)

Commentary

This now concerns civil society. Christians could have said something like: *'I am a citizen of heaven, therefore I owe no debt of allegiance or obedience to earthly government. My only reason for obeying the laws would be to avoid bad consequences.'* Paul says 'No!' Civil authority has a divinely given function of preserving law and order. In general we obey not just from fear of consequences but for conscience sake. 'Should we pay taxes to Caesar?' Jesus was asked. He replied (Matthew 22:21) that since Caesar ran the money system it was reasonable to pay taxes to Rome.

Some obvious issues arise. First, Paul is surely not saying that all present governments are given a permanent divine sanction – some kind of 'divine right of kings'. Most ruling people or groups originally came to power by violent overthrow of a previous regime: Pompey was assassinated, Julius Caesar was murdered, Mark Antony defeated by Augustus, Germanicus and Sejanus were killed, Caligula was murdered in 41 AD, Claudius in 54 AD. Paul's point is about civil authority in general, not that particular governments are divinely ordained.

A second point is that there is no particular Christian sanction or preference for some particular system, such as multi-party democracy. In our own era the naive assumption that this will make everything better for all societies has been plainly shown to be wrong. In Paul's day, of course, there was no democracy, and his words apply to a dictatorship.

A third question is whether a Christian could ever be a revolutionary. Some famous revolutionaries (like Oliver Cromwell and Sun Yat Sen and in a sense Dietrich Bonhoeffer) were Christians. Arguably the question is whether the existing government has gone so far from its proper function to being a 'terror to good works rather than bad' to warrant its removal. The further question is how can you be sure that whatever will result from a revolution will be better?

In general, however, Christians are law abiding people, supporting the civil government in discouraging bad behaviour and encouraging good. We also should *pray for kings and all those in authority, that we may live peaceful and quiet lives in all godliness and holiness'* (1 Timothy 2:2). If we have opportunity to influence this positively, for example by voting, then it would also make sense to do so.

Text 13:8–10

> [8] Owe no one anything, except to love one another; for the one who loves another has fulfilled the law. [9] The commandments, 'You shall not commit adultery; You shall not murder; You shall not steal; You

shall not covet'; and any other commandment, are summed up in this word, 'Love your neighbour as yourself.' [10] Love does no wrong to a neighbour; therefore, love is the fulfilling of the law. (NRSVA)

Commentary

In Galatians Paul insisted that they did not need to do 'works of the Law' but that *all the law is fulfilled in one word, even in this: 'You shall love your neighbour as yourself'* (Galatians 5:14). The 'works of the Law' (particularly circumcision, diet and Sabbaths) are not outworkings of love for others, but have ceremonial significance. In chapter 14, Paul will argue that such things are personal, a matter for individual conscience. But to really 'fulfil the Law' means to fulfil what both its commands and its symbolism are saying – and this is summed up in loving God and loving others. There is a school of theology which says the Law is not for us because (they say) 'Christ is our righteousness and has fulfilled the Law for us'. This is clearly not Pauline, though we are fulfilling what the Law really means, not the purely ritual 'works of the Law'. In Romans 2:14–16 Paul says that some Gentiles who (unlike the Christian Gentiles at Rome) have never heard the Torah but are 'doers of the Law' (Romans 2:13) through their faith, will be justified at the day of judgement. The true 'works of the law', what they really signify, are not external ceremonies, but internal experiences – just as 'true circumcision' is internal 2:28 and someone physically uncircumcised can fulfil what the symbolism of circumcision *means* (2:26).

Questions for Thought and Discussion

- How do these instructions about civil society relate to Western society today? What things might be considered to need the response 'We ought to obey God rather than men' (Acts 5:29)?

- Is there any biblical indication that God prefers one type of government system to another?

Text 13:11–14

[11] Besides this, you know what time it is, how it is now the moment for you to wake from sleep. For salvation is nearer to us now than when we became believers; [12] the night is far gone, the day is near. Let us then lay aside the works of darkness and put on the armour of light; [13] let us live honourably as in the day, not in revelling and drunkenness, not in debauchery and licentiousness, not in quarrelling and jealousy. [14] Instead, put on the Lord Jesus Christ, and make no provision for the flesh, to gratify its desires. (NRSVA)

Commentary

Central to Jewish thought is *halakhah* הֲלָכָה which in literal translation is 'the path that one walks' being derived from a Hebrew root meaning to go, to walk or to travel. In orthodox Jewish practice this was and is interpreted to mean a whole set of detailed ceremonial and moral regulations (which the Gospels also call 'the traditions of the elders'). Paul often uses the concept, but changes its meaning here and elswhere in Galatians 5:16, Ephesians 4:1,17, 5:2, 8, Colossians 1:10, 2:6 and 1 Thessalonians 2:15. He sums it up:

> [2] And walk in love, just as Christ also loved you and gave Himself up for us, an offering and a sacrifice to God as a fragrant aroma. [3] But immorality or any impurity or greed must not even be named among you, as is proper among saints; [4] and there must be no filthiness and silly talk, or coarse jesting, which are not fitting, but rather giving of thanks. [5] For this you know with certainty, that no immoral or impure person or covetous man, who is an idolater, has an inheritance in the kingdom of Christ and God. (Ephesians 5:2–5, NASB)

The 'walk' is about morality coming from the basis of love, not about symbolisms and ceremonials. But Paul always assumes that they have a choice of how to walk. Will it be walking in love and in the power of the Spirit, or walking in the flesh and in failing to keep standards and indulging wrong desires (Romans 8:1, 4)? We are told to put on the Lord Jesus as a conscious choice, basing ourselves on what God has done in Him for us.

Text 14:1–4

[1] Welcome those who are weak in faith, but not for the purpose of quarrelling over opinions. [2] Some believe in eating anything, while

the weak eat only vegetables. ³Those who eat must not despise those who abstain, and those who abstain must not pass judgement on those who eat; for God has welcomed them. ⁴Who are you to pass judgement on servants of another? It is before their own lord that they stand or fall. And they will be upheld, for the Lord is able to make them stand. (NRSVA)

Discussion Topic: Who are the Strong and Weak?

Mark Nanos in *The Mystery of Romans* argues that the strong are 'Gentiles who have come to faith in Christ without attachment to Jewish Law or customs' and the weak are non-Christian Jews. This seems unlikely because:

1. It does actually say 'weak in *the* faith' which perhaps indicates in the Christian faith, though the definite article is admittedly not decisive.

2. Paul identifies himself as one of the strong (15:1)

3. Romans 14:4 refers to them all having the same master – it is hard to see how Paul would apply this to 'enemies of the gospel' (11:28).

4. Though he refers to the unbelieving Jews as his 'brothers' (9:3) Paul qualifies it as 'countrymen according to the flesh' – no such bond would link Christian Gentiles to non-Christian Jews (14:15).

5. Romans 15:5–6 urges them (presumably the strong and the weak) to be of one mind and glorify the God and faith of our Lord Jesus Messiah.

6. Romans 15:7 urges them to 'receive' one another as Messiah 'received' us.

7. The parallel passage in 1 Corinthians 8:4–11 makes it quite clear that these are Christian brothers.

In general, Nanos' (and Sanders') attempts to show that really mainstream Judaism accepted table fellowship with god-fearing Gentiles, and that Gentile Christians freely mingled in synagogues is unconvincing. Peter (who was not a Pharisee) explicitly said: *'You know how unlawful it is for a Jewish man to keep company or go to one of another nation . . .'* (Acts 10:28). It took a special vision before he was happy to associate with the very god-fearing Cornelius.

The parallel Corinthians passage says:

> [4] Hence, as to the eating of food offered to idols, we know that 'no idol in the world really exists', and that 'there is no God but one.' [5] Indeed, even though there may be so-called gods in Heaven or on Earth—as in fact there are many gods and many lords— [6] yet for us there is one God, the Father, from whom are all things and for whom we exist, and one Lord, Jesus Christ, through whom are all things and through whom we exist.
>
> [7] It is not everyone, however, who has this knowledge. Since some have become so accustomed to idols until now, they still think of the food they eat as food offered to an idol; and their conscience, being weak, is defiled. [8] 'Food will not bring us close to God.' We are no worse off if we do not eat, and no better off if we do. [9] But take care that this liberty of yours does not somehow become a stumbling-block to the weak. [10] For if others see you, who possess knowledge, eating in the temple of an idol, might they not, since their conscience is weak, be encouraged to the point of eating food sacrificed to idols? [11] So by your knowledge those weak believers for whom Christ died are destroyed. [12] But when you thus sin against members of your family, and wound their conscience when it is weak, you sin against Christ.
> (1 Corinthians 8:4–12, NRSVA)

The 'weak' here is anyone for whom eating meat offered to idols would be to worship the idol, *and who might copy the act while still in this belief.* This is extremely unlikely to be a non-Christian Jew, but could be either a Christian Jew, or a former pagan. This also seems most likely to be the case here in Romans. It is not that someone might disapprove, but that they might feel coerced or pushed into doing something which to them would be idolatrous.

However, while the emphasis in Corinthians is on the possibility of leading astray, here in Romans the issue is a judgemental attitude. But of course if the strong are judgemental it could again lead the weak into doing things which are against their consciences.

The vegetable diet may be (like Daniel and his friends in the Old Testament) for those continuing practising as Christian Jews to avoid any possibility of eating meat offered to idols. *All right, so don't despise someone like that,* Paul says.

Commentary

The 'weak in the faith' here seem to be those with scruples about eating some kinds of food. These could be because of fears that the food has been offered to idols, or because it is non-Kosher. The 'strong' realise that meat is unaltered in itself if it has been offered to an idol, and that the rules of Kosher meat need not apply. Paul addresses them here (with himself as one of the strong) to be tolerant and not condescending towards those who have dietary scruples.

Text 14:5–12

[5] Some judge one day to be better than another, while others judge all days to be alike. Let all be fully convinced in their own minds. [6] Those who observe the day, observe it in honour of the Lord. Also those who eat, eat in honour of the Lord, since they give thanks to God; while those who abstain, abstain in honour of the Lord and give thanks to God.

[7] We do not live to ourselves, and we do not die to ourselves. [8] If we

live, we live to the Lord, and if we die, we die to the Lord; so then, whether we live or whether we die, we are the Lord's. [9] For to this end Christ died and lived again, so that He might be Lord of both the dead and the living.

[10] Why do you pass judgement on your brother or sister? Or you, why do you despise your brother or sister? For we will all stand before the judgement seat of God. [11] For it is written, 'As I live, says the Lord, every knee shall bow to Me, and every tongue shall give praise to God.'

[12] So then, each of us will be accountable to God. (NRSVA)

Commentary

What are the 'days' here? They could be Roman *dies ferialis*, civic holidays celebrating different gods (or the *Isthmian Games* in Corinth). But had this been the case it would be more likely the 'strong' who celebrated them (ignoring the idolatrous overtones). It would also seem odd (though maybe not impossible) to say that the person 'observes it to the Lord' of a Roman festival. In our view, then, the primary idea here is Jewish festivals and their associated Sabbaths.

Paul's words, also, would seem to extend to the Jewish weekly Sabbath. Some Christians claim that the 'Sabbath' is a 'creation ordinance' because it is introduced in Genesis 2:2–3. From this there are those who claim that it still has to be the Saturday as for the Jews, while others believe that the Christian 'Sabbath' is now transferred to the 'Lord's day' or Sunday. Paul here, however, seems quite clear that it is a matter of individual conscience. The Jews, of course, kept other Sabbaths beside the seventh day, but had Paul intended an exception, surely he would have said so. Moreover we read:

> [12] The Lord spoke to Moses, saying, [13] 'But as for you, speak to the sons of Israel, saying, "You shall surely observe My sabbaths; for this is a sign between Me and you throughout your generations, that you may know that I am the Lord who sanctifies you. [14] Therefore you are to observe the sabbath, for it is holy to you. Everyone who profanes it shall surely be put to death; for whoever does any work on it, that person shall be cut off from among his people. [15] For six days work may be done, but on the seventh day there is a sabbath of complete rest, holy to the Lord; whoever does any work on the sabbath day shall surely be put to death. [16] So the sons of Israel

shall observe the sabbath, to celebrate the sabbath throughout their generations as a perpetual covenant." [17] It is a sign between Me and the sons of Israel forever; for in six days the Lord made heaven and earth, but on the seventh day He ceased from labour, and was refreshed.' (Exodus 31:12–17, NASB)

Genesis does say that God 'rested' though of course this is not literal because 'the everlasting God, the LORD, the Creator of the ends of the earth, neither faints nor is weary' (Isaiah 40:28). But this is transferred to a human 'Sabbath' *specifically for the Jews;* God says: 'it is a sign between Me and the sons of Israel'. The Canaanites are berated for immorality (for example in Leviticus 18:3ff) but not for eating bacon, failing to get circumcised or breaking the Sabbath. These are specifically Jewish ordinances, signs between God and Israel. Both the present authors were brought up in churches which regarded Sunday as a kind of Sabbath, but now our faith is 'strong'! For Christians to meet together is essential, and in our culture Sunday is a convenient day to do this, but not because it is a 'Sabbath' unless you want to make it one. The principle behind the Jewish *Shabbat*, of course, of keeping time for God and for rest, is a good one. But how this is done is for individual conscience. The great Christian missionary and athlete Eric Liddell was right not to run on the Sunday he thought of as a Sabbath, but other Christians may have no issue with it.

We need only to ensure that, in such issues of symbolism, we are able to give our own account to our Lord.

Text 14:13–23

[13] Let us therefore no longer pass judgement on one another, but resolve instead never to put a stumbling-block or hindrance in the way of another. [14] I know and am persuaded in the Lord Jesus that nothing is unclean in itself; but it is unclean for anyone who thinks it unclean. [15] If your brother or sister is being injured by what you eat, you are no longer walking in love. Do not let what you eat cause the ruin of one for whom Christ died. [16] So do not let your good be spoken of as evil. [17] For the kingdom of God is not food and drink but righteousness and peace and joy in the Holy Spirit. [18] The one who thus serves Christ is acceptable to God and has human approval. [19] Let us then pursue what makes for peace and for mutual edification. [20] Do not, for the sake of food, destroy the work of God.

Everything is indeed clean, but it is wrong for you to make others fall by what you eat; [21] it is good not to eat meat or drink wine or do anything that makes your brother or sister stumble. [22] The faith that you have, have as your own conviction before God. Blessed are those who have no reason to condemn themselves because of what they approve. [23] But those who have doubts are condemned if they eat, because they do not act from faith; for whatever does not proceed from faith is sin. (NRSVA)

Commentary

By 'nothing' here (v14) Paul is not talking about food hygiene. He means nothing in the level of ritual or symbol in particular foods. This subjectivity is also about food – not about moral issues like murder or adultery on which he was definitely not a postmodernist.

Paul says he is 'persuaded in the Lord Jesus'. Compare:

– There is nothing unclean of itself . . . all (foods) indeed are pure (Romans 14:14)

– Whatever enters a man from outside cannot harm him . . . thus purifying all foods? (Mark 7:18–19)

Jesus in the context was rejecting the Pharisees' *halakhah* (or 'traditions of the elders'), the over-legalistic interpretations of Torah, but did not intend Jews to stop keeping Torah altogether and start eating bacon butties. For Jesus, faith-relationship was the central part of human-God interaction, so He commends the faith of those who did not keep Torah (Matthew 15:28, Luke 7:9 etc), and while encouraging Jews to keep Torah points beyond to the more important principles (Matthew 23:23). Evidently, though, Paul has picked up the sentiment about food not being inherently unclean, and is reapplying it here in the context of Jew-Gentile fellowship. Bacon is not inherently impure, but for the Jew who feels a conscience in eating it then it is bad. Meat being offered to idols does not change its chemistry, but if to the person eating it this means worshipping the idol then it is wrong. Always with issues that are symbolic it is what it means *to the person doing it* – that is key.

If possible, also, we should avoid our good (for example, free eating of meat which has been offered to an idol) being badly spoken of. But this surely does not mean that the most narrow and legalistic person in a church should rule the others. If we took it thus then we might all finish up as strict teetotal sabbatarians who don't wear makeup, dance or watch television because it is 'worldly'. Some churches coming from a holiness tradition have, alas, finished up like this, but it is not glorifying to God. It is not that the 'weak' in faith person may be *irritated* by the behaviour of the strong or feel judgemental towards them, it is that they may be cajoled into doing something against their conscience.

The 'strong' however, are also not to be judged:

> [16] Therefore do not let anyone condemn you in matters of food and drink or of observing festivals, new moons, or sabbaths. [17] These are only a shadow of what is to come, but the substance belongs to Christ. (Colossians 2:16–17, NRSVA)

The Colossians context is clearly Jewish festivals because they are 'a shadow of things to come'. But Paul, like the writer to Hebrews, sees all these ordinances as types of shadows of the reality that was in Messiah. Paul does not say that they should not keep these festivals if they wish to, but that anyone not keeping them is not to be judged as spiritually inferior. A Jew may perfectly well keep *Shabbat* but no one should be judged or denigrated for not keeping a Sabbath – whether on a Saturday or a Sunday.

Romans 14:23 is sometimes misquoted to try to 'prove' that, for example, all actions done by a non-Christian are sin because they are not done in faith. But this is totally out of context. The context is about symbolic or ritual observance for Christians. In this sense anything that goes against our consciences is wrong – though of course the Holy Spirit may re-educate our consciences over time.

Text 15:1–6

> [1] We who are strong ought to put up with the failings of the weak, and not to please ourselves. [2] Each of us must please our neighbour for the good purpose of building up the neighbour. [3] For Christ did not please Himself; but, as it is written, 'The insults of those who insult you have fallen on me.' [4] For whatever was written in former days was written for our instruction, so that by steadfastness and by the encouragement of the scriptures we might have hope. [5] May the God of steadfastness and encouragement grant you to live in harmony with one another, in accordance with Christ Jesus, [6] so that together you may with one voice glorify the God and Father of our Lord Jesus Christ. (NRSVA)

Commentary

The strong should bear with the scruples of the weak – but this needs to lead to 'edification'. A legalistically bound church is not being edified. But the core issue is that we should want to lead others into liberty – not just act to please ourselves. The core motive should be love for others and love for the Church. How easy it is, though, to slip into pride and self-congratulation that we are amongst 'the strong'. We personally don't have a problem with doing some sport on a Sunday, but the Christian life and character of a man like Eric Liddell puts all of us to shame. In some ways he would be classified as 'weak in the faith' – but for him above all surely God could say (if we are permitted just a little misquotation!) *my strength is made perfect in weakness*. What a man of God!

Questions for Thought and Discussion

- How do we determine which issues are core and which are purely matters of individual conscience?

- How far can we be tolerant of alternative views? How is this to be distinguished from indifference?

Text 15:7–13

[7] Therefore, accept one another, just as Christ also accepted us to the glory of God. [8] For I say that Christ has become a servant to the circumcision on behalf of the truth of God to confirm the promises given to the fathers, [9] and for the Gentiles to glorify God for His mercy; as it is written, 'Therefore I will give praise to You among the Gentiles, And I will sing to Your name.' [10] Again he says, 'Rejoice, O Gentiles, with His people.' [11] And again, 'Praise the Lord all you

Gentiles, And let all the peoples praise Him.' ¹²Again Isaiah says, 'There shall come the root of Jesse, And He who arises to rule over the Gentiles, In Him shall the Gentiles hope.'

¹³ Now may the God of hope fill you with all joy and peace in believing, so that you will abound in hope by the power of the Holy Spirit. (NASB)

Commentary

Messiah has received/accepted Jews and Gentiles. His servanthood (movingly portrayed in Isaiah's vision, though the LXX of Isaiah uses a different Greek word) was to the circumcised to confirm God's promise to Abraham. The words 'has become' imply that in some sense Messiah is *still* a servant to Israel. That promise to Abraham, however, also said that in his seed 'all nations would be blessed'. Paul then cites Psalm 18:49 using the LXX (but missing out the words 'O Lord'). The other three quotations are from Deuteronomy 32:43 (LXX), Psalm 117:1 and Isaiah 11:10 (LXX). All of them are saying that in the Messianic age Gentiles will join in the praise of the God of Israel. But there is also emphasis that it will be 'with His people' and that He is a 'root of Jesse'. Jewish identity and indeed priority in the Church is always assumed, although Gentiles will become equal partners received in like manner by Messiah.

Text 15:14–21

¹⁴ I myself feel confident about you, my brothers and sisters, that you yourselves are full of goodness, filled with all knowledge, and able to instruct one another. ¹⁵ Nevertheless, on some points I have written to you rather boldly by way of reminder, because of the grace given me by God ¹⁶ to be a minister of Christ Jesus to the Gentiles in the priestly service of the gospel of God, so that the offering of the Gentiles may be acceptable, sanctified by the Holy Spirit. ¹⁷ In Christ Jesus, then, I have reason to boast of my work for God. ¹⁸ For I will not venture to speak of anything except what Christ has accomplished through me to win obedience from the Gentiles, by word and deed, ¹⁹ by the power of signs and wonders, by the power of the Spirit of God, so that from Jerusalem and as far around as Illyricum I have fully proclaimed the good news of Christ. ²⁰ Thus I make it my ambition to proclaim the good news,

not where Christ has already been named, so that I do not build on someone else's foundation, [21] but as it is written, 'Those who have never been told of Him shall see, and those who have never heard of Him shall understand.' (NRSVA)

Commentary

Maybe in Romans 15:16 Paul is thinking of his bold admonitions to the Gentile Christians not to be arrogant (11:20), though of course it is much more than this. The NKJV renders 15:18 literally but the NRSVA understanding of the Greek here is also that of the NASB, RSV, ESV and NIV, and is advocated by Cranfield, Dunn and others. Verse 20 may seem a bit paradoxical given his desire to preach the gospel in Rome, but maybe this is because Paul saw Rome as a launching place for new places like Spain.

Text 15:22–32

[22] For this reason I have often been prevented from coming to you; [23] but now, with no further place for me in these regions, and since I have had for many years a longing to come to you [24] whenever I go to Spain—for I hope to see you in passing, and to be helped on my way there by you, when I have first enjoyed your company for a while— [25] but now, I am going to Jerusalem serving the saints. [26] For Macedonia and Achaia have been pleased to make a contribution for the poor among the saints in Jerusalem. [27] Yes, they were pleased to do so, and they are indebted to them. For if the Gentiles have shared in their spiritual things, they are indebted to minister to them also in material things. [28] Therefore, when I have finished this, and have put my seal on this fruit of theirs, I will go on by way of you to Spain. [29] I know that when I come to you, I will come in the fullness of the blessing of Christ.

[30] Now I urge you, brethren, by our Lord Jesus Christ and by the love of the Spirit, to strive together with me in your prayers to God for me, [31] that I may be rescued from those who are disobedient in Judea, and that my service for Jerusalem may prove acceptable to the saints; [32] so that I may come to you in joy by the will of God and find refreshing rest in your company. [33] Now the God of peace be with you all. Amen. (NASB)

Commentary

All this is fairly clear stuff. Paul has been clear in his letter how the Gentiles are spiritually indebted to the Jews, and his strategy has always been to go to the Jew first and through that base reach Gentiles. When he does eventually arrive in Rome (albeit not quite as he planned it!) he still goes first to the Jewish community, even though the opposition (as he here fears) of Jews in Jerusalem has led to him going to Rome as a prisoner.

For us, when plans do not come as we had hoped, it must be some comfort that the one who was perhaps the greatest missionary in history had the same experience!

Paul believes in striving in prayer. As he says in Ephesians, there is a spiritual battle going on in the heavenly places. Through prayer we are a part of this.

Romans 16:1–27 | Personal Greetings and Final Words

Text 16:1–2

[1] I commend to you our sister Phoebe, a deacon [or minister] of the church at Cenchreae, [2] so that you may welcome her in the Lord as is fitting for the saints, and help her in whatever she may require from you, for she has been a benefactor of many and of myself as well. (NRSVA)

Commentary

Paul first commends Phoebe, and as she is so named first she was probably the bearer of the letter. She is a woman, and probably a Gentile as her name comes from one of the Titan daughters of Uranus and Gaia in Greek mythology. The use of the term 'sister' was common in the Early Church. He says she is a minister (*diakonon*) of the Cenchrea church in Corinth from which he writes. The word *diakonos* is sometimes rendered 'deacon' or 'deaconess', but actually is a masculine noun meaning 'minister', and there is no such word as 'deaconess' in Greek. It refers to the office, irrespective of the gender of the person who holds it. Dunn points out that the Greek structure here indicates that it is a position of responsibility: 'the first recorded "deacon" in church history' (*Romans*, p.887). Paul described himself as a minister in Romans 15:16 and in 1 Corinthians 2:5–6 Paul describes himself and Apollos as 'ministers', using the same word.

She is also called a 'patroness' or 'benefactor' (*prostatis*) of many including the great apostle himself (the translation 'helper' in the NKJV and NASB is misleading). The noun is not used anywhere else in the New Testament, but in the LXX the masculine form appears in 2 Chronicles 24:11 and 2 Maccabees 3:4. It means 'one who stands before' and so a 'leader, or 'president' or 'ruler'. Paul uses the verbal form (*proistamenos*) in Romans 12:8 where it is usually translated 'the one who leads' or literally 'the one up front', and Paul says to do it diligently. Young's Literal translation actually has it translated as: 'she also became a leader of many and of myself', and the CEV 'she has proved to be a respected leader for many others, including me'.

271

Arland Hultgren suggests that one can say with certainty:

> He expected her to meet leaders of the house churches in Rome, fill them in on Paul's plans, secure arrangements for his arrival, alleviate any concerns they might have about his coming and being with them, and, above all, interpret the Letter to the Romans among its recipients prior to Paul's arrival. (*Paul's Letter to the Romans*, p.570)

Wow! And it is sometimes said that Paul is a misogynist! We wish all churches today would receive women Ministers in a manner befitting the saints. Yes, all the twelve apostles were free, male and Jewish – but within maybe two decades of Jesus' death we find that a Gentile woman is given this position by the great apostle himself. To the Jew first and also to the Greek, and maybe to the male first and also to the female. In the end, in Jesus the Messiah there is no Jew nor Gentile, slave nor free, male nor female. Maybe we should not be surprised since Paul made the house of another Gentile woman Lydia, a new convert, the base of his very first church in Europe (Acts 15:15, 40).

Text 16:3–16

> [3] Greet Prisca and Aquila, who work with me in Christ Jesus, [4] and who risked their necks for my life, to whom not only I give thanks, but also all the churches of the Gentiles. [5] Greet also the church in their house. Greet my beloved Epaenetus, who was the first convert in Asia for Christ. [6] Greet Mary, who has worked very hard among you. [7] Greet Andronicus and Junia, my relatives who were in prison with me; they are prominent among the apostles, and they were in Christ before I was. [8] Greet Ampliatus, my beloved in the Lord. [9] Greet Urbanus, our co-worker in Christ, and my beloved Stachys. [10] Greet Apelles, who is approved in Christ. Greet those who belong to the family of Aristobulus. [11] Greet my relative Herodion. Greet those in the Lord who belong to the family of Narcissus. [12] Greet those workers in the Lord, Tryphaena and Tryphosa. Greet the beloved Persis, who has worked hard in the Lord. [13] Greet Rufus, chosen in the Lord; and greet his mother—a mother to me also. [14] Greet Asyncritus, Phlegon, Hermes, Patrobas, Hermas, and the brothers and sisters who are with them. [15] Greet Philologus, Julia, Nereus and his sister, and Olympas, and all the saints who are with them. [16] Greet one another with a holy kiss. All the churches of Christ greet you. (NRSVA)

Commentary

Now the greetings. The very first to be greeted are the husband-wife team who *together* undertook the Christian theological education of the famous Hellenist Jewish Rabbi Apollos (Acts 18:26). So much for women having no teaching role in churches! Moreover, Paul here, contrary to ancient custom, names Priscilla first in the pair (using her more official name Prisca rather than the diminutive Priscilla), which would usually indicate greater importance. Paul knew them well, he had stayed with them in Corinth.

There are 28 listed here, though Hultgren suggests that maybe Aristobulus and Narcissus may not have been Christians themselves. We cannot really tell the social mix, nor exactly how many were Jewish (though Aquila, Adronicus and Junia and Herodion clearly were). Some are apparently known personally to Paul: Aquila, Priscilla, Mary, Andronicus, Junia, Amplias, Stachys, Tryphena, Tryphosa, Persis, Rufus and his mum. This makes twelve, who Hultgren says 'would have been persons who could speak on behalf of Paul among the Christian house churches in Rome' (*Paul's Letter to the Romans,* p.577). Seven of the twelve were women, and of the first five named three are women.

The name Ἰουνίαν (*Junian*) in 16:7 is given in the RSV, NEB and NASB as the masculine Junias, though the NRSVA, NIV, ESV and NKJV and others retain the feminine Junia. Actually Dunn cites Lampe that there are 250 known cases of the feminine Junia and none of the masculine Junias in the contemporary literature, and figures like Origen and Chrysostom and the Early Church took the name as that of a woman. The most natural understanding of the language is that they were another Jewish husband-wife team. They were Christians before Paul – probably within a couple of years of Jesus' death, and had also been in prison for their faith. They were 'prominent amongst the apostles', which either means they were held in high regard by the apostles or that they were themselves famous apostles. Dunn says 'The full phrase almost certainly means 'prominent amongst the apostles' rather than 'outstanding in the eyes of the apostles' (*Romans*, p.894), the view also taken by Kasemann, Cranfield and Hultgren. It was taken also by the fourth century Greek-speaking Church Father Chrysostom, who says:

> Think how great the devotion of this woman Junia must have been, that she should be worthy to be called an apostle.' (*Homily 31 on the Epistle to the Romans*)

This does not, of course, mean she was on a level with the twelve apostles, rather the word really means missionary, and is also applied for example to Barnabas (Acts 14:14), Sylvanus and Timothy (1 Thessalonians 1:1, 2:7) and others. Nevertheless, Junia was 'prominent' among the earliest recognised Christian missionaries.

Why do we emphasize this? Priscilla was a teacher, Phoebe a Church Minister and respected leader, Junia a prominent missionary. How is it, then, that some churches today, which restrict women to posts dealing only with women, and deny them preaching, teaching, and leading, believe they are basing themselves on the New Testament? Churches like the Methodists, Anglicans, Salvation Army, Free Methodist, Ichthus and Chinese churches among others, who have suitable women in any and all the church leadership roles, are devoutly following Paul and his Lord. Yes all the twelve apostles were male, Jewish and freemen – but this is not how it was meant to stay and in Christ there is neither male nor female, Jew nor Gentile, slave nor free. In some aspects in society these differences remain, but there is no inherent reason why a female Gentile slave could not be a church leader.

Finally a 'holy kiss'. This was more of a hug, rather than a smacker on the cheek as favoured by some modern politicians. In our British culture it is usually restricted to Christians and footballers!

Questions for Thought and Discussion

- How far do our various churches today reflect the emancipated position of women in the churches of Paul?

- Why is it that many people today seem to regard having 'women ministers' as some kind of compromise with modern politically correct culture?

Text 16:17–20

> ¹⁷ I urge you, brothers and sisters, to keep an eye on those who cause dissensions and offenses, in opposition to the teaching that you have learned; avoid them. ¹⁸ For such people do not serve our Lord Christ, but their own appetites, and by smooth talk and flattery they deceive the hearts of the simple-minded. ¹⁹ For while your obedience is known to all, so that I rejoice over you, I want you to be wise in what is good and guileless in what is evil. ²⁰ The God of peace will shortly crush Satan under your feet. The grace of our Lord Jesus Christ be with you. (NRSVA)

Commentary

The word 'brethren' (*adelphoi*) as previously noted, is often meant by Paul to be gender inclusive, so the NRSVA 'brothers and sisters' is fair enough in modern terms. As always, Paul is wary of smooth talkers, and all too aware that Christians can be led astray. Verse 20 has a vision of the Church as the victorious body of Christ. In Genesis 3:15 God famously prophesied to the serpent:

> And I will put enmity between you and the woman, and between your offspring/seed and hers; he will crush your head, and you will strike his heel.

The offspring of Satan or 'brood of vipers' were not literal snakes, but the human opponents of Jesus (Matthew 12:34, 23:33). Jesus crushed the head of the serpent on the cross, but here Paul pictures the Church, the body of Christ, as crushing the serpent Satan underfoot.

Text 16:21–24

> ²¹ Timothy, my co-worker, greets you; so do Lucius and Jason and Sosipater, my relatives. ²² I Tertius, the writer of this letter, greet you in the Lord. ²³ Gaius, who is host to me and to the whole church, greets you. Erastus, the city treasurer, and our brother Quartus, greet you. (NRSVA)

Commentary

Paul has said his 'amen' but then his friends say 'Hang on a minute!' Timothy is now a 'fellow-worker' – the same term Paul used for us with God in Romans 8:28. Tertius was the amanuensis who wrote the letter at Paul's direction.

In Corinth we know that the church really did mix Jew and Gentile, slave and free, male and female, their communion/meal table is described in 1 Corinthians 11–14. Prophecy and prayer from Jew and Gentiles, men and women, and the city Treasurer Erastus sitting down at table with slaves and maybe some former flute-girls. Amazing. All one in Jesus the Messiah.

Text 16:25–27

> [25] Now to Him who is able to establish you according to my gospel and the preaching of Jesus Christ, according to the revelation of the mystery which has been kept secret for long ages past, [26] but now is manifested, and by the Scriptures of the prophets, according to the commandment of the eternal God, has been made known to all the nations, leading to obedience of faith; [27] to the only wise God, through Jesus Christ, be the glory forever. Amen. (NASB)

Commentary

Many commentators (conservative or otherwise) believe that this doxology was added to the letter at some time in the first 150 years after Paul wrote it, though Longenecker in his commentary argues that Paul himself composed it. In any event it well summarises some of the major concerns in his letter.

Often Christians today think of a 'mystery' as something that does not make sense. When some theologians mistakenly picture God as love and yet as arbitrarily choosing who to make repent, they may say it is a 'mystery'. But the word *mysterion* does not really mean this, it means a secret as is shown here. We now have the mind of Christ, and what before was secret is revealed to us. God's whole plan, as shown in Romans, to deal with humanity, is just awe-inspiring as the secret is now out. The concept of getting the gospel to all the nations for the 'obedience of faith' is in Romans 1:5 and 16:26, and is a kind of beginning and ending of the message of Paul. It is not, of course, about just believing a set of creedal doctrines, but of a faith which is related to obedience. Paul's gospel is a missionary gospel.

Application

Romans & Galatians

Many commentaries you may read on Galatians and Romans would finish here and not expect you to continue on to apply the message. But we believe that theology must be more than a dry intellectual pursuit – if it means anything, it should change us.

Paul's gospel in Galatians and Romans is knit together by the same declaration: the just/righteous shall _live_ by faith (Galatians 3:11, Romans 1:17), and his message is not just a set of theological ideas, but truth to be lived and applied into every area of our lives. Paul reveals the glory of Christ to us, and expects us to be transformed by the renewing of our minds.

In Galatians Paul applies the message which he systematically sets out in Romans to answer the question: 'How do I grow and continue in the Christian life?' However, sixteen chapters of Romans is hard to summarise or express succinctly, and is so rich it is sometimes easy to lose sight of the overall flow of what Paul is saying. We hope the structure we give below will help you to divide up the book in order to begin to apply it.

As you would expect, Romans is Christocentric (focused on Christ) from start to finish: Paul begins with a revelation of the incarnation of Jesus Christ in Romans 1:

> [2] . . . which [God] promised beforehand through His prophets in the holy Scriptures, [3] concerning His Son, who was born of a descendant of David according to the flesh, [4] who was declared the Son of God with power by the resurrection from the dead, according to the Spirit of holiness, Jesus Christ our Lord.

and climaxes the epistle with a Trinitarian statement before his final greetings:

> [30] I appeal to you, brothers and sisters, by our Lord _Jesus Christ_ and by the love of _the Spirit_, to join me in earnest prayer to _God_ on my behalf. (also see 15:12-13 for another Trinitarian statement)

These two statements sandwich the body of the letter, which contains a wonderful series of pictures of the beauty and glory of our Lord Jesus Christ.

If we had to condense Romans down into a couple of sentences then we couldn't do any better than quote Romans 1:16–17. As we have highlighted in different colours, these two verses embody six themes that underpin the whole epistle, and give us a structure to begin to grasp, understand and apply Paul's gospel.

> [16] For I am not ashamed of the gospel, for it is the power of God for salvation to everyone who believes, to the Jew first and also to the Greek. [17] For in it the righteousness of God is revealed from faith to faith; as it is written, 'But the righteous shall live by faith.'

Romans	Theme	Aspect of Christ
1:18–3:20	Everyone Jews and Gentiles need of the gospel	Judge
3:12–5:11	Righteousness of God Justification by Faith	Jesus
5:12–7:6	For salvation Salvation from Sin	One (new) Man
7:7–8:39	Power of God Law of the Spirit of Life	God's own Son
9:1–11:36	To the Jew first . . . The strategy of the gospel in history	Deliverer
12:1–15:13	Not ashamed The New Community	The Christ

Each of these six sections opens up a different aspect of the person of our Lord Jesus Christ. We could write another book just expounding these points, but instead we will leave you to with this as a starting point to delve deeper in to Romans and into your own personal relationship with Jesus.

Reference Material

List of Discussion Topics

Descriptions of Terms and People

Some descriptions of concepts and people, with page references where appropriate.

Accountable	The word *hupodikos* in Romans 3:19 means held to account rather than condemned. [see p.130]
Adam	Adam (*ādām*). In Genesis 1–3 means 'the man' or 'humanity' but later is used as a name. Paul's use is ambivalent. [see p.151]
Adelphoi	'Brothers' but really means 'brothers and *sisters*'.
Adoption	Or 'son-placing' (*huiothesias*) is really in the future but has present implications. [see p.183]
Antioch	City in what is now North Syria from which Paul and Barnabas (later Silas) conducted missionary journeys.
Apocrypha	Jewish writings between the end of the New Testament and the time of Jesus.
Apostle	Means 'missionary'. [see p.90]
Arsenokoitas	Means (a man) having sex with a man. There is no word in Greek for a 'homosexual' (ie someone with an innate attraction for his or her own sex). [see p.101]
Body, Soul and Spirit	Body (*sōma*) soul (*psyche*) and Spirit (*pneuma*) are not precise technical terms and care is needed in interpreting. [see p.161]
Cephas	Hebrew word for 'rock' the nickname Jesus gave his disciple Simon ('Peter' in Greek).
Change of Mind	God sometimes changes his mind according to how people respond to him. [see p.214]
Chiasm	Special structure of six statements. [see p.117]
Covenant Theology	Fits God's dealings with himself and mankind into three covenants. [see p.195]
Covenantal Nomism	Keeping laws to fulfil a covenant.

Dispensationalism	Holds that there are seven 'dispensations': in which God deals differently with humankind [see p.196]
Election	Means choice. Jesus is the elect one and so Christians are elect *in Christ*. Israel was the elect nation, but within it there were a group who had faith and were 'choice' in that they accepted God's grace. [see p.233]
Epimenides	7 – 6th century BC Cretan who is quoted by Paul in Acts 17 and also as a prophet in Titus 1:12. [see p.113]
Exegesis	Principles of interpreting the Bible.
Faithfulness	The word *pisteus* can mean faith or faithfulness. It can refer to God, Jesus the Messiah, or people of faith. The genitive *pisteus Iēsou Christou* always means 'faithfulness of Jesus the Messiah'. [see p.132]
Filled with the Spirit	Can be a specific event (*pleitho*) or a continuous experience (*pleroo*). [see p.181]
Flesh	Flesh (*sarx*) meaning the physical or purely human level. [see p.161, 181]
Foreknowledge	(*proginōskō*) Knowing beforehand or in advance. [see p.189]
Genitive	A noun, pronoun, or adjective, used primarily to express possession, measure, or origin eg 'faithfulness of Christ' or 'love of God'.
Gentiles	Non-Jews. Usually the New Testament word is 'nations' (*éthnos*), though sometimes the word 'Greeks' (*Hellenes*) also means this.
Gospel	Good news. [see p.97]
Grace	Means unmerited and unearned gifts. The term 'sovereign grace' does not appear in Scripture, there is no indication that a person cannot refuse to receive an unmerited gift.
Hillel	Jewish teacher c110 BC –10 AD. He recognised brotherly love as central to Jewish Law. Gamaliel was a Hillelite rabbi who was Rabbi Paul's teacher. [see p.127]
Homosexual	See *arsenokoitas*.
Israel	New name God gave to Jacob, later applied to his descendants. Also occasionally used spiritually [see p.64 & p.195]
Josephus	Famous 1st Century Jewish historian (c37-100AD)

Judaisers	Those in Galatians who were encouraging Gentile Christians to keep the Torah. [see p.39 etc]
Judgement	Can be process of condemning or of calling to account.[see p.107,114]
Justification	Being shown to be in the right or in rightstanding with God. [pp.31, 35,139]
Legalism	Not a view that by keeping certain rules a person can earn God's forgiveness, but rather that a good holy lifestyle consists in keeping a long list of rules.
LXX	The Septuagint. The Greek translation of the Old Testament in common use in the first century, sometimes quoted by Paul.
Messiah	Means 'anointed one' – generally to be a High Priest or King. The Greek word *Christos* means Messiah and is not a name. [see p.9]
Minister/Deacon	The word *diakonon* means a minister of either gender. [see p.271]
Mishnah	The version of the Jewish oral law or 'traditions of the elders' first written down in 217 AD. Jesus (eg Matthew 23) was highly critical of these and indeed the whole approach. [see p.137]
Mystery	Mystery (*mysterion*) means a secret. [see p.245]
New Perspective on Paul	Ideas of eg Dunn and Wright that 'works of the Law' are key ceremonials, and that Pharisees did not believe these 'earned salvation' but rather they were markers of being the people of God.
Old Man	The word *Anthropos* really means old humanity. [see p.159]
Original Sin	Later theological term meaning the sin of the first human. [see p.154]
Paidagōgos	Respected slave who took young mean to their tutors [see p.43]
Pharisees	A 1st century Jewish group who emphasized meticulous keeping of their detailed interpretation of the Jewish Law or Torah as the right way to express being God's covenant people on earth.
Philo	Famous 1st Century Jewish philosopher (c25 BC – c50 AD)
Predestination	Predestination (*proorizō*) means setting out a horizon. [see p.190]

Remnant Theology	Theology that throughout history only a remnant of Israel have been faithful. [see p.217]
Righteous	Of a human it means being in right standing and relationship with God, it does not mean ethically perfect or sinless. [see p.30,98] Of God it means he acts rightly and justly. [see p.134]
Sabbath	The seventh day given specifically to the Jews (who had other Sabbaths) as a day of rest and worship. [see p.263]
Salvation	A salvaging process which has a past, present and future aspect. [see p.98]
Seed	Means descendants or descendant – can be singular or plural in the original languages.
Septuagint	See LXX.
Shalom	Hebrew for 'peace' Goes beyond just an absence of conflict and speaks of wholeness and wellbeing. [see p.147]
Shema	Jewish prayer that begins: *Sh'ma Yisra'eil Adonai Eloheinu Adonai echad* (in Deuteronomy 6:4–6).
Sinner	In biblical terms this means a person not living in right relationship with God. Often it is contrasted with 'righteous'. Christians have all sinned but are 'righteous' not sinners. [see p.8]
Stoicheia	'Elements' – in Paul meaning elementary rules. [see p.47]
Strong and Weak	In this context those with less or more scruples about ceremonial and symbolic issues. [see p.260]
Supercessionism	Supercessionism or 'replacement theology' means the view that the church has replaced Israel as the people of God. [see p.247]
Synoptic Gospels	This refers to the first three gospels, Matthew, Mark, and Luke, which have various pieces of text in common.
Tetragrammaton	The four Hebrew letters הוהי meaning YHWH. [see p.226]
The Potter	Parable in Jeremiah 18, referred to by Paul, has the potter adapting his work according to the reaction of the clay. [see p.212]
Torah	Means the Jewish 'Law': can mean Genesis-Deuteronomy in our Bible or the set of actual commandment/ordinances.
Traditions of the Elders	See *Mishnah*.

Ungodly	LXX *asebesin* – basically means unrighteous and without God. [see p.140]
Walk	The walk (*halakhah*) is a metaphor for the ongoing lifestyle. [see p.259]
Will and Plan	Humans can reject both God's will and plan for them. [see p.192]
Works of the Law	Not good works in general but the key ceremonial marks of being Jewish, particularly diet, circumcision and Sabbaths. [p.30]

Bibliography

Galatians Commentaries

Bruce (1982) F. F. Bruce *The Epistle to the Galatians* Michegan: Eerdmans

Dunn (1993) James D. G. Dunn *The Epistle to the Galatians* London: Black

Jervis (1999) L. Ann Jervis *Galatians* Carlisle: Paternoster

Longenecker (1990) Richard N. Longenecker *Galatians* Dallas: Word

Lyons (2012) George Lyons *Galatians: A Commentary in the Wesleyan Tradition* Kansas: Beacon Hill

Ramsay (1900) William Ramsay *A Historical Commentary on St Paul's Epistle to the Galatians* (rp 1965) Michigan: Baker House

Witherington (1998) Ben Witherington III *Grace in Galatia* Edinburgh: T & T Clark

Romans Commentaries

These are commentaries looked at in preparing this work:

Abasciano (2005) Brian J. Abasciano *Paul's Use of the Old Testament in Romans 9.1–9: An Intertextual and Theological Exegesis* London: Bloomsbury T & T Clark.

Abasciano (2011) Brian J. Abasciano *Paul's Use of the Old Testament in Romans 9.10-19: An Intertextual and Theological Exegesis* London: Bloomsbury T & T Clark.

Barclay (1957) William Barclay *The Letter to the Romans* Edinburgh: St Andrew

Barnes (1842) Albert Barnes *Notes on the New Testament* London: Blackie

Barnhouse (1982) D. G. Barnhouse *Romans* 4 vols. Michigan: Eerdmans

Barth (1968) Karl Barth and Edwyn Clement Hoskyns *The Epistle to the Romans* OUP: Oxford

Beet (1900) Joseph Agar Beet *A commentary on St Paul's Epistle to the Romans* London: Hodder and Stoughton

Bruce (1963) F.F. Bruce *The Epistle of Paul to the Romans* London: Tyndale

Calvin (1834) John Calvin *Commentary on the Epistle to the Romans* (tr Sibson) London: Seeley (originally 1539)

Cranfield (1975) C E B Cranfield *A Critical and Exegetical Commentary on The Epistle to the Romans* Edinburgh: T. & T. Clark

Davies (1990) Glen N. Davies *Faith and Obedience in Romans : A Study in Romans 1–4* Sheffield: JSOT

Dodd (10932) C.H. Dodd *The Epistle of Paul to the Romans* London: Hodder and Stoughton

Dunn (1988) James D.G. Dunn *Vol I Romans 1–8, Vol ii Romans 9–16* Dallas: Word

Fitzmyer (1992) Joseph A Fitzmyer, *Romans: a new translation with introduction and commentary* London: Doubleday

Gaca (2005) Kathy L. Gaca & L.L.Wlborn *Early Patristic Readings of Romans* New York: T & T Clark

Godet (1907) F Godet Tr A Cusin *St Paul's Epistle to the Romans* Edinburgh: T & T Clark

Gore (1899) Charles Gore *St Paul's Epistle to the Romans: A Practical Exposition Vol 1: chapters i-vii* London: John Murray

Greathouse (1975) William M. Greathouse *Romans* Kansas: Beacon Hill

Grieb (2002) A Katherine Grieb *The Story of Romans: a narrative defense of God's Righteousness* Louisville, Westminster John Knox

Griffith Thomas (1966) W.H. Griffith Thomas *St Paul's Epistle to the Romans* Michigan: Eerdmans

Haldane (1958) Robert Haldane *Exposition of the Epistle to the Romans* London: Banner of Truth (originally 1874)

Hay & Johnson (1995) David M Hay & E Elizabeth Johnson *Theology. Vol. III: Romans* Minneapolis: Fortress

Hodge (1876) Charles Hodge *The Epistle to the Romans* Michigan: Eerdmans

Hultgren (2011) Arland J. Hultgren *Paul's Letter to the Romans* Michigan: Eerdmans

Ironside (1928) H A Ironside *Romans* Neptune: Loizeaux

Jewett (2007) Robert Jewett, Roy D Kotansky, and Eldon Jay Epp (ed) *Romans: A Commentary* Minneapolis: Fortress,

Kasemann (1980) Ernst Kasemann, and Geoffrey W Bromiley, (tr) *Commentary on Romans* London: SCM

Kruse (2012) Colin G. Kruse *Paul's Letter to the Romans* Apollos: Nottingham

Lloyd –Jones (1970) D Martyn Lloyd-Jones *Romans 3:20–4:25* London: Banner of Truth {Lloyd-Jones did a whole series of commentaries but we will not list all of them}

Longenecker (2016) *The Epistle to the Romans* Michegan: Eerdmans

Luther (1954) Martin Luther, and J Theodore Mueller (tr) *Commentary on the Epistle to the Romans* Michigan: Zondervan

Lyons (2008) George Lyons and William Greathouse *Romans 1–8* Kansas: Beacon Hill

Moo (1996) Douglas J. Moo *The Epistle t the Romans* Michigan: Eerdmans

Morris (1994) Leon Morris *The Epistle to the Romans* Leicester: IVP

Moule (1893) H G Moule *The Epistle of Paul to the Romans* London: Hodder

Murray (1968) John Murray *The Epistle to the Romans: the English text with introduction exposition and notes* Michigan: Eerdmans

Nanos (1996) Mark D. Nanos *The Mystery of Romans* Minneapolis: Fortress

Nygren (1949) Anders Nygren *Commentary on Romans* Philadelphia: Fortress

Pelagius (1997) Pelagius and Theodore Dr Bruyn tr *Pelagius's Commentary on St Paul's Epistle to the Romans* Oxford: OUP

Sadler (1888) M F Sadler *The Epistle to the Romans* London: Bell

Sanday & Headlam (1900) William Sanday and Arthur C Headlam *A critical and exegetical commentary on the Epistle to the Romans* Edinburgh: T. & T. Clark

Schreiner (1998) Thomas R. Schreiner *Romans* Michigan: Baker

Stuhlmacher (1994) Peter Stuhlmacher Tr Scott J. Hafemann *Paul's Letter to the Romans* Knox: Kentucky

Stott (19914) John R.W.Stott *The Message of Romans* Leicester I V P

Talbert (2002) Charle H. Talbert *Romans* Georgia: Smyth & Helwys

Witherington (2004) Ben Witherington III *Paul's Letter to the Romans* (Michegan-Cambridge)

Wright (2002) Ed L E Keck *The New Interpreters Bible* vol 10 Nashville: Abingdon

Wuest (1955) Kenneth S. Wuest *Romans in the Greek New Testament for the English Reader* Michigan: Eerdmans

Ziesler (1989) John Ziesler *Paul's letter to the Romans* London: SCM,

Philippians Commentaries

Fee (1995) Gordon D. Fee *Paul's Letter to the Philippians* Michigan: Eerdmans

O.Brien (1991) Peter T. O'Brien *Commmentary on Philippians* Michigan: Eerdmans

Other Books and Papers

Other books on specific aspects can be found in the bibliographies of our *God's Strategy in Human History* where come of the issues are dealt with in more depth.

There are also general books on Paul's background and other issues, for example:

Bruggen (2005) Jakob Van Bruggen and M Van der Maas tr *Paul* New Jersey: P & R

Dunn (1990) James D. G. Dunn *Jesus, Paul and the Law*

Edersheim (1883) Alfred Edersheim *The Life and Times of Jesus the Messiah*

Hengel (1991) Martin Hengel *The Pre-Christian Paul* Philadelphia: Trinity

Howard (1967) *On the Faith of Christ* HTR 60 (1967) pp.459-465

Klein et al (1993) William W. Klein, Craig L. Blomberg & Robert L. Hubbard. *Intoduction to Biblical Interpretation* (Dallas: Word)

Longenecker (2015) Richard N. Longenecker *Paul, Apostle of Liberty* (2md Ed) Michigan: Eerdmans (first edition 1964).

Marston (2000) Justin Marston *Jewish Understandings of Genesis 1–3 Science and Christian Belief* (2000) 12 (2), 127-150

McGrath (1998) A. McGrath *Justitia Dei: A History of the Christian Doctrine of Justification* [2nd edn]

More (2016) Jacques More *Deleting 'Elect' in the Bible* Tonbrige: Jarom

Stendahl (1963) K. Stendahl *The Apostle Paul and the Introspective Conscience of the West* HTR 56 (1963) pp199-215

The Dictionary of New Testament Theology (5 vols) Edited Colin Brown (1986)

Witherington (1998) Ben Witherington III *The Paul Quest* Illinois: IVP

Wright (1997) N. T. Wright *What St Paul Really Said* Oxford: Lion

Wright (2009) N.T. (Tom) Wright *Justification: God's Plan and Paul's Vision*

Wright (2013) N. T. Wright *Paul and the Faithfulness of God* London: SPCK

Wright (2015) N.T. Wright *Paul and His Recent Interpreters* London: SPCK

Copyrights

About the Authors

Roger Forster has an MA in theology and mathematics from Cambridge University. He is leader of the Ichthus Christian Fellowship, and is known internationally as a preacher, speaker and evangelical leader. He has been a member of the Council for the Evangelical Alliance, Vice President of TEAR Fund, and Administrator and founder of the March for Jesus movement.

Together Roger and his wife Faith have written *Women and the Kingdom*, and his solo books include *Suffering and the Love of God – The Book of Job*, *Prayer – Living in the Breath of God*, *The Kingdom of Jesus*, *Trinity*, *Saving Faith; Fasting*, and *Saturday Night, Sunday Morning . . .*

Paul Marston has a BSc (Econ) and an MSc in statistical theory from LSE, an MSc in the history and philosophy of science, an MA in holiness theology, and a PhD which concerned science, methodology and Christian faith. He is a Senior Lecturer in the University of Central Lancashire. He has also spoken at conferences, Christian Unions and at Word Alive on issues of science and faith.

His solo books include *The Biblical Family*, *God and the Family*, *Christians, Divorce and Remarriage*, *Understanding the Biblical Creation Passages*, *Women in Church Leadership and in Marriage*, *Gay Christians and the Jesus-Centred Church* and *Great Astronomers in European History*.

Paul and Roger have co-authored a number of books including: *Yes But . . .*, *That's A Good Question*, *Reason and Faith*, *Christianity, Evidence and Truth*, *Reason, Science and Faith*, three editions of *God's Strategy in Human History* and most recently *Christianity: The Evidence*.